THE IMAGE OF THE AMERICAN CITY
IN POPULAR LITERATURE,
1820-1870

Kennikat Press
National University Publications
Interdisciplinary Urban Series

General Editor
Raymond A. Mohl
Florida Atlantic University

ADRIENNE SIEGEL

THE IMAGE OF THE AMERICAN CITY IN POPULAR LITERATURE

1820–1870

National University Publications
KENNIKAT PRESS // 1981
Port Washington, N.Y. // London

Manufactured in the United States of America

Published by
Kennikat Press Corp.
Port Washington, N.Y. / London

Library of Congress Cataloging in Publication Data

Siegel, Adrienne.
    The image of the American city in popular literature, 1820–1870.

    (Interdisciplinary urban series) (National university publications)
    Bibliography: p. 186
    Includes index.
    1. American literature–19th century–History and criticism. 2. Cities and towns in literature. 3. Popular literature–United States. 4. Cities and towns–United States. I. Title.
PS217.C57S56   810'.9'321732   80-19277
ISBN 0-8046-9271-8

FOR MY FATHER
Who Made It Possible

ACKNOWLEDGMENTS

This book owes much to the invaluable guidance of Bayrd Still. It was he who first aroused my interest in urban history. His lively discourse on the ways in which Americans reacted to their cities sparked my curiosity to investigate this subject further. His generous encouragement and critical intelligence helped me over innumerable difficulties. Thus what often has been considered a most trying rite, that of authorship, became a most pleasurable experience. I am grateful, too, to Paul Baker and Carl Prince of New York University, whose judicious observations and suggestions helped to guide me in an early draft of this work. To Mary DeDeka I would like to express my sincere thanks for her skillful editing of chapter 6. To Manfred Weidhorn I am deeply indebted for carefully reading the entire manuscript and, as a true friend, prodding me to make numerous stylistic and textual changes. The present form of this book owes much to his gentle but persuasive criticism. Any merit this work may possess is due largely to his promptings; the faults are my own.

The decision to undertake a lengthy scholarly enterprise would hardly have been possible without the encouragement of family and friends. Few deserve more credit than my father, Dr. Nat Spitzer. His own joy in learning and his disciplined work habits spoke eloquently to me as a child of the pleasure of a life devoted to intellectual inquiry. Equally important, his constant support of my endeavors convinced me that I had the power to achieve. I know of no other father who got up at 4 A.M. to awaken his daughter for one more dress rehearsal with her notes before an examination. Nor can I neglect to record the debt I owe to my mother, who took me as a child weekly to the library and helped me to delight in a world of books. She too saw me over innumerable bouts of academic stage fright but, unfortunately, did not live long enough even to see me get my first diploma, from junior high school. Without my sister Deanna and brother-in-law Stanley the preparation of this book would have been much more painful. Their sense of humor and genuine interest in my work leavened isolating hours of research and composition. I am grateful for the many days spent writing in their home in East Hampton, where they allowed me both the privacy and good fellowship I alternately craved. I would especially like to express my appreciation to my husband, Martin, whose own commitment to historical research has done so much to generate an atmosphere in our home of both the playfulness of ideas and the sense of excitement that comes from original discovery. During the many years it took to prepare this book, he understood when I was unavailable, but was there when I needed him. His candid criticisms were most helpful in sharpening my own thinking on many of the historiographical problems posed by this study.

Parts of this book have appeared as articles in the *Journal of Popular Culture* and the *North Dakota Quarterly*.

CONTENTS

THE IMAGE OF THE AMERICAN CITY
IN POPULAR LITERATURE,
1820–1870

ABOUT THE AUTHOR

Dr. Adrienne Siegel is a historian for the New York City Board of Education and is an adjunct professor of history at Long Island University. She has received awards and fellowships, and is a member of the Institute for Research in History. She is the author of *Philadelphia: A Chronological and Documentary History* and articles on urban history in the *Journal of Popular Culture* and the *North Dakota Quarterly*.

1

INTRODUCTION

In the period 1820-70 Americans voted with their feet for urban life. As increased opportunities for industrial employment, improvements in transportation, and a torrent of European immigration pulled people to cities, the United States experienced the most dramatic urban boom the nation has ever before or since known. In the four decades which preceded the Civil War, cities with over 2,500 inhabitants swelled in population ninefold, and those over 50,000 rocketed more than twelve-fold.[1] Most startling, the decade of the 1840s witnessed the unprecedented increase in urban population of over 92 percent, a rate of growth three times as high as population increments for rural areas. The watershed in American demography which brought the most significant shift in population from the farm to the city was not the fratricidal American Civil War, but rather what Walt Rostow has called the decades of economic takeoff in the antebellum era.

Before 1820 towns held little appeal for Americans. Contemporaries identified the destiny of their nation with the abundance of opportunity on the land. The farm, and not the city, was home for 95 percent of the populace. Consequently, during the colonial and early national periods the growth of cities barely kept pace with national population gains.

Starting in 1820, however, people poured into cities with a magnitude that was unprecedented. In the half-century between 1820 and 1870, urban population spiraled more than 1,300 percent, as compared to an overall population augmentation of approximately 300 percent. From that time forth the urban population ballooned at a rate so rapid in comparison with the whole national population that it signaled the transformation of the United States from an agricultural country to a commercial and industrial one. A nation which in 1820 was less than 8 percent urbanized became within fifty years a country with more than 25 percent of her people city dwellers. During these five decades of crucial urban development, towns grew into cities and cities into metropolises. Whereas in 1820 only New York and Philadelphia contained more than 100,000 inhabitants, by 1870 the number of large cities had mounted to fourteen, and New York City had evolved into a metropolitan agglomeration exceeding a million residents. While in 1820 no section of America was more than 25 percent urbanized, a half century later Massachusetts, Rhode Island, New York, and the District of Columbia had more than 50 percent of their citizens dwelling in cities.

The swelling current of newcomers to the city not only intensified the size of existing municipalities but also spawned new cities in every section of America. By 1870 the United States had ten times as many urban centers as had existed fifty years earlier. Already the Old Northwest had become 25 percent urban. Whereas formerly New Orleans was the only American city of more than 10,000 which did not hug the Atlantic coastline, by 1869, with the completion of the first transcontinental railroad, seven cities, each containing a population of more than 100,000, extended across the trans-Allegheny West. This constellation of regional cities, stretching to the Pacific, served to unify the national economy.[2] Thus by 1870, no matter how contemporaries might detest cities, they could no longer brush them aside. The drift townward had become a permanent and far-reaching change in American life.

During this half-century of galloping urban growth, the modern city took shape. Improvements in mass transit transformed once-compact, spatially diverse pedestrian towns into segregated business areas and downtown slums surrounded by sprawling residential suburbs. Within the city during this fifty-year period, the more affluent separated themselves physically from congested wards in the heart of the historic city and occupied distinctive neighborhoods which segregated them from the poor. The growth of urban-based factories imparted to cities with a strong commercial orientation a new and significant industrial dimension. Chaotic growth and the unprecedented onrush of foreigners to American shores changed once-homogeneous, well-ordered communities into teeming, physically dangerous centers unable to protect their citizens. Thus the half-century between 1820 and 1870 witnessed not only the establishment of every important American twentieth-century city but also the birth of the all-too-familiar unruly modern metropolis.

In what frame of mind did people uproot themselves from traditional moorings in the countryside to face life in a startling, new environment?

In what way did they adjust to the traumatic displacement from a known universe to one unknown?

In their pioneering book *The Intellectual versus the City*, Morton and Lucia White show how the intelligentsia reacted to the challenge posed by urbanization. In the Whites' opinion, America's literary heritage has consisted of fear and revulsion toward metropolitan life. Whether writers were romantics who rhapsodized about the beauties of a natural landscape or urbane men who embraced the values of a civilized society, the American city was a failure. It was either a decadent artifact or a stunted child of civilization. It would seem from the assembled evidence that any prospective migrant to the American city, after reading the books of the nation's literary giants, would have felt dread at the thought of leaving a benighted arcadia for "commerce, crime, crowds and conventionalism" in the nightmarish metropolis. Nor would readers find much comfort in the prospect of urban relocation if they read American poetry. For, according to the scholar Robert Walker, the nation's bards presented the metropolis as a chamber so reeking with vice that their rhymes formed a brief that encouraged farmers "to stay behind the plow."

Yet the census returns belie such conclusions. One wonders how such an enormous demographic shift could have occurred without some intellectual energy behind it. How could succeeding generations have kept coming to the city if no cultural forces eased the pain of adjusting to a new home? Did the attitudes of an alienated intellectual elite really reflect the opinions of society at large? Historians are beginning to recognize the need to examine not only the works of recognized literary luminaries but also the writings of leaders of popular culture. Frank Freidel has suggested that if historians were to dig into a lower tier of intellectual activity they would in fact find an enthusiastic response to the city. In spite of the shibboleth that America has been saddled with an antiurban tradition, Charles N. Glaab has argued that ordinary reading fare reveals an exuberant celebration of the American city as a symbol of progress and growth. Blaine A. Brownell has gone so far as to contend that, until most recently, popular thought throughout American history has viewed the city as the best of all possible worlds.

This book will test these various hypotheses by scrutinizing pulp literature in an era of dramatic demographic dislocation—namely, the period 1820-70. It will demonstrate that literary hacks offered a view of the city that was often at odds with the somber images painted by writers of belles-lettres. We will see how, to a significant degree, popularizers whetted the appetite of Americans for city life.

The publishing industry was attuned to the march townward between

1820 and 1870. During this half-century of accelerated urbanization the presses saturated the market with books that presented a hungry readership with information about the burgeoning cities of America. In fact, while in the entire span from 1774-1839 only 38 urban novels were published (20 of these being written in the 1830s), in the single decade of the 1840s writers flooded the market with 173 works of city fiction; in the 1850s, with yet another deluge of 167 books; and in the 1860s, will still another 97 novels. Equally significant, in this heyday of the western frontier more than three times as many books were written about life in the city as about conditions beyond the Appalachians. We may logically infer, then, that these urban books, disseminated to a mass audience, exerted a more powerful influence on fashioning the popular conception of the American city than the remote philosophic and literary disquisitions of intellectual men of letters.

Certainly, the drift of the population to urban centers signaled not only a new ecological reality in America but also an important affective one. As the sociologist Robert Park early realized, "the city [was] something more than . . . a mere constellation of institutions and administrative devices. . . . [It was] rather a state of mind."[3] Yet only a handful of scholars have studied the ideological dimension of urban history. As we have seen, the Whites have illuminated the antiurban attitudes of America's intellectuals and Robert Walker of the nation's poets. Sociologist Anselm Strauss in *Images of the American Cities* has revealed, embedded in writings which range from booster pamphlets to Protestant sermons, a variety of beliefs about different types of urban communities. Literary critic George Dunlap in *The City in the American Novel* has focused on conditions of city life described in novels set in New York, Philadelphia, and Boston, which he considered to have permanent artistic value. In contrast to his lack of concern with implicit psychological and social attitudes toward urbanization, literary analyst Janis Stout in *Sodoms in Eden* has appraised the response of antebellum belletristic and subliterary authors to the city as an "emblematic . . . moral landscape." None of these investigations, in spite of their many merits, has explored the way in which literature directed at a mass audience mirrored actual conditions of American urban society.

This work, which examines books written for the common man, has used a source long neglected by scholars with a traditional elitist bias. It takes stock of the fantasies of silent classes, people who are mute about their own experience. It analyzes a subliterature which Russel Nye in *The Unembarrassed Muse* considers remarkable for its unusual sensitivity to "the attitudes and concerns of the society for which it is produced." Thus, by tapping sources which we may safely presume shaped the

consciousness of ordinary men and women, it will attempt to reconstruct the image of the American city from the bottom up.

The books selected for investigation have been drawn at random from
a substantial portion of the urban prose listed in Lyle Wright's biblio-
graphic survey of American fiction. Of 462 books listed by Wright which
seem to deal with urban themes, I have selected 336 for historical analysis. However, in spite of its title, the compilation indiscriminately cites
many works that are not of a strictly fictional nature. For example,
Wright includes the "confidentials" of New York life narrated by
George G. Foster but excludes the equally important nonfictional
accounts offered by popular writers such as James Dabney McCabe,
Junius Henri Browne, and Matthew Hale Smith. I have, therefore,
examined well-known exposés not contained in the Wright bibliography
as well as the equally popular Horatio Alger stories. These tales, regarded by Wright as children's literature, nevertheless so strongly parallel
the plots and points of view of novels labeled as adult fiction that they
merit attention. Finally, plays performed on the urban stage offer more
data for analyzing recurring themes of city literature at mid-century.
To ascertain whether a different genre of popular culture corroborated
the picture of urban life presented in pulp prose, I made a limited
sampling of theatrical literature.

Examination of these various genres reveals a rather lopsided coverage
of American cities at mid-century. Approximately 50 percent of the
books written about urban life in this period were set in the Empire
City. Of 468 books written about life in the period 1820–70, including
those not listed in the Wright bibliography, 230 were specifically set
in New York. The only other metropolitan center to receive any comparable treatment was Boston, the locale of 59 works of popular prose.
Philadelphia, which won third place in literary attention, was the scene
of a mere 23 novels. Other urban centers received even scantier recognition. Our analysis of the image of the American city in pulp literature
must of necessity, therefore, rely upon sources which often focused
upon New York to the exclusion of other cities. In spite of my desire
to examine a roster of books set in various urban communities in the
period 1820–70, the preponderance of my illustrative examples are drawn
from literary descriptions of the largest and most important metropolis
in the western hemisphere.

The overwhelming majority of these books make few claims to
artistic merit. In contrast to the contemporary works of Nathaniel
Hawthorne, Edgar Allan Poe, and Herman Melville, the publications
examined for this study can most aptly be categorized as what Stuart
Hall and Paddy Whannel call "kitsch literature"—an essentially

"conventional art which restates in an intense form values and attitudes already known."[4] Written for the most part by professional authors who could churn out several novels in a year with little regard for delicacy of style or artistic invention, these books consistently used hackneyed plots, cardboard characterizations, improbable situations, and platitudinous language. One of these writers, Edward Zane Carroll Judson, authored a 610-page book in sixty-two hours. He said, "I push ahead as fast as I can, never blotting out anything and never making a correction or a modification." Another, Joseph Holt Ingraham, wrote 7 novels in 1843, 8 in 1844, 26 in 1845, and 11 in 1846. Henry Wadsworth Longfellow wrote of him, "A new American novelist has arisen; his name is Professor Ingraham. . . . He is tremendous—really tremendous. I think we may say that he writes the worst novels ever written by anybody. But they sell."[5]

Yet, according to such students of the mass media as John Cawelti, Dwight MacDonald, and Irving Howe, it is exactly books of this nature that best articulate a culture's continuing set of values. For unlike an elite literature which presents the reader with the personal vision of an artist and with disturbing new information about the world, pulp publications, manufactured impersonally by technicians for a mass audience, comfort the public by incorporating familiar, shared images and repeating received opinions. A collective product of society rather than the unique creation of an individual sensibility, they are cemented to the ideological clichés and sociological conditions of the culture in which they are produced. In contrast to literary masterpieces, which demand reflection on the part of the reader, the easily comprehended stereotypes and stock emotions in popular books reinforce the existing attitudes of the majority. Thus, according to sociologists Diana Laurenson and Alan Seingewood, they enter the public consciousness with a minimum of cerebral resistance.

For these very reasons the potboilers dismissed by literary critics because of their lack of artistic merit are of value to the social historian. As Arthur Schlesinger, Sr. pointed out in 1928, they can exert a more powerful impact upon society than the belletristic relics prized by the literary custodians of our culture. Serving as a mirror of the fears, frustrations, anxieties, and aspirations of the people who read them, they allow the historian to decipher the imaginative symbols by which the American urban community of the mid-nineteenth century sought to understand itself. For embedded in these long-neglected books are the attitudes and assumptions, the illusions and shared daydreams, of a society in crisis.

A word of caution. In our society reading is usually a solitary activity which leaves behind few traces useful to the historian. We have no archives to throw light on the way a piece of literature affected an earlier generation. Even where notations in a diary preserve the feelings of an individual about a particular book, we cannot infer that such a reaction was typical of the public at large. To the extent, then, that the response of mid-nineteenth-century audiences to popular urban literature is shrouded in obscurity, we cannot with certainty reconstruct the meaning that these books held for the people who read them. Despite this limitation, we can gauge the climate of opinion toward the city by examining a multitude of books whose configurations so astonishingly duplicate each other that we get a "Gallup poll" of "what readers accept[ed], what they excus[ed], and what they forb[ade]."[6] Clearly, repeated bombardment with certain images in the mass media indicates both "large public interest" and sufficiently wide circulation to ensure "effects on a wide scale."[7]

Until 1895, when *Bookman* began a list by checking with 100 book-shops in thirty different cities for their leaders, there were no reliable figures on the popularity of a publication. Newspapers did not yet keep accurate records of best sellers, and the records of most publishers of urban literature during the mid-nineteenth century are no longer extant. Thus the historian cannot know exactly how many people read a book or, for that matter, who read it. A classic could be purchased to serve as a status symbol in a properly equipped library or to be read avidly by many members of the family. Nor can one know whether pulp urban books were directed primarily to a rural or city audience or whether they were read by the group for whom they were intended. Likewise, the researcher faces the question of whether hack authors wrote on city themes in reaction to the popular interest in urban life or in response to the environment which was most familiar to them.

Equally confounding is the problem of the motivation of authors in writing exposés of city conditions. For instance, did an author reveal the vices of the metropolis in order to warn readers of the dangers in the town or to exploit sensational subject matter that would boost the sale of his books? Did he exhibit the hazards of urban conditions to frighten potential migrants from relocating in the metropolis, or did he disclose the cankers of the city in order to promote reform? Even if a writer did state a high-minded motivation in the preface or text of his book, can one be certain that this was his true purpose? No less problematic is the impact of these books on the behavior of contemporaries.

However intriguing these considerations, they go beyond the scope of this topographical survey of popular urban literature. Because we are dealing with social and psychological attitudes, we will not use a strict chronological approach. Nor will we probe the biographies of books about which so little can be known. Instead we will allow publications written for a mass audience to serve as a window through which we can view the cultural mentality of a generation shaken by accelerated and disruptive urbanization. Although we recognize that this window is clouded with the prejudices of the people who wrote about the city, we are less interested in finding a literal transcription of the social and physical ambience of mid-nineteenth-century cities than in examining refractions of an emerging urban self-consciousness.

In a day without movies, television, radio, and comic strips, books provided the most common form of leisure entertainment. Already at mid-century *Harper's Magazine,* in a congratulatory mood, proclaimed, "Literature has gone in pursuit of the million, penetrated highways and hedges, pressed its way into cottages, factories, omnibuses, and railroad cars, and become the most cosmopolitan thing of the century."[8] Reading was becoming a national habit. While population and national income nearly doubled during the decades of the forties and fifties, the value of books more than trebled, and the number of titles multiplied twenty-fold. Samuel Goodrich, the publisher, estimated gross sales of books in America at $2.5 million in 1820; $12.5 million in 1850; and $20 million in 1860. The *Western Literary Journal* called the United States "a nation of . . . novel readers." In 1854 the author George W. Curtis declared that almost as soon as a book was printed it reached a circulation of five thousand.

The era of the common man resounded not only in the cries of "Tippecanoe and Tyler, too!" but also in the coming of age of the popular book. For the first time economical methods of production and distribution enabled a mass audience to have access to the printed word. Beginning in 1842, books began to be printed at a low price. Technological innovations such as type casting, the rapid Napier and Hoe cylinder press, and inexpensive paper produced by Foundrinier machines all reduced the cost of production. The developments of stereotyping and electrotyping, combined with folding and sewing machines for binding, further lowered the cost of printing so that, by mid-century, books could be produced as efficiently as clothes and hardware.[9] The transportation revolution meant that literature could be distributed to a farther-flung audience, while the growth of cities in the West provided retail facilities for bringing books to a much larger market than was possible on isolated farms. Oil lamps and gas lighting further democratized the book by increasing the possible number of reading hours each day.

When engineering was combined with sharp business practice, savings could be passed on to the reader. Printed as "extras" of a newspaper, fiction was mailed out in coverless editions that took advantage of low postal rates. To meet the paperback challenge, book publishers like Harper and Brothers cut prices to twenty-five cents for soft-cover books. Further incentive for cheap publication came in 1845 when Congress reduced the price of mailing books. Although dime novels did not flood the market until 1870, enterprising publishers like Dick and Fitzgerald, Peterson, and Harper and Appleton continued to compete with each other in the years that followed the bargain book outburst of the early forties by offering reading fare at prices under one dollar.[10] Such houses knew how to exploit readership potential by adjusting their titles and prices to various audiences, advertising in national magazines and newspapers, and distributing their wares through subscription agents and specialized booksellers, as well as by sponsoring authors who pandered to popular tastes. In 1855 the *American Publishers' Circular* commented on the zeal for reading among chambermaids and sewing women and concluded, "In no other country in the world is the condition and prospects of the book publisher so secure as this. . . . Whatever, in the shape of a book is printed here, will find a market."[11]

Only when new publishing techniques mated with democratic social reform, however, could a mass media entertainment industry be sired. By the nineteenth century writers were liberated from aristocratic patronage and could cater to a growing urban middle class with sufficient leisure time to read. With authors' royalties booming at 33 1/3 percent in 1857, writing evolved into a profession which yielded its practitioners a respectable income. Literary production spurted between 1825 and 1850, when the extension of free public schools accompanied a threefold increase in the number of circulating libraries. The development of lyceums brought thousands in contact with spokesmen of middle-class culture. Proliferation of other educational facilities like reading rooms, night schools, secondary schools, women's academies, and colleges helped create the most numerous reading public the world had ever known. These people were eager to improve their mind and turned to the printed word as a means of becoming what was generally thought of as cultured. Consequently, books assumed an importance in the life of the average person as never before. The growth of a numerous but uncritical reading audience had an unprecedented impact upon the publishing industry which Arthur Schlesinger considered "comparable only with the invention of moveable-type printing in the middle of the fifteenth century."

The spectacular increase of population in cohesive urban units made it even easier for a growing corps of professional writers to communicate with a large audience: "Bookstores could prosper in the cities but seldom in the country; an urban culture was more hospitable to reading than a rural one" and assured "a mass readership capable of escalating faster than its own numbers."[12] The book became a product suitable for mass consumption. Hacks, commissioned by book publishers to satisfy the leisure time needs of a new mass audience, aimed to please the customer and saturated the marketplace with entertaining tales of the city.

2

HAZARDS OF CITY LIFE

American popular books during the period 1820–70 chronicled the stormy uncertainties of urban life. As we have seen, during these decades the urban population expanded at the most frenzied rate the nation had ever known. Cities were growing feverishly, mindlessly. In unprecedented numbers migrants from the countryside and foreign lands elbowed into the core of the historic city, quickly straining available housing space. The crush of newcomers also overwhelmed existing public services. The streets were snarled with traffic; police and fire protection were woefully inadequate; water and sewerage failed to provide elementary standards of hygiene. Spiraling crime, violence, and pauperism plagued urbanites. Juvenile delinquency skyrocketed; mountains of garbage accumulated; riots ripped once-cohesive communities apart. The impact of a proliferating and increasingly heterogeneous population, mushrooming rates of internal residential mobility, and the failure of middle-class norms to control the poor all baffled urban societies. In short, by 1820 sprawling, diverse, inflammable cities had replaced the well-regulated, stable urban order of an earlier era.

Popular literature written during this period of exploding urban growth expressed the pain and anxiety of a society in motion. It warned a people who were uprooting themselves from familiar rural surroundings that a world of woe might await them in the strange and frightening cities of the land. For a readership that was hungry for information about the rising metropolitan centers of the nation, it catalogued many problems of municipal life. Whether fire or crime, riots or pollution, the "shadows" of urban existence were exposed in lurid detail by hack writers. Yet, as we shall see, these very hazards made the city a living theater—part melodrama, part romance, and part farce.

In cities afflicted by haphazard growth a basic human requirement like satisfactory shelter was a scarce commodity. Slums scarred the urban landscape. Housing construction could not keep pace with galloping population increments. As real estate costs spiraled, the poor crammed themselves into incredibly small spaces, occupying converted warehouses, abandoned private homes, and jerry-built tenements. Although rents were high, apartments were dark, staircases tottering, windows broken. Dwellings lacked even the most basic rudiments of sanitation. In the rear stood filthy toilets which lacked doors and were usually out of repair. Here children played, and women hung up wash which dangled into excrement from the overflowing privies.

Those not constricted by indigency to the slums nevertheless found themselves in a housing vise. Unable to afford marble-fronted mansions and unwilling to live in blighted buildings, many people with moderate incomes had to secure lodgings in hotels and boarding houses. Indeed, this practice became so widespread in the mid-nineteenth century that urbanites were sometimes labeled a boarding people and New York City a vast boarding house. Popular books did not neglect to unfold this particular misery of urban life. They relieved the reader of the delusion that such accommodations would provide him with decent quarters and companionship. To judge from the fate of fictional boarding house dwellers, his health would be injured by irregular meals, his manners and morals by an ever-present bottle of liquor at a communal table, and his peace of mind by enforced association with a menagerie of inmates living in an "indiscriminately gotten-together community." He might be assigned to a narrow room on a high floor with a thin partition and a lumpy mattress that gave shelter to an army of bedbugs. At night he could amuse himself killing cockroaches.[1] Nor would residence in overbooked hotels increase his comfort. He could be treated to a bed in a public parlor or to a room that had to be shared with strangers. Even if he secured private rooms in a first-class hotel, he might sacrifice his health and marriage to a round of glittering, dissipated parties.[2]

Popular literary descriptions of the dining fare offered in city restaurants and boarding houses corroborate the claim of Robert Riegel, the social historian, that American food during this period was bearable only if bolted down quickly and flushed out with whiskey. The journalist George G. Foster alleged that the typical commercial eating house was perfumed with burnt grease and decorated with tablecloths that looked as if they "had done duty in a surgeon's dissecting room."[3] An anatomist of boarding house life, Thomas Gunn, asserted that the bill of fare in that institution offered nothing more palatable than greasy soup, tough meat served with a gravy made from the fragments left on the boarders' plates, and potatoes "with more eyes than Argus."[4]

The middle-class urbanite who sought to escape the hazards of residence in a hotel or a boarding house found other frustration in the rental of a private house. After hunting through a maze of brick edifices, he would find only overpriced quarters. To make ends meet, he would have to sublet part of his dwelling to another party.

Nor could he rest once he located a decent home. As Peter Knights has demonstrated, the antebellum urban American was a person on the move, at least geographically. In New York City, in particular, house hunting was an annual ritual. The expiration of all leases on May 1 allowed landlords to demand a staggering hike in rent. Seba Smith's *May-Day in New York* and Lydia Maria Child's *Letters from New York* humorously explored the May Day plight of the residentially mobile city dweller. The tenant foolish enough to resist the landlord's greed was obliged to spend his leisure hours searching for new quarters only to find his own home invaded by hordes of prospective occupants. Now forced to vacate his dwelling for one less comfortable and more expensive, he had to battle an entire metropolis to secure a moving van on May Day. Once in his new flat, he found that peace still eluded him. For there he would collide with the old tenants, still packing their household belongings. Yet to the writer Junius Henri Browne this "annual vacation of abode" represented something more than a needless discomfort of urban life; it embodied in excess America's "fondness for change."

While the search for housing space in crowded cities spurred the citizens into frenzied activity, the problem of providing urbanites with satisfactory sanitation service stirred municipal authorities to adopt measures which can be described charitably as torpid. According to historians Lawrence Larsen and John Duffy, who have examined public health policies in mid-nineteenth-century urban Amrica, antebellum cities were overwhelmed by a "sea of garbage." They exuded a bucolic stench. Tenements adjoined stables, distilleries, and bone-boiling establishments. Their yards teemed with dogs, chickens, horses, and swine. The most congested areas were without adequate sewage. Cesspools overflowed, and human wastes drained into alleys where children played. Tenement dwellers, unaccustomed to personal hygiene, littered the gutters with their garbage. The air reeked with the smells of slaughter houses, gasworks, and the uncollected bodies of dead animals. In wet weather mud choked the thoroughfares, and in dry, clouds of dust enveloped the streets. Horses, the mainstay of public transportation, excreted mounds of manure which swarmed with flies. Removal of wastes was left to private contractors, who permitted the excrement they collected to spill back onto the streets in order to allow their horses to move more quickly with a lighter burden. Battalions of pigs, which served as an adjunct to the sanitation department, matched the swinishness of human scavengers. Charles Dickens, as well as many other visitors, was appalled by the swarms of hogs that came and went as they pleased in American cities, "mingling with the best society on an equal, if not superior footing."[5]

Popular novelists documented the scandalous problem of urban pollution. They depicted the city as an unwholesome environment plagued by filth, odors, and traffic congestion. With its putrid smells, dark smoke, and knee-deep filth, it seemed to be a hatchery of poisoned air. Writers like Edward Zane Carroll Judson, Ann Sophia Stephens, Henry Morford, and Horatio Alger, to name but a few, noted that, despite the great wealth of the American city, its sanitation service was dependent on the hit-and-miss collection activities of wandering city hogs; their unsystematic eating patterns allowed heaps of garbage to accumulate on the streets. Novelists pictured the city in its most fearsome aspect during the sweltering heat of the summer, when a foul miasma arose from the reeking gutters, creating clouds of poison over the city.[6]

In such an environment epidemics became another scourge. Among the most dreaded was cholera, the "poor man's plague," endemic to those living in filthy hovels. While the rich idled the warm months away in fashionable watering resorts, those who could not escape the noisome atmosphere of the city became subject to the fatal pestilence. Novels like A. Sylvan Penn's *My Three Neighbors in the Queen City*, Richard B. Kimball's *Undercurrents of Wall-Street*, and Azel S. Roe's *Like and Unlike* accurately recorded the disproportionate death toll suffered by the urban poor. William A. Caruthers in *The Kentuckian in New-York* depicted New York during the cholera epidemic of 1832 as a silent city, forsaken by its residents: "The throng, and hurry, and . . . the pleasure of business have changed into the throng and hurry and misery of fear. Carts that formerly bore merchandise . . . are now carrying [the furniture] of flying families to their country seats. . . . The theatres and places of amusement are closed. . . . The only business which thrives is that of the apothecaries and coffin-makers" (pp. 22-23). While the Asiatic plague struck down the unfortunate inhabitants of metropolitan cities in the North, Edward Durell in *New Orleans As I Found It* recounted how yellow fever ravaged urban dwellers in the South.

In a novel published one year after the devastating cholera epidemic of 1849, Charles Averill vocalized the anger many Americans harbored toward the medical profession during the scourge. We know from the research of Richard Shryock and Charles Rosenberg that the conduct of numerous doctors during the pestilence brought their prestige to a new low. Averill, capitalizing on the public's eagerness to believe a rumor that doctors had spread the disease to elevate their income and reputation, charged in *The Cholera-Fiend: or The Plague Spreaders of New York* that a quack doctor and an unscrupulous clergyman had secretly opened the coffins of cholera victims, thereby allowing deadly vapors to poison the metropolis.

The fiction of the day informed readers of the hazards not only of air contamination but also of noise pollution. The hero or heroine who embarked upon a journey to the metropolis was awed by the hum of municipal life.[7] Din continually poured forth from the concentrated human activity—the craftsman at his workbench, the newsboy hawking his papers to the passers-by, the cartmen clanking their drays through cobbled streets, or vendors peddling their wares to the passing throng.

In the dirge of complaints about the city, traffic represented yet another insufferable irritant. The streets were choked with vehicles. Whether one was a pedestrian crossing the street or a passenger riding an omnibus, one risked life and limb in the helter-skelter madness of urban congestion. To traverse a famous street like Broadway was a veritable feat, in the popular book. Wherever one looked, one saw handcarts snarled between drays and stages. To judge from urban novels like Alger's *Rough and Ready*, Winter Summerton's *Will He Find Her?* and Henry L. Williams's *Gay Life in New York*, Victorian etiquette did not extend to proper manners on the congested streets of the city. In these books drivers exchanged oaths and blows when stalled cabs, coaches, and stages collided on packed metropolitan thoroughfares. Yet the commotion of the city was not without charm. While Edgar Allan Poe in his *Doings of Gotham* found the shrieks of fishmongers, charcoal-men, and organ grinders jarring to his nerves, more obscure urban novelists like Roe, Mrs. Elizabeth Oakes Smith, and Charles Gayler celebrated the aural commotion of the metropolis as a man-made phenomenon that rivaled the "roar of the sea." Their descriptions of massive traffic jams and the rumble of the multitude conveyed a sense of wonder at the incredible tempo of urban life.

While frontiersmen might ride wild horses on the western prairie, the city resident who entered an omnibus faced perils which made him an adventurer in broadcloth. Popular writers alerted their readers to the hazards of urban America's first mass transit system, a system which historian Glen E. Holt agrees was uncomfortable, overcrowded, and unsafe. James D. McCabe, Frank St. Clair, and Edward S. Gould revealed that the passenger's dignity was assaulted by rude conductors, his eyes by filthy cars, his purse by pickpockets, his person by rough passengers who threatened to press him to death at rush hour, and his life by drivers who whirled their cars at dizzying speeds through the city. For someone seeking sensations a 6 1/2-cent investment bought an omnibus ride, a dangerous race over slippery pavement between drivers of rival lines.

Transit also offered those who relied upon private conveyances the excitement of reckless driving. Warren Baer in *Champagne Charlie* depicted dapper men-about-town racing their trotters along Broadway. A bet to surpass all previous records spurred them on, even if it meant dashing into handcarts, colliding with trucks, and knocking down pedestrians.

To ride a cab, one needed a guidebook, as hackmen were one more brigade in the army of urban scoundrels. Often in the pay of unscrupulous hotelkeepers, they would, for a commission, steer the ignorant immigrant to outrageously priced lodgings where the newcomer was cheated of all he possessed. Others charged the "verdant" for a tour of the entire metropolis, when all the stranger had requested was a ride that necessitated passage through a few short streets. Yet anyone who took the trouble to acquaint himself with the practices of the city could discover in George Foster's *Fifteen Minutes around New York* that the municipal authorities were anxious to protect the tourist. If a passenger felt that he had been overcharged, he could report the offender's number, receive a refund, and enjoy the satisfaction of seeing the trickster fined five dollars.

Popular exposés not only unfolded for the reader the numerous ways by which urban existence could rob a person of his peace of mind but also revealed the countless criminal practices which could deprive him of both his purse and his life. Lawlessness was obviously no preserve of the frontier. While James Fenimore Cooper successfully employed the drama of the forest, other novelists wrote adventure stories of cities filled with ruffian gangs, impoverished families, and ruthless criminal organizations. As lower-class types of crime accounted for an increasing number of arrests between 1820 and 1870, popular writers exploited the public's fear of violence and flooded the market with books concerning law-breakers bred in the slums.

Novelists, startled by the high incidence of mugging in mid-nineteenth-century cities, showed that citizens had to arm themselves if they wanted to step out at night. City streets were dark. According to both Edgar Allan Poe and Charles Swan, the gas companies were at fault. The profit-hungry utility firms neglected to illuminate the sidewalk lamps whenever the almanac predicted a full moon, in total disregard of actual weather conditions. Consequently, thieves found cover on dark city byways. Novelists like George Thompson, Charles Burdett, and J. Wimpleton Wilkes, as well as many others, suggested the sinister quality of urban life in their numerous scenes of criminals garroting men and raping women after sundown.[8]

Sometimes, though, popular authors portrayed crime on the streets as an undercover operation. In Benjamin Barker's *Clarilda* and John Neal's *True Womanhood,* pickpockets waited for the unwary on crowded corners and public vehicles, and even in church. In fact, according to confidential writer McCabe, the Catholic houses of worship were a favorite haunt for purse snatchers. While ladies kneeled devoutly in prayer, rogues relieved them of their valuables.

At a time when burglary was swelling to a flood tide, popular writers reinforced the contemporary stereotype which viewed the sophisticated house thief as an uninhibited individual who took what he wanted when he wanted it. This glamorous villain reduced robbery to a scientific operation, obtaining wax impressions of the locks on supposedly secure doors and timing his entry to avoid detection. A case in point is the character Bristol Bill, an English burglar whose exploits were celebrated not only in New York newspapers and the *Police Gazette* but also in the novels of George Thompson, a Boston journalist who, after a personal interview with the crack thief, embroidered romantic tales with his gallantry, expertise, and daring.[9]

In a period of booming lawlessness the existence of covert crime excited the wonder of writers no less than did the flamboyant capers of a Bristol Bill. Popular writers like Burdett, Joseph Holt Ingraham, and Robert M. Bird, to mention but a small sample, showed the adeptness of white collar workers at embezzlement and defalcation. In the urban novel trusted employees frequently falsified books and forged notes in order to enjoy a glamorous life. Even eminent bankers siphoned depositors' funds into their own purses, replacing the stolen monies with counterfeit coins. In fact, counterfeiting seemed to be as commonplace as embezzlement. Esteemed men were portrayed cooperating with criminal cohorts to pass fraudulent bills into circulation.[10]

Among the metropolitan centers of the nation New York City was considered the capital of crime. Here ruffians could rob men in broad daylight, sexually assault women in horsecars, and dispose of mangled corpses in the East River. According to Henri Foster's shocker *Ellen Grafton,* it was a city where men undertook any job for money, even if that job were murder. In fact, John D. Vose in his journalistic exposé *Seven Nights in Gotham* alleged that sixteen murders had occurred in the Empire City in the short space of nine months.

In addition to the increased incidence of homicide, organized crime grew alarmingly. Uprooted vagrants, drifting from smaller urban communities to great metropolitan centers, caused gang membership to soar. In 1855 an official report estimated the number of hooligans affiliated with criminal groups in New York City to be approximately thirty thousand. With impunity these thugs terrorized the city, plundering stores and residences.[11] Such writers of sensational urban fiction as Judson, Thompson, and Isaac Baldwin, responding to the public's interest in this phenomenon, gingered their stories with the ganglanders' patois and conspiracies. They showed that syndicated criminal organizations hired outlaws to commit arson and murder, steal horses, and hold up banks. Quite accurately they depicted many of these professional thieves as English. They did not blame the Irish, whose record of arrests was soaring for petty infractions but not for professional, serious offenses.

Even more disturbing than the rise of professional crime was the lack of safety on the streets. As urban communities disintegrated under the impact of population growth, ethnic diversity, and an eroding family structure, the incidence of public disorder mounted. Citizens became increasingly nervous about the rise of juvenile delinquency. Gangs of savage youngsters, spawned in the slums, banded together as Plug Uglies, Bowery Boys, Dead Rabbits, and Roach Guards. They periodically plunged cities into uncontrollable violence, rioting against flour merchants, blacks, abolitionists, the Irish, and hapless citizens who wished to exercise their own judgment at the polling booths.

Pulp writers were as impressed as Charles Loring Brace, founder of the Children's Aid Society, with the threat to the community posed by these aimless youths, the "dangerous classes" who stomped their rivals with hobnail boots, gouged out eyes, and tore off ears. They were a portent of social anarchy, a sign that the American dream of an affluent, harmonious society had run aground. Like Brace, popular authors acknowledged that juvenile desperados were victims of overcrowded tenements and parental neglect; but they were as interested in exploiting a sensational contemporary phenomenon as they were in reforming it. Butcher boys, clad in undershirts and armed with iron pipes, brickbats, and razor-sharp knives, provided a savage human component to the "mysterious" city.

Equally ferocious were the women attached to the gangs. Authors did not have far to look for models of women who mocked the idea of the gentler sex. Edward Zane Carroll Judson, a habitué of gangland and cohort of the Bowery Boys, used female celebrities of the New York waterfront—amazons like Gallus Mag, Sadie the Goat, and Hellcat Maggie—

o show that in the depraved environment of the city women too were
a lawless element, expert at wielding a bludgeon or pistol.

Although these books, curiously, ignored the spectacular labor riots,
ich-poor riots, and race riots that erupted in Philadelphia, Cincinnati,
and New York City during this period, scenes of young hooligans fighting
or fiefdoms within the city confirmed for readers that violence was
becoming endemic to the urban community. In Boston gangs battled
or territorial hegemony over the Commons. In Philadelphia hoodlums
defaced the city with graffiti. In New York's Astor Place a mob, lurching
"like wild animals blinded by passion," hurt innocent bystanders when
it protested a supposed insult to the nation's honor. But no matter the
city or the gang, popular books that ranged from Ingraham's *Alice May
and Bruising Bill* to William Ritner's *Great Original and Entrancing
Romance* branded the volunteer fire "laddies" as wild Indians who were
bringing armed warfare to the city's streets.[12]

Numerous eruptions of mob violence and a spiraling rate of urban
rime convinced contemporaries that unpaid, un-uniformed, unpro-
essionalized police departments were failing to protect the physical
ecurity of citizens. What had worked for homogeneous colonial communities was no longer viable in heterogeneous mushrooming cities. A
mall constabulary body lacked the manpower to patrol all the streets.
Officers in mufti, claiming that uniforms would debase them into
"liveried lackies," frequently ran away from dangerous situations. A
itizen force designed to protect eighteenth-century Americans from
tanding armies and paid bodies of government officials lacked the
raining for crowd control. When riots broke out, municipalities had to
ummon the militia to restore order.

Although the job of maintaining law and order was becoming much
more demanding by the mid-nineteenth century, as James F. Richardson
and Roger Lane have shown, police departments lacked the autonomy
ecessary to serve the public good. They functioned as creatures of the
arty in power. To obtain appointment to the force, a man was
equired to bribe the captain or alderman of his district. Poor health,
ge, or illiteracy was no bar to service. Once he was on the force, the
olitical machine determined an individual's tour of duty, retention,
and promotion, and it could also protect him from disciplinary action;
ut when the party lost its control of City Hall, he was out of a job.
ew appointees remained long enough to learn their jobs well.

Nor did municipalities train officers or keep records of meritorious
ervice. Indeed, officers too vigilant in enforcing the law found themselves

assigned to trivial tasks. What mattered most for a successful police career was to curry the favor of the political group in power, a feat most readily accomplished by remaining blind and deaf to violations of the law. Thus despite a welter of antivice legislation, saloonkeepers, prostitutes, abortionists, and gamblers flourished in American cities. As Seymour Mandelbaum has ably demonstrated, bribery was the grease that oiled the political machine. The police, left with discretionary authority, selectively enforced the law, raiding only those brothels and bars that failed to support the politicians.

Few patrolmen viewed their job as a calling of disinterested service. Until the 1830s the gifts of grateful citizens constituted the patrolman's only renumeration; thus, the only way of making a living was to restore stolen property. Those who concentrated on preventing crime and apprehending thieves had virtue as their only reward. Those who dedicated themselves to furthering their private interests were ingenious in enhancing their incomes. By allowing criminals to turn over their booty and then go free, for instance, they received payment from both the thief and the victim; by colluding with burglars to hold up stores, they easily recovered stolen merchandise and split the reward with their underworld cohorts.

Little wonder, then, that a large body of popular literature pictured the police as prone to crime as those they were hired to thwart. In the eyes of Ritner and Judson policemen were cowards, loafers, and grafters who openly winked at lawbreaking, "looking at crime through *golden spectacles.*" Claimed Judson in *G'hals of New York,* "Thief-catching-while it [was] a perfectly *safe* business, [was] in a pecuniary point of view, a far more profitable calling than the criminal profession itself" (pp. 128–29). In his *Mysteries and Miseries of New Orleans,* it was difficult indeed for pickpockets to earn their daily bread in peace, so plagued were they by "sharks" in blue uniform demanding a cut. In order to escape arrest, they were obliged to disgorge almost all of their booty, and when released by one corrupt officer they were certain to be held up by yet another, demanding due compensation for silence. In New York City law-enforcement officials were active in chasing homeless orphans from the streets and passive in protecting the citizenry from dangerous riots. The writer Augustine Joseph Hickey Duganne, who shared the Protestant reformers' scorn for a force which did not enforce antivice statutes, sniped at policemen for "loitering in the purlieus of taverns . . . winking at open violations of the law . . . , suborning corruption in the ballot box" and absenting themselves when "riot endangered [the] peace of the . . . city."[13]

Popular writers, echoing a common sentiment of the day, usually considered watchmen to offer as little protection as the municipal police

Charged with the task of protecting the city from sundown to sunrise, they could not cope with their increased responsibilities in the 1830s and 1840s. Understaffed and underpaid, the watch recruited poor men who worked during the day and ne'er-do-wells who had little shame about receiving fifty cents to a dollar a night for getting drunk and sleeping on the job. To obtain appointment, a man simply had to give loyal service to the party in power. The leatherheads—so called for the leather caps they wore—were infamous for neglecting their duty, and a popular expression of the day was "lazy as a leatherhead." Their incompetence was matched by their venality. When they roused themselves from their torpor, they concentrated on earning supplementary witness fees by arresting the poor for trivial offenses.

Popular literature registered the public's disgust with this obsolete institution. It presented the watch as merciless to pathetic women and homeless children, tender and obsequious to the rich. "Worshippers of Baal," they valued people by how much they could pay. In popular novels like Duganne's *Two Clerks,* St. Clair's *Six Days in the Metropolis,* and Alexander Lovett Stimson's *Easy Nat,* they were visible in packs of three or four on well-lit corners, while totally absent from dark, dangerous streets.

Significantly, during the 1850s, when criticism of the police was reaching epidemic proportions, popular books focused on a dishonest constabulary as a favorite explanation of urban disorder. In George Foster's novel *Celio* a policeman allows a crucial witness in a murder case to go free for a fee, although this may send an innocent man to the gallows. In anonymously authored *Old Haun* a law-enforcement officer allows a kidnapper to escape for a $200 charge even though such connivance may endanger the life of a child. In Osgood Bradbury's *Female Depravity* a constable with a name suitable for the profession, Grabwell, in consideration for payment from the girl's parents rescues their virginal daughter from the clutches of a madam. He then collects a second commission by threatening to send the harridan to the Tombs unless she bribes him and his fellow arresting officers.

Popular literature assailed policemen not only for dishonesty but also for cowardice. Despite the outstanding reputation enjoyed by the Boston police by the 1850s for their professionalism and maintenance of civic order, for example, Stimson remained unimpressed. In *Easy Nat* a Boston policeman, hired to find an assassin, gives up the chase after a week even though his client will be executed if the true murderer is not brought to justice. Similarly, Thompson in *City Crimes* and Justin Jones in *Big Dick* echoed the oft-repeated jibe that one could never find a constable when danger struck. Their protagonists, despairing of effective police protection, chase after criminals in slums where patrolmen dare not penetrate.

While contemporaries lashed out against the police in the 1830s and 1840s for their corruption and inability to maintain law and order, by the 1850s and 1860s they inveighed against them for their brutality. They were acting like an alien army in the slums, showing little respect for the civil liberties of the poor. Unable to command respect by the dignity of their behavior, they tried to impose it by force. Popular novels such as the anonymously authored *Match Girl* and Eleanor Ames's *Up Broadway* reinforced the stereotype of the policeman as an individual who extracted bribes from brothelkeepers, smoked "segars" on duty, and bullied the poor.

In particular, the Irish recruits to the police force, although as yet only a minority, were linked with official violence. Popular writers pictured these appointees as stupid hirelings of the party in power, likely to provoke riots by their insolent, swaggering behavior. Uneducated and brutal, they persecuted helpless children, infirm women, and native Americans who had committed no offense. A portrait of Finnigan, one such Irishman in Thompson's *The Brazen Star,* revealed a vulgarian who "never arrested a brother Irishman, if he could possibly avoid it. Armed with a cane, and generally rather more than half drunk, he lost no opportunity to display his authority, committing savage assaults upon little boys who were playing in the streets, and ordered peaceable men to 'move on' with the air of a monarch" (p. 23). Thus, despite several reforms inaugurated in the mid-nineteenth century to professionalize police work, many popular authors regarded law-enforcement officials as unreliable, corrupt bullies who belonged on "a hangman's rope."

Examination of pulp urban literature reveals, however, that the image of the mid-nineteenth-century policeman was neither one of unrelieved villainy nor of untarnished virtue. Already the detective story was becoming the Iliad of urban fiction and the sleuth the Hector of the metropolis. As cities established detective bureaus in the 1840s, the criminal investigator became a glamorous figure about whom the public wanted to learn more. A school of popular authors sought to satisfy this curiosity and wrote romantic detective legends, showing how the sleuth combined intelligence and daring in his struggle against crime. Fearless in his discharge of duty, he traced thieves to their dens and joined cutthroat bands incognito. A master of cloak-and-dagger ploys, he shadowed suspects with his hat drawn low and collar raised high, confounding his enemies by using a disguised voice and false whiskers. A pioneer in applying technology to the service of law enforcement, he used the telegraph for setting up a dragnet of wanted persons and the daguerreotype for establishing a rogues' gallery of desperate characters.[14]

Nor was the detective the only exemplary guardian of the law. As Lane has demonstrated, the police, more than any other civic agents, were in close contact with the misery of the rupturing metropolis and could help the slum dweller with prosaic social problems. This fact was not lost upon some popular authors, who took inventory of the important community work performed by the police department. Novelists like Alger, James Maitland, Ann Sophia Stephens, and John Bell Bouton, as well as other writers, cast law-enforcement personnel in the role of welfare workers who provided shelter and food to the destitute. Such characters tramped the sidewalks of the city at all hours and in all types of weather, spending their off hours in nighttime vigils to prevent crime and their days in efforts to rehabilitate the wayward.[15]

While it would await the twentieth century for a professionalized, politically independent force to emerge, by the 1860s municipalities had instituted reforms to correct the vagaries of individual policemen. Inspired by the new prestige of the army during the Civil War period, the police adopted the ideal of a paramilitary organization with uniforms and military titles for officers. Cops—so called because of their use of star-shaped copper insignia in lieu of uniforms—were replaced by professional, uniformed officials, and the force was removed from the control of corrupt aldermen. As guardians of the metropolis, forced to meet satisfactory character requirements, pass a rigorous examination, and adhere to a strict system of discipline, policemen gained new stature in several popular books. St. Clair congratulated the Boston police for their efficiency, intelligence, and humanitarianism. Novelist Judson and non-fiction writer McCabe both applauded the New York metropolitan police for making an essential municipal service into a model of political independence and professionalism. The near-best-seller *Sunshine and Shadow in New York* by Matthew Hale Smith bragged in 1868: "No city in the world, except London and Paris, has a police which, in efficiency, discipline and character, equals that of New York. . . . New York is the home of the most daring and desperate criminals, who come from all parts of the world. Over two thousand men, efficient, brave and well disciplined . . . guard our homes, make life safe, and property secure" (pp. 183–84). Indeed, as the values of authority, discipline, and standardization assumed growing importance in the post–Civil War era, popular books accorded a new respect to the more vigorously constituted law-enforcement departments.

Even if police service improved, municipal government seemed a conspicuous failure of urban life. As both Mandelbaum and Alexander Callow have demonstrated, cities had outgrown their administrative structures. Urban governments were little more than patchwork quilts of independent sovereignties not accountable for their policies or subject to any central authority. Power was fragmented and lines of responsibility a tangled web of overlapping jurisdictions. Aldermen and supervisors ran their districts like feudal duchies. Such administrative muddle invited dishonesty, and political machines moved in to fill the vacuum. The boss could provide the services the official government had failed to render. By giving extralegal doles to the swelling legions of the poor and bestowing franchises on urban construction projects to entrepreneurs who saw the mushrooming metropolis as a field of economic profit, the boss would both enrich himself and make of municipal government an engine of power and graft. Making the slums his political citadel, he traded jobs, relief, and good times for the vote of the immigrant. Finding urban improvements a lucrative source of extortion, he exchanged contracts for paving streets and establishing transportation lines for the bribes of businessmen.

The cost of government skyrocketed, and the dishonesty and violence used to control the electoral process disturbed contemporaries. Bruisers packed the primaries. The scum of the city intimidated peaceable citizens into voting the party line, and on election day gangs of ruffians slugged at each other for control of the polls. Repeaters caused more votes to be returned than there were registered citizens. From their headquarters in the saloons, ward heelers set up naturalization factories to turn out the immigrant vote and recruited cartloads of men to cheer at mass meetings, march in parades, and serve as "shoulder-hitters." The police, dependent for their own tenure on the good will of aldermen, allowed gang leaders to be above the law.

Long before Lincoln Steffens indicted city politics for dishonesty, many popular authors exposed the schemes of political rings to feed from the public trough. Anticipating the reformist impulse of civic organizations like the Citizens' Association and the Union League Club formed in the 1860s, novelist Gould spoke of "sneaking scoundrels" who robbed honest citizens "under the cover of law."[16] Laying bare the mesh of municipal improvement programs which provided politicians with kickbacks, novelist Gayler and nonfiction writer McCabe both asserted that men in positions of public trust were selling city property at bargain prices, awarding to friends contracts that had not yet been legally advertised, and purchasing worthless goods from confederates at an exorbitant cost to the city treasury. They showed how liberal loans to the mayor, aldermen, and councilmen allowed enterprising citizens to obtain public transit franchises. Satirist William W. Howe revealed that contracts for paving streets could provide amazingly high returns. All an ingenious gentleman need do was to find an obliging official who would alter a few figures on the number of avenues that were actually paved: "Surely it [was] not stealing to draw lines with a quill dipped in ink" (p. 88).

The machine politician of the city figured as a familiar character in popular urban literature. The composite portrait that emerges is one of a scoundrel willing to grovel his way into high office. Unctuous and openhanded to voters in his ward, at least before election day, he was overbearing and tightfisted to distressed people who were without the franchise. Such officials, according to both Stephens and the anonymous author of *Florence De Lacey*, won their posts by hiring Irish toughs to scatter the opposition from the polls. In addition, "a judicious distribution of money and liquors, a notoriety for street fights, a singular talent for profanity, and an unstinted adulation of the basest classes of the community won for [them], in succession, some of the best prizes of the Municipal lottery."[17]

While urban America was sinking into more degraded levels of political opportunism, popular writers singled out New York City for its more numerous battery of audacious and incompetent civil servants. In Howe's view, its customhouse was operated by officials who possessed the following prerequisites for their post: "1. An entire ignorance of any of the more showy branches of learning; it being most democratic to be a man of few words, and to utter these with a liberal disregard of grammar. 2. Very short hair, affording the slightest possible grasp for an antagonist in case of a passage of arms. [3.] Physical ability to drink confusion to the opposition at all times, in all places, and in every sort of beverage" (pp. 122-23). Books like Williams's *Gay Life in New York* and George William Curtis's *Trumps* charged that the councils of state in the largest city of the land were in the hands of Tammany Hall, a machine which selected candidates for office by their ability "to see things from a particular point of view."

What most frightened many novelists was that a ring of vulgar, grasping men could so easily control the urban electorate. Writers who easily stooped to vulgar sensationalism in their own literary productions climbed a patrician pedestal when they evaluated municipal politics. Sympathetic with the old ruling classes who had been evicted from City Hall, they registered an elitist contempt for corrupt machines that were enriching the "wrong element." Both Howe in *The Pasha Papers* and the anonymous author of the novel *The Three Golden Balls* accused the sachems of Tammany Hall of buying votes, altering ballots, and ensuring their tenure in office by hiring red-necked "b'hoys" whose job was to decide how the "Dear People should vote."

In Cornelius Mathews's *The Career of Puffer Hopkins,* Tammany employed more subtle methods on election day. By judiciously distributing counterfeit coins to the poor, ward heelers convinced the slum dwellers that a vote for the machine was a vote for good times. Dispensing with any serious discussion of issues that confronted the electorate, demagogues vied in outlandish promises to the ignorant masses: "As [election] day approached its close, the creed of the two parties ... became ... more liberal; their affection for the poor ... more devoted and fraternal ... [so] that certain poverty-stricken and simple-minded gentlemen who stood by listening with greedy ear ... voted for one ticket or the other according as they preferred the fare, lodging and accommodations held out by either party" (p. 187). But while Mathews delighted in satirizing the trumpery of a new breed of urban politicos, he ignored the fact that the appetite of upper-class politicians had been limited by the smaller opportunities for graft in the old compact city.

Like the reformers of the period who wanted to return to smaller economic government, writers like Mathews, Howe, Curtis, and Williams did little more than mouth platitudes. Looking to a simpler yesterday when the right sort of people ruled, they failed to see that the political boss was providing essential municipal services and defusing political tensions. Their Jeffersonian biases were irrelevant to the needs of cities that required positive government. Instead of assaulting the root problems of urban malaise in their books, they implied that the metropolis would return to normality once respectable citizens routed the "Shiny Hat Brigade" from City Hall.

In spite of salvos at the city boss, many novelists agreed that the cesspool of urban politics mirrored the vulgarity, opportunism, and materialism of American life. If machines bowed to expediency, was not the Republic itself devoted to seizing the main chance? If the city brought into focus electioneering based on self-aggrandizement, was not the federal government elevating into national policy the slogan "To the victor belong the spoils!"? In the not-too-dim past, when Whigs were railing at a president like Andrew Jackson for usurping authority from Congress and the Supreme Court, novelists were likening the mayors of America to Russian czars.

With the rise of Fernando Wood to the mayoralty of New York in 1854, control over the giant city had fallen to an individual who, in the estimation of ex-Mayor Philip Hone, belonged in state prison rather than in an honorable office. Wood, whose organization of henchmen was a forerunner of the Tweed Ring, was a suave political buccaneer who according to modern scholars, exceeded all previous records of corruption, extravagance, and malfeasance in office. No underhanded scheme was beneath his dignity. As Gustavus Myers demonstrated in his *History of Tammany Hall,* Wood openly sold political favors, used underworld thugs to stuff the ballot boxes, and transformed the police department into an instrument of his personal power.

This record was not lost upon writers who wanted to reveal the shadows of urban life. We may infer by the 1855 date of her novel *The Old Homestead* that Stephens had Fernando Wood in mind when she condemned the chief magistrate of the city not only for his excessive exercise of power but also for his ruthless use of the spoils system. She alleged that the mayor enjoyed totalitarian control in deciding whether an individual, regardless of merit, was to be hired or fired. "He is judge—juror. He is the *law* in these cases" (p. 89). With such capricious authority, little wonder that those employees most knowledgeable about the wants of the populace were kept impotent.

Among the accusations contemporaries leveled against city government was that its very agencies of justice had become criminal tools. The judicial system was an open scandal; the law, a matter of politics. Magistrates were political hacks expected to pay for their appointment by returning the right decisions. If the supporters of the machine were arrested, machine judges would acquit them. Popular books, then, were not exaggerating when they condemned the courts for driving the innocent to prison while allowing the guilty to break the law daily. Henry Edwards's *The Belle of Central Park,* Judson's *B'hoys of New York,* and Maitland's *The Watchman* echoed the oft-heard refrain that if an intoxicated brawler belonged to the upper class his case was instantly dismissed, but if a poor seamstress wandered the streets she was condemned as a vagrant and consigned to a cell with hardened prostitutes. They showed that when an Irishman apprehended for incitement to riot was discovered to have voted the "right ticket" his case slid through, while an inoffensive man known as a supporter of the opposition party was quickly indicted for disturbing the peace.

Nor did jury trial offer much protection for those seeking retribution. According to Duganne in *The Knights of the Seal,* the courts of great cities were up for sale: "Acquitted for murder, of course. Jury lived like fighting cocks during the trial and went home, better and richer men! ha, ha! . . . Justices and juries are cheap; excessively cheap; and governors uncommonly tender hearted. ha, ha!" (p. 129). Williams's *Gay Life in New York* pictured those who administered justice as coarse, sensual men who were no better than the prisoners they condemned. Deaf to the problems of the poor, they handled the rich with kid gloves and the penniless with an iron fist.

One of the most criticized aspects of municipal administration in popular literature was the practice of requiring victims of crime and other witnesses in a trial to post bond or be shipped to prison. In Stimson's *Easy Nat* and Stephens's *Fashion and Famine,* persons too poor to produce the bonding fee were consigned to cells with murderers and thieves. Even children, the offspring of condemned female convicts, were incarcerated with a vice-ridden community.

The prisons of the city offered another glance at the cankerous condition of urban life. The Tombs of New York City, in particular, loomed as an ominous physical reminder of injustice. Popular American writers were as appalled as Charles Dickens by "this dismal-fronted pile of bastard Egyptian, like an enchanter's palace in a melodrama."[18] Novelists like Gayler, Stephens, and Maria Maxwell decried the fact that in its dark and filthy confines boys and men aged twelve to sixty were intermingled indiscriminately. They assailed the city for schooling those still innocent in vice; for exposing prisoners booked for a trifling misdemeanor to death from rats or poisoned air; for providing a degraded urban populace with the spectacle of executions.

Fire posed another nightmare of urban life. The rich attempted to escape it by building in brick and marble, but most city residents, living in flimsily constructed wood buildings that were huddled cheek by jowl, could readily become homeless victims of ravaging flames. To an audience seeking thrilling books, fire ranked almost with the seduction of a fair maiden. Descriptions of crowded quarters in flames, shrieking tenants unable to escape, cherished children hurled out of windows, firemen struggling to bring their engines through narrow, impassable alleys, and homeless refugees shivering in the cold as they watched the ruin of their apartments and the destruction of their scanty belongings allowed the reader to experience in a city novel the anxiety of a gothic tale of horror. His heart could beat faster as he saw firemen, confounded by steep stairs, complicated passages, and flimsy walls, fighting untiringly against inexorable flames. His pulse could throb as he watched a "sublime spectacle" of tenants crushing each other in desperate attempts to escape down dilapidated staircases, and horses, maddened by the danger, breaking through stable doors, trampling those who did not flee in time.[19] Just such a disastrous blaze in Pittsburgh in 1845 provided a terrifying episode in Samuel Young's novel *The Smoky City.* This fire reduced twenty square blocks of the most valuable part of the city to cinders and ravished two-thirds of the community's wealth.

In a place with expanding economic opportunities a city fire was a great leveler, helping to break and make men's fortunes. John B. Jones in *The Spanglers and Tinglers* showed how merchants in the boom towns of the West could work hard, yet be suddenly wiped out as a blaze destroyed hastily slapped-together wooden structures. Even if a businessman had been lucky enough to empty his store before the onslaught of flames, he still faced the menace of looters. In the *Mysteries and Miseries of San Francisco,* an anonymous author chronicled the actual depredations of the Hounds, a lawless gang who set fire to the wooden city in 1851 in order to plunder shops and homes during the blaze. Thus fire, a common urban hazard, could create an inversion of the American dream.

Nevertheless, this shadow of city life, along with slums, swindles, pollution, and dangerous streets, lent the metropolis an aura of excitement. The city might not be a safe place, but it was a thrilling one. When a lad living on its outskirts "heard the heavy reverberations of the fire-bells from afar and the deadened roar of the engines . . . and saw the lurid light in the sky, he longed to be there, to take a part in the exciting scene."[20] In the fantasy life of village youth the fire engine, the "Metamora," was a technological wonder which lured to the metropolis those hankering for adventure.

Fire meant two enemies—the blaze itself and a rival volunteer engine company, and popular novelists captured the usual brick-throwing squall that accompanied fires. Joseph Clay Neal's novel *Peter Ploddy* and Miss M. C. Montaigne's short story "The Fireman," for example, showed how restless teenagers, thirsting for recognition as heroes, raced after the engines while simultaneously clubbing, punching, and pelting volunteers from all other hook-and-ladder houses. What mattered most to these shrieking fire laddies was to gain the glory of extinguishing the flames first, and if this entailed breaking the engines of one's opponents, placing plugs over hydrants until one's own "musheen" arrived, or knocking all rivals into insensibility this was but part of the manly pleasure of the struggle.

Fires in contemporary city fiction allowed the urban resident not only to engage in the joy of battle but also to participate in collective heroism. Rescue parties could be organized spontaneously: "A hundred hands are outstretched, a hundred noble hearts would prostrate themselves upon the pavement to save, to break the fall of a beggar boy whom they would have kicked out of their path the day before."[21] For all the accusations of callousness leveled against city inhabitants, then, a fire inevitably brought out their noblest qualities. Facing a common peril, the people brought to the crisis a sense of communal cooperation that rivaled the community spirit so famous among pioneers. Even writers who embroidered their novels with incidents of urban depravity also portrayed episodes of self-sacrifice at fires. In Foster's *Celio,*

Judson's *Three Years After,* and Solon Robinson's *Hot Corn,* men hurled themselves into tottering buildings to save strangers. The doors of rich and poor alike opened to the homeless victims of the disaster. Fire, an ominous urban hazard, thus became in tales of derring-do the cement that bound disparate city types and classes. It provided urban dwellers with a folklore of common identity and concern.

The peril of fire, in addition to creating a mythology of the city as a community, also produced an original folk hero, the fire boy who valiantly braved death to save his neighbors, finding "no danger too fearful to face, no hazard too daring for them to brave." The conception of this indigenous stock character owed much to Jacksonian ideology. The typical firefighter was identified as a man with rough hands and a kind heart. A hardworking citizen, a mechanic without the polish of a refined education, he appeared in popular literature as a man of instinctive morality who, like Old Hickory, could become capable of violence when roused to indignation at injustice. In contrast to a leisured class of stock villains who idled their hours away in dissolute pleasures, this urban Galahad risked his own life to save others. Shrewd and unaffected, he seemed a modern noble savage—an urbanite with generous impulses and manly mettle.[22]

Popular authors did not have to look far to find a model for the fire volunteer. Mose Humphreys, a butcher and leader of the Bowery Boys in the 1840s, was already a legendary figure among the masses in his own lifetime. A Paul Bunyan of a man, he was reputed to be a seven-foot giant who had jumped across the Hudson River, uprooted an oak tree, and blown ships down the East River. Waving a bludgeon and a butcher's cleaver, he was known to be as much a terror when battling rival engine companies as he was a daredevil in extinguishing fires. Urban novelists, as we have seen in many other instances, were quick to exploit subject matter easily identified by ordinary readers, and when they needed a heroic firefighter they named him Mose and accompanied him with his equally famous sidekick, Syksey.

The appearance of this urban folk hero was not confined to the printed page. "Mose the Fireboy" became an outstanding attraction of the New York stage. Garbed in a plug hat, red shirt, and turned-up trousers, he became the embodiment of the impudent and exuberant child of the city, the Bowery boy. In the epidemic of Mose plays which followed the successful production of Benjamin Baker's *A Glance at New York,* the hero inevitably battled against a rival in a hostile ladder company and capped his exploits by dragging a hose across the stage to quench a ravaging blaze.

In the city itself, however, the picturesque yielded to the professional, and popular writers applauded the efforts of urban residents to create improved fire prevention programs. By the time the guns had quieted at Appomattox, New York had transformed its fire department from a haunt of rowdies, "more wild than South American revolutionaries," into a first-class, full-time force under an almost military discipline. The state legislature, as anxious to court the good will of the business community as it was to deprive the city's Democratic machine of an important source of political support, had allowed lobbyists to persuade it that the undermanned, politics-ridden, autonomous volunteer companies could not cope with their burden. On March 30, 1865, Albany set up its new Metropolitan Fire Department—to the delight of the fire insurance companies. In place of the hangers-on who had enjoyed carousing at the engine house, racing after the machines, and plundering stores under the guise of saving property, the members of this new fire-fighting service were sober, exemplary citizens who quietly performed their heroic duties. Celebrants of city life like Junius Browne and Matthew Hale Smith praised them accordingly.

The chaotic conditions and dangers of mid-nineteenth-century cities provided the stuff of urban "romances." The fanciful titles of popular novels suggest a far-fetched subject matter, but, as we have discovered, enterprising authors used some of the actual catastrophes and disruptive changes of the time to embroider their adventure stories. Like the Protestant sermon, which for centuries had been an outgrowth of the immediate experiences of the congregation—its losses due to war, sickness, fire—the popular urban novel now provided a propitiative balm to disruptive flocks whose ties to church had loosened. By placing seemingly inchoate experiences within the context of a rational plot with identifiable villains—the quack medical practitioner, gangster, machine politician—pulp books gave readers an easily comprehended, moralistic explanation of baffling tensions. They externalized the problems of urban life.

In contrast to the hazardous environment of cities, the countryside provided a natural, tranquil, and fulfilling world. Certainly, an important element in the pulp fiction of this period was a nostalgic longing for rural jobs: "Blest rural life! Thy homely fare, thy simple pleasures, thy manly toil, and thy calm retreats may be despised by the flutterers in the thronged and splendid mart; but keep to thy plain and homeborn virtues, maintain thy jealousy of pomp and state."[23] In a tradition as venerable as Virgil's *Georgics* and Hesiod's *Works and Days,* many mid-nineteenth-century urban writers, perplexed by the complexities of life in America's adolescent cities, beat a retreat to the supposedly simple village green. Frightened by the nation's radical departure from its familiar agrarian ways, they registered the cultural shock of those forced to face unwanted changes and anticipated the animadversions toward the city expressed by writers during the Gilded Age. Echoing many readers' suspicions that the metropolis was a fearsome, wicked place, a backward-looking literature articulated the values of an earlier culture and confirmed the validity of its mores. By presenting a chamber of urban horrors, it reassured its audience that a rural residence offered a security and dignity denied those who had sought greener pastures in a brick-and-mortar wilderness.

In what amounted to a collective ritual, a reading public could confirm its need for historical continuity at a time when rapid economic development was threatening the stability of village folkways. By reinforcing rural readers' prejudices about the city, popular literature of this ilk allowed an older culture to perpetuate itself a while longer. By voicing the familiar fears of those dreading dislocation, urban books provided an agricultural people with reassurance that they need not be ashamed for remaining on the farm. With the menace of crime, the danger to health, and the terror of fire, why should they not stay put and count their blessings?

Revelation of the problems of metropolitan life did not, however, necessarily imply a condemnation of urbanization itself. Protest against corrupt political machines, traffic congestion, and inadequate police service can be interpreted as an attack on known evils in need of correction rather than as an indictment of urban values themselves. Like others in this age of humanitarian reform, novelists frequently sought to ameliorate many monstrous problems of city life. By dramatizing the difficulties of the day, writers of pulp prose took an important first step in elucidating for the public the aspects of the battle still to be won.

Furthermore, by revealing creative, communal responses to urban hazards and by praising initial efforts at collective action, novelists may well have spurred city residents in their combat against major metropolitan ills. Equally important, by creating new folk heroes—the detective and the firefighter—literary hacks helped urban dwellers to see themselves as pioneers who were conquering a new and challenging frontier.

Pulp writers presented the perils of city life so colorfully that the very shadows of the metropolis endowed it with charm. Where else could one find both daily excitement and near-catastrophe? Where else existed such a concentration of novel sights and sounds? We can assume that, for those stunted by the known regimen of farming activity, books that glamorized the dangers of crime or fire, the ghastliness of housing conditions, or even the hair's-breadth hazards of a mundane ride on public transportation created an image of the city as adventuresome as the high seas or wilderness.

Such reading material also suggested to city inhabitants the vitality and variety of their environment.

The enormous repertoire of experiences found in the town became the stock in trade of writers of novels and nonfiction exposés alike. Their books were mid-nineteenth-century counterparts to the more familiar television news broadcasts and disaster movies of our own era. By dramatizing physical hazards, they allowed people to experience the sense of adventure sorely lacking in their regimented lives. By sensationalizing urban pathology, they created an image of the city as a place that defied the boredom of the clock. Likewise, as we shall now see, by unfolding for the reader's delectation the prevalence of vice in the metropolis, albeit under the guise of moral outrage, they invited respectable citizens to pore over pornography.

3

THE CITY UNDERGROUND
Sinful Spots of Forbidden Pleasure

A persistent theme in the mid-nineteenth-century novel was that the American city was fast becoming like Sodom or Gomorrah. As the traditional bulwarks of authority—the church and the family—began to crumble and urban discipline to erode, innumerable books echoed the contemporary fear that the metropolis was becoming a haven for all sorts of immoral behavior. Yet popular authors often uncovered underground spots of forbidden pleasure gratuitously for the curious readers of their smug exhortations against urban sin. Like English working-class fiction of this period, which tried to rivet the attention of semiliterate audiences on melodramatic romances set in houses of assignation, gilded tap rooms, and gambling hells, popular American literature gave a means of secretly indulging their lurid fantasies to a reading public constricted by a Victorian regime of overt respectability.

One of the most serious indictments of the city in popular literature was the easy availability of sex outside of the legal bounds of matrimony. To a society which saw the pits of hell yawning before sinners who enjoyed mating without benefit of clergy, the city was an emblem of guilt. It openly harbored a large number of bordellos. Girls might have been seduced and abandoned on the farm, but sex became a business operation only in the city. No matter what his proclivity or purse, the man in search of erotic amusement could, according to sensational writers, gratify his desires in cities which had become new frontiers for uninhibited sexuality.

Whether one sought a private residence overflowing with gorgeous courtesans, a discreet chamber of assignation for an affair with a married woman, or a readily available "bed house" with public bawds, the metropolis was a land of plenty. Indeed, in a locale that fostered visible social distinctions, sin became subject to class stratification. Thanks to the police department, which, according to Edward Zane Carroll Judson's *G'hals of New York,* served as an unwitting chamber of commerce for the illicit pastimes of the city, houses of ill fame were classified. They ran the gamut from the exclusive hideaway requiring a special introduction to the democratic house of ill repute which served a clientele indiscriminately.

The deluge of episodes set in richly furnished "parlor houses" suggests that what covertly leering readers wanted was to learn more about the "other Victorians"—the respectable financiers who left their wives on pedestals of Christian otherworldliness to pursue more earth-bound women in "shrines of vice." In church the middle class heard ministers denounce supposedly decent family men for patronizing prostitutes, but in books with windy subtitles like *Legends of New York. Being a Complete Expose of the Mysteries, Vices, and Doings, As Exhibited in Fashionable Circles of New York. Including the Haunts of the Gamblers. Their Names, Places, and Visitors. Also, the Names, Places, and Visitors at the "Fashionable Houses of Fashionable Prices" with a Full Development of All the Ways and Mysteries of the Upper Ten Thousand* and *Mysteries of Upper Ten-Dom; Being a Spirit Stirring, a Powerful and Felicitous Expose of the Desolating Mystery, Blighting Miseries, Atrocious Vices and Paralyzing Tragedies Perpetuated in the Fashionable Pandemoniums of the Great Empire City* they could learn more explicitly about the sexual adventures of the wicked rich. Popular writers unfolded for their readers scenes of upper-class debauchery. The anonymous *Mysteries of Philadelphia* and John Vose's *Seven Nights in Gotham* showed how in elegant and discreet surroundings gentlemen of means sipped champagne, conversed, and fornicated with beautiful, cultivated women.

Among the exposés of moral corruption was Judson's popular novel *Three Years After,* which described mysterious houses of assignation where wickedness was so rife that a husband and his veiled wife could cross paths in their rendezvous with illicit sweethearts. James D. McCabe's *Secrets of the Great City* instructed the reading audience on the subtleties of the advertising sections of newspapers in this respect. Announcements of "rooms to let to quiet persons" or "rooms for a strictly private family where boarders are not asked impertinent questions" were said to trumpet to those sophisticated in vice the availability of quarters for amorous adventure.

The proliferation of red-light districts into respectable areas of the city was a source of concern to contemporaries. Bishop Simon of the Methodist Episcopalian Church announced to an audience at Cooper

Union in 1866 that New York City was disgraced by the fact that it contained as many prostitutes as it did members of the Methodist church. The superintendent of police, John A. Kennedy, felt compelled to quiet public fear and gave his own body count of 2,123 harlots. As we might expect, urban confidentials favored the churchman's more alarming figure. According to the reports of Vose, McCabe, and Junius Browne, Gotham could boast, as one of its tourist attractions, at least ten to twelve thousand strumpets.

Who were the women who so brazenly offered themselves for public consumption? According to a host of writers, poverty drove many into this occupation. Prevented from earning an honorable livelihood by employers who refused to pay even a subsistence wage, girls could either slowly starve or traffic themselves in the city's fleshpots. Others, surrounded by vice in the slums, might at twelve years of age exchange their virginity for a pretty dress. Yet not all harlots were necessarily drawn from the most wretched classes. Some were attracted to such a life by their aspirations for an elegant standard of living.[1] In this sense, to use Daniel Bell's phrase, prostitution in the mid-nineteenth-century city served as "a queer ladder of social mobility." Presumably many status seekers appreciated the material advantages of illicit sex, for according to wag Junius Browne, the number of strumpets was continually growing.

For the moment, popular writers did not blame the increase in this ancient profession on the foreign element in the city. Prostitution was a native occupation. Indeed, the countryside was one of the most important recruiting grounds for new talent. Girls "ruined" in a supposed arcadia saw in the city a refuge from village gossips. In novels such as Lambert Wilmer's *Confessions of Emilia Harrington*, Tom Shortfellow's *Annie*, Joseph H. Ingraham's *Frank Rivers*, and Osgood Bradbury's *Ellen Grant*, prostitution provided to deflowered unmarried females both anonymity and a means of earning a livelihood. In this sense, the metropolis allowed girls who had deviated from the norms imposed by village life to find a means of economic and psychological survival.

Obviously, not all country lasses entered the ranks of whoredom voluntarily. Most often pulp authors showed them to be ensnared by runners the moment they arrived in the metropolis. In Judson's *Mysteries and Miseries of New York*, an innocent is trapped by a hackman who offers to bring her to an honorable boarding house only to take her instead to a dishonorable bawdyhouse, where she is kept under lock and key until inducted into a life of sin. In *Caroline Tracy* "ropers" promise fresh immigrants good jobs only to bring them to hags who hold them until they are ruined. In McCabe's *Secrets of the Great City* girls are lured to dance halls where they are drugged and dishonored. They are prisoners of the proprietor, their clothes owned by the establishment; when they try to escape, they are arrested for stealing and sentenced by courts upholding the rights of property. In shockers like *The Three Widows* and *Arrest, Confession and Suicide of Almira Cathcart,* harridans moving from city to city in search of fresh talent pose as benefactors only to prove procurers: "Men treat all these poor girls as children treat toys. The fresh and beautiful are admired, then barely tolerated, then kicked aside to make room for a fresh set. Hence all the arts that cunning, vile women know of are used to obtain new toys for their customers."[2] Like merchants needing to freshen their inventories, procurers for houses of prostitution were ingenious in finding young girls to serve to their patrons. Such palpably sensational schemes extended beyond the realm of the lurid writer's imagination. In New York City "Red Light Lizzie" and "Flora" were notorious procurers who sent scouts to the country to lure young girls to the metropolis with the promise of good jobs. Once enticed to one of their establishments, the farmer's daughter would be drugged and raped.

A standard scene in many books set in the city was the abduction of a fair maiden to a den of prostitution. There she was held in captivity by villains and hags who trafficked in human flesh. This formula was hardly novel; popular writers simply transferred to a new milieu, the city, the old story of atrocities committed by savage Indians on their captives. In the mid-nineteenth-century urban novel the city was as dangerous as the frontier. If Indians stalked the woods ready to pounce on virtuous pioneers, cads waited on city streets plotting the ruin of innocent girls. Significantly, Judson, the famous writer of Buffalo Bill tales who published many novels under the pseudonym Ned Buntline, moved easily from the frontier wilderness of the West to the urban wilderness of New York and New Orleans. In his blood-and-thunder novels, *Mysteries and Miseries of New York* and *Mysteries and Miseries of New Orleans,* lust was as much a danger as any tomahawk.

Houses of ill fame not only serviced a debauched urban populace but provided an important attraction to out-of-town visitors, who could enjoy in the city freedom from the restraints imposed in a rural village. Indeed, the *Revelations of Asmodeus* alleged that three-fourths of the demand for New York's prostitutes came from the tourist population. Often, however, these men, like their rustic female counterparts, became the victims of sharpsters. Their search for fun in the sinful city frequently ended in their undoing. No match for a cunning "hooker," the male greenhorn might be stripped of whatever money he had on his person or, more seriously, become involved in a lifetime of blackmail. Matthew Hale Smith and the anonymous author of *The Mysteries of Philadelphia,* intent upon alerting readers to the dangers of the metropolis, repeatedly warned against a clever confidence operation known as the panel game. In this swindle a prostitute lured a victim to her den and had him undress; while his attention was absorbed, a confederate, concealed behind a panel in the room, removed the panel and, along with it, the unsuspecting customer's possessions.

McCabe revealed another scheme. A prostitute would bring a customer to her room, obtain payment in advance, and then allow her victim to be alarmed by frantic knocks at the door. Predictably, she would tell her client that it was her dangerously irate husband. The dupe then thankfully escaped through a back door bereft of the money he had paid for a service never rendered.

If unsophisticated men were trapped by feminine sharps, the cosmopolitan libertine found a natural ally in the nefarious stock character of city fiction, the hag abortionist. A model for this character existed in the notorious Madame Restell of New York City, who conducted her operations in an elegant brownstone and advertised openly in newspapers. Dubbed by contemporaries the wickedest woman in town and Madame Killer, she served in George Lippard's novel *New York* and McCabe's confidential *Secrets of the Great City* as a female embodiment of urban depravity. For a fee she would protect the respectability of her wealthy clientele. If a young girl died on the operating table, a bribe could silence the harridan. If an expectant mother chose to have her child instead, the harpy would provide secluded, tasteful rooms for her patient's confinement. She also would worm her way into her charge's confidence until she discovered the name of the mysterious father, who had to pay dearly to keep his good name.

Even Broadway, despite its image as an aristocratic avenue, often appeared in popular literature as a national highway of sin. Its elegantly dressed ladies, gilded amusement halls, and marbled stores might look appealing, but popular books quickly instructed readers that many of the handsome women who promenaded on this crowded thoroughfare were in reality painted strumpets bearing their wares to every passer-by. The God-fearing man who wanted to walk the path of righteousness was informed in George Foster's *New York by Gas-Light* that he would encounter numerous invitations to bed if he took a stroll along the nation's most famous avenue.

While vice displayed itself openly on Broadway, it also assumed many masks. A seductive amusement which appeared for the first time in the 1840s was the strip show, euphemized as tableaux vivants. Here, according to a lurid description in H. M. Rulison's *Mock Marriage,* artistes performed dances in almost complete nudity, swaying lasciviously to the music.

Foster's *New York Naked* revealed that such shows could be seen at the Franklin Museum. Foster further described the dancers as destitute country girls whose appetites had become so "exaggerated" from their "abhorrent profession" that they inevitably moved from the stage "to the brothels, the hospitals, the penitentiary and the grave."[3]

Even attendance at the legitimate theater could prove to be a source of corruption, warned James Rees in *Mysteries of City Life.* If the tableaux vivants exhibited naked women in the guise of statues and paintings, the plays, pretending to show "life as it is," presented pornographic comedies about seduction and adultery. Moreover, according to John Vose and the anonymous author of *The Three Golden Balls,* the stalls were filled with abandoned women who plied their trade publicly. The third tier in particular was "a storehouse of prostitution" where "scores and scores of painted, drunken, lascivious females" bartered themselves at bargain prices.

Dance halls represented yet another circle of the metropolitan inferno. Located in the worst quarters of the city, they provided amusement to the most degraded element of the population. Situated "sixty" feet below the ground, they appeared in Vose's *Seven Nights in Gotham* as "headquarters of overgrown rats." Here fallen women, bloated with drink and disfigured in appearance, paraded themselves in low-cut red dresses. In this racially integrated urban institution black women mingled with white rowdies who were armed with a wide assortment of weapons. The most savage sight of these dens was the dance floor. Here a person seeking adventure could witness a bacchanal of dancers contorting their bodies and accompanying their convulsive motions with screams and shouts of laughter as they leaped "frantically about like dervishes." These "temples of depravity" were dangerous, and readers were warned not to purchase drinks; for once swept into the revelry, they might well be drugged and stripped of all their valuables.[4]

A legion of writers also admonished their audience to be wary of concert saloons, a new type of establishment that appeared in the 1860s. They might seem like centers of harmless conviviality, but they were, according to books like Bradbury's *Ellen: The Pride of Broadway,* William Sikes's *One Poor Girl,* and Browne's *The Great Metropolis,* "immoral mushrooms," "underground hells" scattered throughout the city "in frightful numbers." Frequented during the gaslight hours, they were "noisome cellars, thick with tobacco smoke," reeking with the smell of cheap liquor. Equally jarring were the musicians; they fiddled on squawking violins, thumped on asthmatic pianos, or bellowed strident minstrel songs.

In many respects urban potboilers endowed the concert saloon of the mid-nineteenth-century city with attributes that make it a forerunner of the familiar western frontier saloon of a latter-day popular genre. In John Brougham's play *The Lottery of Life,* saloons were decorated with tawdry ornaments and salacious paintings and patronized by savage men who thought little of pulling out pistols at a moment's provocation and holding a shootout inside the premises. A stranger had little chance of leaving unscathed from such a place, for in the scenario he would be treated to drugged drinks, then robbed, and even murdered for his money.

The most piquant feature of these noisy musical taverns was the staff—"unchaste nymphs" who served drinks in "scanty" costumes that revealed their shoulders and ankles. These "waiter girls," unperturbed by Victorian restraints, served alcoholic drinks to men until the early hours of the morning. Many who came to these places innocent succumbed to the leering advances of patrons and earned overtime pay in their bedchambers. When clergymen wished to gather material for their sermons on the iniquities of the metropolis, they visited these thinly disguised houses of prostitution.

Other notorious pleasure haunts were the gambling hells, where men chanced easy gain with the shuffle of a deck of cards or the spin of a roulette wheel. Popular writers, responding to growing public concern over the unprecedented proliferation of gaming resorts in the city, warned that one trifling bet could metamorphose a respectable man into an addict. Loss would only lure him on, and before long he might end up a drunkard in the gutter or a lunatic in an asylum. Thompson, Williams, Anna Fitch, and many other writers, anxious to instruct potentially wayward sheep, tirelessly catalogued the tricks of "blacklegs."[5] A favorite gambit used by gambling establishments was to hire a roper, who offered to show a newly arrived bumpkin the iniquitous sights of the city. The "pigeon" was plied with liquor, brought to lewd theatrical spots, and then, as the capstone of the evening's entertainment, guided to an opulent gaming den, where he was feted free of charge with gourmet delicacies and rare wines served in crystal glasses. Here the greenhorn was introduced to a practiced gamester, who pretended to be an innocent who knew nothing about cards and who could be persuaded only reluctantly to take his chances with the deck. The victim was allowed to win until he became so confident that he staked all his money on one hand. On this occasion luck inevitably would go against him, but, convinced that he could retrieve his loss, he would write a note on his home for the last gamble, only to lose all.

The out-of-towner was not the only victim of the gambling fever. In *The Gambler* Charles Burdett described the degeneration of a once-respectable urban merchant, who was persuaded by a former classmate to sip a glass of champagne in an elegant gambling house. Here the acquaintance, now a polished confidence man, reveals to his long-lost friend how easy it is to win at faro. Claiming to be without his pocket-book, he requests a loan, promising to share the winnings but to take the entire loss upon himself. Lured by such a generous offer, a man who never dreamed of risking money at games of chance insists that he share both the losses and the gains. The newly formed team wins at first, then loses, until an enormous sum is relinquished in one evening. The once-sober merchant returns each night to the green cloth tables, hoping to make up his losses. After exhausting his own funds, he borrows from friends, and when that money is also depleted he draws from his respectable firm until it too becomes bankrupt.

Many sensational books suggested that gaming infested all levels of city life. In anonymous novels like *The Mysteries of Philadelphia* and *Nick Bigelow* as well as in Judson's *Mysteries and Miseries of New York*, store clerks, lured by the promise of excitement and riches, wagered their week's salary, and when that was lost, "borrowed" funds from their employers, altered the books, and forged checks. Wall Street brokers staked the winnings of their legitimate business enterprises on roller-coaster speculation in fashionable casinos. From the pages of *Ella Cameron*, William R. Smith's *As It Is,* and John Ellis's *The Sights and Secrets of the National Capital,* readers learned that in Washington, D.C., senators and statesmen mixed freely with notorious gamblers who were above the law. And even struggling workingmen, according to Burdett's *The Gambler,* squandered their wages on seemingly innocent raffles.

The gambling disease was accompanied by the drinking mania. Many mid-nineteenth-century writers indicted the alcohol bottle as an important cause of poverty, crime, and disorder. Like the reformers of the period who indulged in moralistic analysis of social problems, authors of urban fiction joined the crusade for prohibition legislation as a remedy for pauperism and mob violence. Although one of the most widely read reform books of this period, *Ten Nights in a Bar-Room, and What I saw There* by Timothy Shay Arthur, was set in a small village where demon rum destroyed its victim, a host of popular books portrayed the city as a place where a low groggery or a "gilded den of perdition" beckoned the weak to moral dissolution.[6]

With the highminded zeal of antislavery agitators, popular writers who espoused the cause of temperance reform alerted their audience to the offers of seemingly solicitous bartenders to warm themselves with a free cordial on a cold winter day and cautioned them against accepting the invitations of friendly strangers for soda water at a saloon. They advised the teetotaler to resist the hospitality of tavernkeepers, whose offers of free lunches, cool ice water, and a comfortable armchair were intended to tempt him into tasting that perilous first glass. They warned that the spirited conversation at coffeehouses was often stimulated by the spirits served; that the sports most frequently indulged in at bowling and billiard parlors were drinking and wenching.

The oyster bars, a traditional culinary attraction of the metropolis, were portrayed in popular books like Foster's *New York by Gas-Light* and Winter Summerton's *Will He Find Her?* as emphasizing the fruit of the vine over the fruit of the sea. Underground centers of vice and crime, they provided an Aladdin's cave of mirrored arcades, erotic paintings, marble bars, and silver pitchers. Here customers could refresh themselves with oysters and liquor and then amuse themselves with adulterous intrigues or games of rouge et noir and twenty-one. These cellars, warned Lippard in *The Quaker City,* were places where "youth [went] down laughing merrily" and came up with "his ruddy cheek wrinkled and his voice quivering with premature age" (pp. 9–10).

The theater itself could prove to be an induction into a fatal first glass. At intermission time the spectator might follow the crowd to a splendid marble room with a bar, where he might appreciate the bottle at the expense of the stage performance; or the fashionable urbanite might enter a gorgeously ornamented temple of Bacchus to mingle with the swells of the town and sip sherry cobblers. Before long, though, he would crave a more potent brew and participate in brawls.[7] Even an ice-cream parlor like the famous Taylor's in New York was, in the eyes of Solon Robinson, a gilded snare which would lure unsuspecting ladies with "health-destroying luxuries." Youngsters too could become alcoholics. Rum dealers, alleged P. H. Skinner in *The Little Ragged Ten Thousand,* peddled sweet brandy-drops to tots and forced children to swallow their brew as an initiation rite into slum society.

In the slums, especially, haunts of alcoholism were ubiquitous. If the reign of King Alcohol meant the moral decay of those in high life, it spelled destitution to low-life drunkards. Once addicted, the inebriate would allow a dying wife to go without medicine, a hungry child without food. Painting the progressive degeneration of those who succumbed to the "man-traps" of the metropolis, writers typically pictured a once-industrious member of the working class indulging from cup to cup until he became unfit to earn a livelihood, bestial enough to cripple or kill his own child, and dehumanized sufficiently to end his days in the gutter or as a madman in an asylum.[8]

Yet the very temptations of an urban milieu created challenges to moral people. If alcohol could destroy the prospects of the poor, it could also inspire Christian missionaries to clean up the nation's cities. It could allow the concerned to convert tap houses into "freedom houses," where inebriates would sign the pledge. Imbued with an unfailing optimism, reformist fiction like Julia Wright's *The Corner Stall* promised that the Bible could be brought to the savage areas of the city and drunkards freed from their bondage to the bottle.

Fashioners of the popular imagination adorned their books with titles that promised to take the reader on a tour of the mysteries of city life. These exposés of urban vice provided information about an environment that was exposing increasing numbers of farm youths to new moral dangers. Like the evangelical preachers described by Anselm Strauss in *Images of the American Cities*, novelists warned readers of the traps which could ensnare the weakminded. By showing the newcomer the shoals of the city, they allowed him to steer clear of danger.

Yet we may consider these urban confidentials as more than Polonius-like enjoinders from the old to the young, for they provide the modern scholar with an oblique guidebook to the anxieties of an earlier epoch. To that generation, with its acute sense of the power of vice and the danger of anarchy, the mushrooming of bars, whorehouses, and gambling hells signaled impending social chaos. Already society was brimming over with temptations to corruption and initiating the young into vicious habits. Many popular writers, unable to understand the economic forces which were creating widespread dislocation in cities, focused on old-fashioned moral issues. Ignoring root causes, they dwelt instead on symptoms and implicitly equated the physical disorder of the metropolis with eroding standards of personal rectitude.

Fear of disorder galvanized the guardians of Christian morality. Melodrama would purge the city of sin. The popular book would uplift the city morally, salvaging it from social disintegration. Like the evangelical organizations of the period that were formed to close down bordellos and saloons, pulp authors prodded urbanites to cleanse their house and to shield dangerous classes from temptation. In a humanitarian if somewhat self-righteous spirit that paralleled the reform crusade of the antebellum era, a melioristic literature often exposed the secrets of the city in order to restore stability and traditional decency to an urban society engulfed by disorder.

Notwithstanding all these potentially highminded purposes, however, writers of pulp books were probably more interested in telling a good story than in providing rural dwellers with ammunition against the city or, for that matter, urban residents with a prod to moral regeneration. The city provided a perfect backdrop for hairbreadth escapes from the clutches of evil. The enchanted kingdoms of gothic fiction could be translated into the mysteries and miseries of the metropolis. Rustics and regimented city dwellers alike could enjoy vicarious visits to dance halls, gambling hells, strip joints, bars, and houses of prostitution. As Simon Lesser has argued in *Fiction and the Unconscious,* they could safely identify with the transgressions of womanizers and blacklegs, displacing their lusts and aggressions onto fictional villains and, at the same time, assuage their guilt by seeing the terrible punishment that awaited sinners.

Thus while some popular authors echoed a fear expressed by the Universalist minister Edwin H. Chapin, who bewailed the way certain urban facilities were exposing people to new excitement and allowing them to delve into recesses of their nature better left undisturbed, other writers so graphically described the seamy side of the city that they made vice attractive. Their exposés of sin were little more than guidebooks for the uninitiated. Behind the moralizing facade they provided the names and locations of the urban underground. Undoubtedly, many readers purchased these books, not to hear pious platitudes, but to obtain exact addresses of forbidden palaces of pleasure.

4

SWEET CHEATS OF THE METROPOLIS
Enticements to Corruption in the City

Even though explorations of urban vice in popular literature fell back
upon Biblical images of the city as a Sodom, Gomorrah, or Babylon,
hack writers were prisoners of a prescriptive narrative formula which
required the righting of wrongs and the punishment of evil. If the city
housed sin, it also harbored heroes who could discover scoundrels' plots.
Repeating a theme found in John Milton's *Paradise Lost,* in which Adam
learns to differentiate between inner light and the dazzling glare of opulent
cities like Rome and El Dorado, a conservative American literature taught
that the pious Christian could find a Celestial City in the modern
American metropolis. In a seesaw play between treachery and deliverance,
a worthy protagonist was catapulted from one harrowing situation to the
next until a long-lost relative or friend providentially brought rescue at
a moment of near calamity. The preposterous became axiomatic. As
Herbert Ross Brown has stated, readers of the sentimental novel who
believed in the daily intervention of Providence suspended disbelief
and accepted the most improbable coincidences.

Yet what was uncanny was that this shopworn recipe could survive
with new ingredients. For characters to be miraculously rejoined with
long-lost relatives in the country where neighbors knew one another
intimately was one proposition; for city dwellers to discover a missing
mother or father in the far-flung reaches of a crowded city quite another.
The incredible number of recognition scenes in the urban novel of this
period suggests that the metropolis was less an anonymous milieu of
alienated individuals than a place of concerned people linked by the
traditional bonds of family and friendship.

As in much of the popular fiction written from the 1820s through the 1860s, Osgood Bradbury's *Female Depravity* contains both urban treachery and redemption. A debauched man in his fifties, Captain Robinson, wants to seduce fifteen-year-old Fanny Dumond while concurrently marrying a wealthy widow, Mrs. Melville. Fanny is threatened with a caning by her wicked female guardian if she refuses to submit to the captain. A nephew of the captain who is a newcomer to the metropolis, Charles Henderson, asks a well-mannered young lady directions to his boarding house. Little does he suspect that the cunning creature is directing him to a den of vice. Having succumbed to Clara, he is overcome with guilt; he thinks he has seduced an innocent girl and feels he must make amends by marrying her.

The author, after carrying worthy characters like Fanny and Charles to the ledge of the moral precipice, rescues them from the abyss of urban sin. Fanny, begging pennies on the streets, encounters a generous couple, Mr. and Mrs. Hapgood, who become concerned with her fate, invite her to live with them, and adopt her as their daughter. Later, when she is abducted to a brothel, they hire a policeman who rescues her in the nick of time. Nor is Captain Robinson beyond redemption. Conscience-stricken at his son's death from alcohol poisoning, he reforms and devotes himself to helping others. Now he marries the charitable widow, Mrs. Melville, the friend of poor Fanny. Even for Charles Henderson all is not lost. Clara repents her former follies and through the love of this virtuous man becomes a respectable wife.

The city, the author suggests, may be a place of traps, but it need not entrap. Fanny, exposed to the gazes of the libertine, does not become a streetwalker. Her personality, undamaged by the brutality of her formative years, remains gentle and lovable. Even the fallen can rise from their former depravity. Clara easily becomes transformed from wanton into wife; Robinson, from lecher into benefactor.

New York City becomes in this novel an intensely personal place—in fact, an extended family. No country village could rival the connectedness of its inhabitants. Captain Robinson, the debauched pursuer of Fanny, is also the suitor of Mrs. Melville, who, in turn, had always tried to help Fanny. Charles Henderson, the fiancé of the reformed prostitute, is the nephew of the rakish captain who had been one of Clara's lovers. Everyone in Gotham seems to know or have heard of the captain's black servant. When Fanny is abducted, the police officer knows the ruffian hired by Robinson like a book. What is more, Fanny finds that Mr. and Mrs. Hapgood, the strangers who sought to adopt her, are her long-lost parents. Mrs. Melville is the long-lost sister-in-law of the Hapgoods. The largest city in the United States, at least in the world of this representative popular book, was one big, happy, reunited family. Certainly, one would gather that, far from being afflicted with alienation and anomie, the mid-nineteenth-century urban community successfully accommodated the values of Christian fellowship to secular materialism, feminine purity to social mobility.

Although Fanny is saved from betrayal, many fictional women suffered a fate which contemporaries considered worse than death. In novels patently modeled after Samuel Richardson's *Clarissa,* but with an added urban dimension, young girls were seduced and abandoned by upper-class rogues. The sad fate of the deflowered female was an object lesson to young girls who might be enticed from the safety of the farm. It also permitted readers to equate the growth of sexual immorality in the mid-nineteenth century with the emancipation of women. Already, time-honored restrictions on females were crumbling. By the 1840s state legislatures were conferring upon women more liberal property rights, colleges were opening their doors, factories offering opportunities for an independent livelihood. As women acquired new freedom and dignity, sentimental authors enshrined the pure maiden and pious mother. Instead of coming to grips with the economic and social forces which were transforming institutions like the family and the social status of females, they focused their rage on the seducer and on weak women. Resorting to a moralistic sleight of hand, they allowed these fictional characters to stand as hostages for the perplexing changes undermining the stability of urban society.

According to popular writers, seduction was not the only peril to young women in the city. In a place where "adventurers [swelled] the vampire crowd attracted by the 'golden calf,'"[1] marriage could be another gilded snare. In Anna Cora Mowatt Ritchie's *The Fortune Hunter: A Novel of New York Society,* Brainard, a penniless profligate, sees marriage as a means of gratifying his appetite for elegant clothes, fast horses, and champagne dinners at Delmonico's. He seeks a match with a flighty belle, but when foiled in this courtship attempts to redeem his fortune by marrying an acerbic spinster, Miss Adair, who he believes compensates in cash for what she lacks in charm. But Miss Adair, full of pretensions, is herself without money and marries Brainard under the delusion that he is wealthy. Juxtaposed with these two shallow urban dwellers are a homely girl, Rachel Clinton, who has asked her parents to disinherit her so that she will not be courted for her money, and a rich man, Mr. Allen, who has been a misogynist because he hated women's selfishness. The plain girl and the truthful man marry. Once again the urban novel implicitly suggested that, though the city abounded with loveless marriages, it also had its share of honest relationships.

Amidst the epidemic of male fortune hunters in popular fiction were the women who put themselves on the auction block at fashionable watering places, displaying as much of their wares as they possibly could while still maintaining pretensions to respectability. Once married to rich men, they devoted their lives to spending the wealth their husbands had toiled to accumulate. Edward Sherman Gould in the serialized novel *John Doe and Richard Roe* portrayed one such conventional match. Helen, a beautiful young woman, aspires to riches rather than romance. She ensnares an affluent old man, Richard Roe, and has him settle a fortune on her. Once she has obtained an independent income, she sheds her subservience to her spouse's authority and flees to Paris.

Not all urban literature, however, depicted matrimony in the city as high-class prostitution. Many authors, utilizing the now-familiar Dickensian image of the home as a refuge from the cares of a commercial society, juxtaposed the emptiness of fashionable marriages with the homely pleasures of domestic love. Even Nathaniel Hawthorne, labeled by Morton and Lucia White as antiurban, in *The Blithedale Romance* considered a happy family circle in a Boston boarding house as "a prettier bit of nature [than] in all my summer in the country."[2] Less-renowned writers, too, celebrated the constancy of the urban hearth. In the novel *Nancy Waterman; or Woman's Faith Triumphant* the heroine, a resident of New York City, is a modern Penelope besieged with rich suitors while her husband, an escaped convict accused of murder, hides in the woods. Nancy resists the blandishments of her tempters and awaits the return of the man she knows to be guiltless. Similarly, the novel *Isabella; or Filial Affection* depicted an unselfish child laboring to bring a disgraced parent back to the family fold. Whether devoted wife or daughter, the woman was the linchpin in holding the family together.

Just as the city offered schemers an opportunity to cheat in love, it also afforded them a chance to swindle for property. Pulp writers, echoing the cautionary sermons and business journals of the period as well as a popular formula found in contemporary English working-class fiction, recounted tales of bumpkins caught in the net of urban sharpsters. George Foster's tale of Zerubbabel Green in *New York by Gas-Light* is typical of this genre. In it the newcomer from upstate New York escapes cabmen, hotel runners, and pickpockets only to meet a gentleman who promises to introduce him to New York's "upper ten-thousand." Taken to a place filled with beautifully dressed courtesans, he is plied with drink and led to believe that one of the harlots is the Countess of Astoria. His companion then suggests that, before sampling some of Gotham's exciting night life, they deposit their money in a safe with the "chief of police," an idea to which he readily agrees. Once in a bar, they realize that they lack money to pay for the drinks. Zerubbabel quickly draws upon the extra supply of cash in his secret money belt. After being aroused by scenes of naked women dancing, he is taken to an oyster bar, where a wager costs him his watch. He finally passes out in a drunken stupor and awakes the next morning in the streets, robbed of everything. To compound his difficulties, a vigilant policeman hauls him to the Tombs for drunkenness and loitering. This story, recycled in numerous contemporary versions, flattered the city reader whose sophistication protected him from such schemes, while it tutored the would-be urbanite on how to avoid disaster.

Like Henry Fielding, in whose *Joseph Andrews* a country footman must withstand the temptations of gambling, drinking, and genteel vices in London, popular American urban authors of the mid-nineteenth century represented the city as a testing ground of a person's moral mettle as well as a school in the ways of the world. Those who read these books presumably would become so imbued with middle-class virtues that they could avoid the reefs and shallows of city life. The long-winded title *Harry Harefoot; or the Three Temptations, A Story of City Scenes, Showing the Allurements to VICE, with the incentives to VIRTUE, which a Metropolis offers to all young Adventurers and how the one may be attained and the other avoided* by the prolific author Joseph Holt Ingraham states baldly the purport of his book. Two young men from New England embark on a journey to Boston. One, Harry Harefoot, finds employment as a shop clerk; the other, Pierce Wentworth, apprentices himself as a mechanic. Although Harry was an upright person in his native town, the city stimulates in him a desire to appear genteel, hide his country origins, and imitate the manners of suave young gentlemen. His occupation in a business dedicated to appearances puts him in contact with the wrong acquaintances. Like many a character in the early American sentimental novel, as well as in didactic success manuals of the 1840s such as *Hints to a Tradesman* and *The Young Merchant,* this rural youth becomes friendly with a dissolute young clerk who leads him into vice. Once Harry is persuaded to quaff a drink, he becomes susceptible to all types of depraved revelry. Taken to a gambling hall, he acquires a debt to a fast young man and agrees to be panderer to his new creditor. Sinking lower into vice, he becomes the paramour of a loose woman, steals from his employer, and finally robs a bank. He dies a raving madman, his conscience overpowering him.

But for those who could avoid the three temptations of the city, "wine, the play and the grosser pleasures of the senses," the metropolis did not have to be a place of corruption. Pierce Wentworth, although only a carpenter's apprentice, studies at night and subscribes to an apprentice's library. Imbued with the Protestant ethic and uninterested in aping fashionable society or in indulging sensual appetites, he works hard at a useful trade, studies, saves, and eventually, becomes a recognized, brilliant architect who builds a European palace. During a period when the self-improvement book was being consumed by people anxious to elevate their status, novels like this served as subliterary manuals for rising above the temptations of the city.

Many mid-nineteenth-century hack writers adapted the archetypal theme of a young man's initiation into the ways of the world to the new setting of the American city. Instead of placing the hero on an enchanted island or in a sea of monsters, popular authors put their young gallants in the mysterious world of the metropolis. Those who succumbed to the city's Sirens were doomed. In another novel, *Paul Perril,* Ingraham demonstrated that incorruptible youths could stop their ears to the bewitching songs of Boston's tempters. When Paul, a virtuous lad from Maine, visits Boston, he is shocked to see how the city has turned his brothers from God-fearing folk into Sabbath-breaking heathen: "They smoked cigars, drank wine at soda shops, and visited place where vice and profligacy nightly held their licentious levees" (p. 14). But Paul resists the blandishments of his wayward companions and remains faithful to the morality of his country home.

While the hero of Herman Melville's novel *Redburn* can be initiated into the mysteries of London by a ne'er-do-well and yet remain incorruptible, the namesake of A. L. Stimson's potboiler *Easy Nat* is not an athletic enough Christian to stand up to the "wayward ways of Boston bars and New York novelties." He can keep his virtue only by living on a farm. But his friend Edwin Fairbanks, who is firmly cemented to the Protestant ethic, receives his first lucky break when he leaves an abusive country home for the city. There he finds the opportunity to learn a trade, help the poor, and study at Harvard Law School. His adherence to the teachings of Poor Richard brings him knowledge, higher social status, and even true love.

V. M. Griswold's novel *Hugo Blanc, The Artist* varied the theme of the city as a spiritual proving ground. The idealistic hero goes to New York City to pursue his dream of becoming a painter. But Hugo finds that in the artistic capital of the nation ignorant businessmen act as arbiters of public taste. They patronize artists who use cheap, stylish histrionics, while ignoring men of true ability. Despite these tinsel values, Hugo does not compromise his talent. Providentially, he wins recognition when a long-lost, rich relative becomes his sponsor. Once he becomes wealthy, posturing collectors of art pound at his door, overwhelming him with commissions. In the realm of fiction the metropolis allowed a youth with refined sensibilities to unleash his artistic genius and to receive the acclaim of the multitude.

The city thus accommodated itself with plasticity to both good and evil. Graveyards were often the gothic setting for the latter. Sensational books like George Lippard's *The Nazarene,* Charles Averill's *Secrets of the Twin Cities,* and George Thompson's *City Crimes* pictured Philadelphia, New York City, and Boston as infested with daring groups of body snatchers. In Charley Bowline's *The Iron Tomb* grave robbers bring their booty to a gigantic Negro who stirs a caldron filled with flesh, bones, and liquid. The body snatchers sell the cleaned skeletons to doctors. Such a repulsive activity was allegedly one of the profitable occupations of urban life: "Strange, strange as it is yet it is but one of the many mysteries conducted in [the] city." Bowline injected further morbid excitement into his tale by moving from the tomb to the medical laboratory. There a doctor is about to dissect the body of his betrothed, brought to him for an anatomy lesson. Just at the point of disaster the physician looks at the face of the corpse, stays his knife, and then learns that his fiancée has only been drugged. The sentimental formula with its compulsory triumph of good over evil obviously could survive the new setting of the city.

Despite the deluge of patently absurd happy endings many urban novels of the mid-nineteenth century unconsciously revealed distrust of a newly emerging business civilization. In metaphors reminiscent of Milton's *Paradise Lost* and Bunyan's *Pilgrim's Progress,* these books warned pilgrims to the modern American metropolis to raise their field of vision from the glittering fair of Beelzebub to the purer atmosphere of the Celestial City. Although set in the prosaic atmosphere of mercantile establishments, such books envisioned the urban environment as both City of Destruction and City of God. Written as cautionary tales to reinforce traditional Christian morality, they dispensed with any critical analysis of social and economic institutions and focused instead on the problem of making money while maintaining personal morality.[3]

An anonymous writer devoted his novel *Herbert Tracy; or, The Trials of Mercantile Life, and the Morality of Trade* to what he considered one of the crucial questions that faced mid-nineteenth-century Americans—namely, was "it possible for a Christian to be a successful merchant?" The answer of the author was an emphatic no. Herbert Tracy comes to New York from Tarrytown to seek his fortune. He finds in his uncle's shop that it is "old-fashioned" to be honest. His uncle advises him, "Make the world believe that you are an out-and-out Methodist, or a long-faced Presbyterian, if you choose, but in business transactions all you have to do is manage and keep on the right side of the law" (p. 86).

In his mercantile apprenticeship Herbert finds mean-spirited men whose whole purpose in life is to make money. But he and an earnest clerk, Longfellow, decide to set up their own business and still maintain their principles. They put their faith in heaven and, when the panic of 1837 strikes, are bankrupted. Bible morality, it would seem, has no place in business. Herbert goes back to Tarrytown to lead a contented life as a tiller of the soil.

Although the author advises his readers to suppress ambition and be satisfied with the "noble," "manly," and "honest" profession of farming, the plot of the story belies its message. For even though the protagonists fail in business, they are not morally contaminated by their migration to the metropolis. While Herbert retreats to the homestead of his forebears, Longfellow remains in New York, where he succeeds as the editor of a city newspaper. Both men also find true love in the city. Herbert meets his Fanny, a pious girl who visits the dens of the poor to relieve affliction. Longfellow is happily united with Herbert's sister, who has taken the providential step of leaving her country home to mix in city society. Thus while the city did not provide material rewards it did offer human gratifications for principled men who fought against greed.

Not all fictional characters maintained their honesty in urban literature of this period. Popular writers described the game of the votaries of Mammon. The first rule was always to lie to the customers. An overstocked merchant was to say this was the very last article he had in the shipment. The second rule was to show a country merchant a sample and then send a different product after it was purchased. The third rule was to capture the trade of a country businessman by offering merchandise at less than the fair trade price and then to provide him with overpriced trash. The fourth rule was to line the front of the store with empty cartons to give potential clients the impression that they were dealing with a firm with heavy orders. The fifth rule was to adulterate products. Coffee was to be mixed with damaged beans, oil diluted with cheap whale sperm, and liquor with water.[4] A sixth was to expose patrons to the disreputable haunts of the metropolis: "As Religion maintains ministers of purity and truth to recall the wandering into paths of peace, so does Commerce support an infernal priesthood to entice the weak into wickedness."[5]

Business chicanery was not a special preserve of the metropolis, however, and books like James Fenimore Cooper's *Home As Found* and V. M. Griswold's *Hugo Blanc* accused village storekeepers of charging the poor higher prices than the rich, shortchanging customers and padding their bills, and presenting worthless, adulterated products as quality merchandise. Dollar worship was a national virus.

Yet no place in America evoked more terrifying mystery than Wall Street. In the popular imagination it was the seat of a power that could ruin the entire country. It was the scene of ruthless machinations remote from popular control. There bogus companies sold shares in nonexistent oil wells and gold mines. There gentlemen financiers watered stock to profit those on the executive boards. "Every operation is a conspiracy to defraud, by rogues who ought to be serving the State in Sing Sing. Where the thief steals a few dollars, and the common gambler wins a few tens or hundreds, this aristocratic villain plunders thousands."[6] At a time when the skulduggery of prominent families on the stock market was ruining small investors, Frederick Jackson in *A Week in Wall Street* and *The Victim of Chancery* indicted men on the "Change" for making two hundred percent profit on other people's money, thereby accumulating such enormous fortunes that they could control the destiny of the American people. Lippard, a prototypic populist, also blamed bankers for reaping a harvest from the ruin they sowed. In his novels *The Nazarene* and *New York,* economic depressions were the handiwork of these princes of paper who conspired to flood the cities with notes and forced businessmen to lay off laborers.

By the 1850s some popular authors grudgingly began to recognize that personal rectitude would not ensure success in the city. Richard Kimball's own experience as a lawyer on Wall Street convinced him that financial forces beyond the control of any individual could destroy the accumulation of many years. In his novel *Undercurrents of Wall-Street* he portrayed his protagonist, Charley Parkinson, plunged into bankruptcy, not through intemperance or wild speculation, but through the failure of houses to which he had extended credit. First in 1837 and then again in 1847, a business panic sends his fortune skidding. If he is to keep a roof over his family's head, he must learn to lie, manipulate, and swindle—all legally. He hates his work on Wall Street but has no choice. Yet Kimball in the end, like many other popular writers, could not refrain from employing the stale device of rewarding virtue. Mr. Parkinson, who labors at a humiliating occupation, gains little from his efforts. But a one-time college friend uses Parkinson's repayment of a loan to invest in city real estate. At a strategic moment of need the erstwhile acquaintance reappears with $30,000 to save the hero from poverty. Thus an author who sympathized with the plight of the "reduced rich" and the values of a bourgeois society could not resist reuniting the victims of Wall Street with their former wealth.

Even where a protagonist could make his millions, his creator asked, *Was He Successful?* In a novel written in 1863 Kimball portrayed the son of a Connecticut farmer, Hiram Meeker, who longs for fame and fortune. Although raised in the supposedly virtuous countryside, Hiram develops into a calculating, shrewd materialist who knows how to maintain a facade of piety. It takes no city to corrupt this oily hypocrite. Like many Yankees of the period who were assuming a commanding position over New York City's commerce, Hiram finds that Gotham is the natural arena for his talents; thus he migrates to the metropolis. Within a year he achieves a position of importance in New York mercantile life and becomes engaged to a girl whom he considers to be a sound investment. However, when his fiancée's father is bankrupted he speedily breaks the relationship.

Later, he marries an heiress despite her sour disposition and unsightly appearance. By shrewdly investing in city real estate her fortune of $200,000, he becomes one of the richest men in the Empire City, worth five to ten million dollars. But Hiram must pay in his later years for his arrogance. His daughter runs off with an Italian would-be count, actually a penniless member of an opera troupe. His son leaves for Europe in disgrace to avoid criminal prosecution for forgery. Hiram is paralyzed with a stroke. He is a multimillionaire, but his worldly success is mere veneer. Yet the author never blames the city for Hiram's undoing. He contrasts his defects of character with the selflessness of his brother Frank, who as a physician in the city utilizes his talents to save the lives of the poor. Once again, then, we see that in an age of rampant individualism the popular book propounded the notion that the individual was free in the city to choose a life of acquisitiveness or altruism.

Quite as important as the Sodom and El Dorado motifs was the image of the city as a Babylon inimical to the nation's spiritual and political ideals. Urban novelists frequently depicted ministers as hypocrites and their parishioners as rogues. Repeating the charges made by evangelical reformers that the church in the city was failing to reach large portions of the urban population, popular books like Mary Eastman's *Fashionable Life*, Augustine Duganne's *Tenant-House*, and Kimball's *To-Day* pictured the poor congregating on Sunday on the wharfs of the city, where they amused themselves drinking, smoking, and cursing; the rich, meanwhile, sat back in velvet-cushioned pews where they could hear music and sermons which eased their self-satisfied consciences. William Wirt Howe used barbed rhyme in *The Pasha Papers* to ridicule à la mode worship in the city:

O men! who have store of money and meat,
And women whose souls are pure and sweet:
O worshipping thousands! who meekly meet,
And prayer and praise and text repeat: ...
Tell me, I pray you, if tell you may,
    In Charity's name
    Are you to blame,
    That in a street of a Christian city,
    With none save God to see or pity,
    A fair young girl yields up her breath,
        Frozen to death? [pp. 151–52]

The metropolis might erect gorgeous mansions to the glory of God, pay large salaries for its ministers, and donate vast sums for foreign missions, but in the image conveyed by Lippard's *Quaker City* and Duganne's *Knights of the Seal* its heart was hardened to the misery in its very midst. Yet, as we shall see in chapter 12, this negative view contrasts sharply with another school of popular writing which celebrated missionary activity in the slums.

Popular books pilloried clergymen not only for numbing their congregations to the blight of the city but for hiding lives of sin behind religious robes. Lippard, the writer of sensational exposés who had trained for the ministry in the Methodist church but dropped out because of his disillusionment with the actual practice of the faith, in the popular shocker *Quaker City* told of seemingly pious parsons going to Monk's Hall to revel in midnight orgies. Within five years the book was in its twenty-seventh edition. In his novel *New York, Its Upper Ten and Lower Million,* one of the army of urban savages is Herman Barnhurst, spiritual leader of a wealthy congregation. He "was a minister for the sake of a large salary, fine carriage, a splendid house." Although a man of the cloth, he seduces a young girl, forces her to have an abortion—which brings about her death—and murders her father. One of his colleagues, the Reverend Bulgin, is also a lecher, adept at seducing the women in his congregation.

The cherished ideals of the Republic could become as hollow in the city as the professions of its ministers. At a time of ultimate danger, the Civil War, the writer Henry Morford exposed the perfidy of speculators who sought profits while their nation was in danger. In his novels *The Day of Shoddy, Shoulder-Straps,* and *The Coward,* New York, the center of commercial operations of the continent, becomes the central point of corruption. Shoddy textile merchants sell to the Union uniforms "upon which whole generations of moths [had] run riot." Dishonest businessmen lease vessels for combat at a monthly cost equal to the whole value of the ship. Others sell horses used for dragging dirt on the city's streets as steeds for service in the cavalry. Citizens, anxious to receive bounties for recruiting men for military service, organize gangs of street sweepers, drunken vagabonds, and even convicts into regiments. Men who have no intention of fighting take commissions so that they might have "Colonel," "Major," or "Captain" attached to their name. Officers desert their commands but nevertheless sport their uniforms of "unimpeachable blue and gold" in order to enjoy the adulation of women as war heroes. "Sunshine soldiers" draw pay for raising brigades which exist only on paper. In short, a "shoddy" aristocracy trades upon the nation's crisis, supplying the Union with "shoddy coats, shoddy shoes, shoddy blankets, shoddy tents, shoddy horses, shoddy arms, shoddy ammunition, shoddy boats, shoddy beef and bread, shoddy bravery, shoddy liberality, shoddy patriotism, shoddy loyalty, shoddy statesmanship, shoddy personal devotion."[7]

Yet despite the existence of such leeches, Morford did not indict the entire city for profiteering and showed that shoddiness was no monopoly of the metropolis: "Many of the good people of the country believe in the exploded nonsense about green fields making mankind more honest . . . than pavements,—and who do not know that . . . there is no exclusive patent for goodness or even for wickedness existing in a particular spot . . . because it happened to be capped with a flagstone or tufted with a few blades of grass."[8] Though New York City sheltered cads, it also contained patriots ready to lay down their lives for the Union; though it harbored spies from "the brothel to the brownstone," it also housed volunteers like the New York Zouaves, a fire brigade that battled the flames of rebellion without flinching.

In summary, popular literature carried the flat-footed message that metropolitan centers abounded with dangers to traditional morality. They teemed with villains who would sully the purity of women, wreck the financial security of families, dishonor religion, betray the ideals of the nation. But, significantly, popular books did not picture the city itself as a threat to American values. The city was too much a talisman of material progress to be totally cast in moral shadow. Instead, novelists allowed urban schemers to carry the burden of evil. In a period of rapid economic expansion with temptations to untrammeled individual expression, readers could displace their lusts and aggressions onto these wicked characters. In the realm of imagination they could, as Simon Lesser in *Fiction and the Unconscious* has indicated, fulfill their unsanctioned wishes by identifying with the villain who trampled on a code of restricted behavior and, at the same time, expiate their guilt by seeing such ne'er-do-wells punished.

Quite as important as the abundance of knaves in urban potboilers was the prevalence of fools. Most often these characters were young and country-born. Vulnerable to the sweet cheats of the metropolis, they suffered some terrible retribution for their flaccid commitment to Christian virtue. Their sad fate served as a reminder to young people that the standards of behavior espoused by their elders were still relevant. Like an oft-repeated Sunday service ritual, the typical scenario reassured the public that in a time of dramatic demographic change old values could survive in a complex, new setting. In novel after novel the obligatory betrayal was followed by an obligatory rescue and reunion. Protagonists who clung to a familiar code of conduct emerged triumphant in a locale filled with danger. How could the reader escape the conclusion that even in an environment as sinister as the city he need not fear to tread? The triumphant bourgeois ideology of laissez-faire, which envisioned harmony amidst the strife of the marketplace, found a counterpart in popular tales which suggested a reconciliation of conflicting interests and classes within the city.

In contrast to the literature of the post–Civil War era, popular writers of the mid-nineteenth century did not yet conceive urban society as a place of crushing defeat—a habitation that brought loneliness, alienation, personal disintegration. Rather they perceived it as an exciting locale which challenged the mettle of the moral man and woman. Ironically, at a time when the prescient foresaw the doom of the old rural order, hack authors fell back on the ethical clichés of the seventeenth century and provided reassurance that cherished values could survive in the city. To use Marcus Hansen's concept, they gave first-generation immigrants, caught between two cultures, a vital link with familiar traditions. By emphasizing the strength of old-fashioned virtues—abstinence, piety, and industry—as armor against the perils of urban life; they offered to the uprooted a sense of cultural continuity with the past. Such cultural ballast could cushion the psychological shock of transplantation: it allowed disoriented newcomers to bridge the chasm between their country traditions and new urban realities. Furthermore, by charting the terra incognita of the American metropolis, the writers of "dreadfuls" helped would-be pilgrims to acquire the knowhow for grappling with the challenges of a magnetic but strange society. The urban writer thus provided more than a sensational story; he offered a blueprint for survival.

5

THAT OH-SO-WICKED HIGH SOCIETY
The Urban Aristocracy

So far we have seen how mid-nineteenth-century popular literature preached a conservative message. Written at a time when cities were caught in the eddies of onrushing change, it tossed out an anchor of time-honored values. Strict adherence to tradition, it taught, would preserve urbanites from marital, business, religious, and political deceits. It would also strengthen them, as we shall now see, against a new menace—the rise of a conspicuously wealthy elite.

Between 1820 and 1870 the rich became much more visible and lavished upon themselves a standard of living that anticipated the conspicuous consumption of the Gilded Age. De Tocqueville's observations of an egalitarian society notwithstanding, we now know, thanks to the work of Edward Pessen and other revisionist scholars, that in the cities of America a privileged minority representing less than 5 percent of the urban population owned about 50 percent of the community's wealth. Enjoying an opulent standard of living that compared well with that of the Southern planter aristocracy, this urban oligarchy built marble-fronted townhouses which they staffed with retinues of servants and decorated with elaborate furnishings of mahogany and gilt. Where once they had lived on streets in proximity to their poorer neighbors, by 1845, encouraged by improvements in intraurban transportation, they had moved from the heart of the business district to distinctive neighborhoods occupied by their social equals. Where once they had enjoyed a comfortable but unostentatious manner of life, they now paraded themselves before the masses in costly garments and handsome private carriages. Experiencing a splendor that sharply separated them from the vast majority of ordinary citizens, they vacationed at expensive

61

watering spots, sat in special boxes at the theater, and socialized with each other in exclusive clubs.

How did contemporaries react to the growing power, position, and wealth of a charmed circle of urbanites? Were all observers as blinded by the nation's surface prosperity as De Tocqueville? When we examine the commentaries of other foreign visitors, like Harriet Martineau and Frances Trollope, as well as the writings of American authors like Ralph Waldo Emerson, James Fenimore Cooper, and Edgar Allan Poe, once again we find perpetuation of the myth that in the United States the urban masses enjoyed unrivaled opportunities for material abundance. However, when we inspect long-neglected books manufactured for the common man, we discover that ordinary Americans were scouring reading fare which voiced concern about the increasing concentration of wealth in the nation's cities. Repeating the successful formula used by Charles Dickens in *Sketches by Boz* (1836), which emphasized the contrast between plenty and poverty in London, hack writers in the United States indicated that America's urban communities were reproducing the glaring social distinctions of Europe.

If the popular arts are a seismograph which records the shock waves buffeting a society, as authorities on the mass media contend, then books which invite condescending mirth from a literary point of view, provide us with an invaluable instrument for measuring the reactions of Americans to the ever-widening chasm which was separating the rich from the poor. They furnish us with a collective record of the cultural mentality of a society rankled by an accelerating maldistribution of wealth. For their images of the urban oligarchy document intuitively what cliometricians have only recently discovered—namely, that inequality of condition was the rule in the nation's cities during the mid-nineteenth century.

To judge by the welter of newspaper articles describing the extravagant costume balls of society's luminaries and the vogue of compendiums cataloguing the fortunes of wealthy men, a ready market existed in the mid-nineteenth century for publications which allowed readers to peep into the world of high society. Between 1820 and 1870 enterprising authors produced no fewer than seventy-five books which promised the public an inside look at the urban plutocracy. Paradoxically, these productions delighted in detailing the material abundance enjoyed by the city's upper class and, at the same time, courted the common man by ridiculing the excesses of a new moneyed elite.

Many popular writers, anxious to profit from the materialistic interests of the age, exploited the theme of the growing splendor of the American city as a new sort of magical, satanic domain. Instead of carrying their audience to castles in Spain, they spun stories of a glamorous urban universe inhabited by belles and beaux. For palaces they substituted palatial brownstones; for fair princesses they created fashionable ladies clothed in silks and satins. No ball in a land of make-believe could outshine the scenes in urban novels of people dancing through the night in stately townhouses.[1]

Even those writers who satirized the follies of fashionable society also provided a window on the world of the idle rich, filling their accounts with details of fine food, silken sofas, stunning costumes, and dazzling soirées. They might poke fun at epicureanism, but they also permitted their audience vicariously to sip champagne and feast on partridges and vol-au-vent. They might condemn the extravagant carriages and clothing of the rich as unbefitting a democratic republic, but at the same time they chronicled for a curious public the consumption patterns of a sybaritic urban society.[2]

Some writers recognized that what many readers wanted was information on the social code of fashionable society. Manuals of etiquette, instructing aspiring social climbers on decorum, were already an important part of the book trade. Many Americans, imbued with the ideology of limitless social mobility in their nation, wanted to acquire the manners which would hasten their advancement in society. Novels which described the elegant ways of genteel people and satirized the vulgarity of status seekers paralleled this literature. They allowed readers to distance themselves psychologically from financially successful fools and concomitantly to learn the rules of good taste practiced by an aristocracy of merit.

In spite of the fact that recent quantitative scholarship has indicated that only 2 percent of the upper class in northeastern cities during the second quarter of the nineteenth century actually came from humble origins, numerous satires on the noveaux riches uncritically accepted the idea popularized by Moses Yale Beach in *The Wealth and Biography of Wealthy Citizens of the City of New York* that fashionable society consisted primarily of self-made men. Dazzled by the more ostentatious lifestyle of the cities' leading families, popular authors attributed the new, flashy exhibition of wealth to arrivistes. They contrasted the constructive manner in which the old Whig gentry expended its fortune on behalf of the city's unfortunates with the wasteful self-indulgence of the new moneyed class. They compared the tasteful refinement, the unobtrusive demeanor of the Knickerbocker aristocracy with the vulgarity, the ludicrous excess, of "small potato patricians."

The advent of a parvenu oligarchy seemed a threat to America's twin founts of wisdom—John Calvin and Benjamin Franklin. What would happen to the vaunted national virtues of energy and enterprise if a leisured elite could enjoy wealth without work? How could the wisdom of Poor Richard guide future generations if financiers, scorning honest labor, could flourish from manipulating a phantom universe of notes and securities?

In ridiculing the excesses of the city's very rich, popular writers often utilized the effeminate male of the metropolis, the dandy, as a stock figure in their tales. Unlike the farmer whose hands were rough and heart was soft, the gay blade of city life hid his smooth hands behind soft kid gloves and his calloused heart behind a flow of facile talk. For him it was unthinkable to appear without a high stand-up collar, a flowing cravat, a Genin hat, two fancy rings, and patent leather boots. If he were to make the grade of "blood," he had to parade himself in extremely tight pants, keep his mustache artfully curled, and scent himself with perfume. The true occupation of his existence was to promenade on Broadway at the correct hour. He had to know how to sneer at everybody, consume pâté de foie gras ardently, smoke strong cigars, discourse on vintage wines, dash horses, and act gallant with the ladies. He had to be a familiar face at fashionable brothels, saloons, and gambling dens. If his father were a rich man, he went on $900 evening sprees, and if he possessed a very rich parent, he distinguished himself with $2,000 fêtes. Even if he had but slender resources, he was adept at gratifying his large appetites. A gentleman with a ready wit and a proper ebony cane went far if he prattled about the arts with an amorous, rich married woman. He could even obtain his regulation uniform if he knew the right tailor. In exchange for a discount on his dashing clothes, he could introduce his friends to the obliging tradesman.[3]

Equally ludicrous was the belle, a product of the new wealth and leisure available to upper-class women in the city. With men now working in business establishments separated from their homes, the rich woman had little to do other than devote her efforts to fashion. Popular authors, who we may infer were addressing a less carefree audience, ridiculed these privileged women, portraying them as delicate creatures who wore the finest furs, rode in the most stylish equipages, and knew the latest French dances and the newest French millinery, but who knew nothing of housekeeping and cared even less for child rearing. Such a woman might be graceful, witty, and charming, but she was, in reality, an affected, empty-headed individual whose "accomplishments . . . [were] merely dabbled in" and who expected "to be supported in a sumptuous style, until her dying day."[4] She might appear elegant in her corseted, bustled costume, but readers of Frank Hazelton's *Mysteries of Troy* and Edward Dixon's *Scenes in the Practice of a New York Surgeon* learned that a woman who was a slave to fashion was a likely candidate for consumption, melancholy, indigestion, constipation, and atrophy of the maternal organs. When a belle invited people to her home, it was not for a party but for a con- versazione. If a visitor were impolitic enough to comment on the weather, he was dismissed as a ruffian, but he triumphed with such a comment as,: "When we alighted from our sleigh . . . I noticed how firmly the edge of the street was pressed down by the feet of the hundreds who have called on you; and I could but not think how truly that white surface upon which the prints of so many boots were beautifully blended, typi- fied the purity of motives which brought the owners of those boots to your door."[5] In short, the belle was a counterfeit woman, a beauty with brains but no heart, intelligence but no morality.

Popular authors pilloried the urban nouveaux riches not only because they corrupted their own lives with tawdry splendor but also because they reared a generation of indolent misfits. At a time when concerned citizens were emphasizing the need for firmer control in cities shaken by social upheaval, literature written for the common man attacked the rich for raising their offspring without puritanical, patriarchal discipline. Books like Nancy Lasselle's *Annie Grayson,* Maria Lamas's *The Glass,* and Mary Torrey's *City and Country Life* revealed that fashionable women found the duties of motherhood tedious and abandoned their children to servants. By the time such pampered youths could walk, they were adept at controlling their nurses and abusing their parents. Introduced early in life to gay society, they sipped champagne, whiffed mild cigars, and dressed outlandishly. In a comedy written by Eugene Raux for the stage in 1846, *The Road to Fortune,* an old-fashioned, hardworking man laments the unruliness of a younger generation of would-be gentlemen: "Instead of being active and industrious, they waste their time . . . in lounging, in dissipating, in indulging in vicious propensities. . . . What a sad picture, indeed! . . . the inheritors of our free and glorious institutions so degraded and effeminate—contaminated with idleness and dissipation!" (p. 10). Thus popular authors, writing in several genres, fell back on a contemporary bromide which explained mounting social disorders in terms of overindulgence within the family.

As the rich increasingly isolated their children from the rest of society by sending them to exclusive boarding schools, where they acquired the refinements necessary for moving in a selective social circle, popular books upbraided the leisure class for training its young in fatuous accomplish- ments. According to Joseph Alden's *Elizabeth Benton,* Catherine Williams's *Aristocracy,* Margaret Smith's *What Is Gentility?* and Rhoda White's *Mary Staunton,* among other books which upheld the puritan ethos of a useful, moral education, the daughters of the elite learned French, not as a means of understanding the culture, but because Society deemed it pleasant to utter commonplaces in a foreign language; they were taught music, not to express spiritual yearnings, but because it was helpful in capturing suitors. William Wirt Howe in his satire of New York mores, *The Pasha Papers,* deplored the fact that what young ladies learned in private schools was to "have good children, good looks, good manners, and Nothing To Do" (p. 59).

Popular authors contended that the morality of an older generation would prove ultimately triumphant. Their stories broadcast the commonly held, if erroneous, belief that the rich would be impoverished by their rash speculations. Just at a moment in American history when the wealthy were enhancing their economic strength and the less fortunate were finding it increasingly difficult to improve their financial status, an important segment of popular fiction fed the national myth that this was a socially fluid age in which "fortunes rose and fell mercurially." In the typical scenarios of this school, fictional embodiments of Poor Richard ethics gained affluence by their productive labor, while the leisured elite suddenly lost its ill-gotten riches. As Herbert Ross Brown has pointed out, in a day of ledgerbook morality literature written for the masses suggested that Christianity would reward with earthly dividends those steeped in traditional virtues.

In a characteristic morality tale, *Hartley Norman,* the novelist Allen Hampden contrasted the crude nouveaux riches with hardworking families ennobled by their labors. While the hero's pious mother, Mrs. Norman, must sew tirelessly to earn a mere subsistence, her employers, the Shavers, are "purse-proud parvenus" who live for display and long for recognition; but an upstart aristocracy of this sort, the reader was assured, was perched on the edge of disaster. Unlike those who meekly labored, the speculator could lose his mansion by one mistake on the market. Thus the Shavers, untrained in a useful trade, ultimately lose their gaudy splendor and must eke out a pitiful existence in the slums. On the other hand, Hartley Norman, who has steadily worked at humble occupations, earns a fortune and wins the hand of a beautiful and genuine aristocrat from Latin America.

At a time when the distractions of the metropolis seemed to threaten older values, popular fiction reaffirmed the religious attitudes of America's self-denying forebears. Nathaniel Hawthorne expressed his distress over the literature that was winning the favor of the common man in the 1850s. In a letter to his publisher, Ticknor, he wrote, "America is now wholly given over to a d------d mob of scribbling women, and I would have no chance of success while the public taste is occupied with their trash—and should be ashamed of myself if I did succeed."[6] These "female scribblers" inundated the press with domestic novels which sought to prove the value of religiously based virtues. To a generation perplexed by diminishing economic opportunities, such books carried the reassuring message that inner peace was the only worthwhile wealth. In these novels the beau monde becomes a place where "music, laughing, dancing, fashion and display ... gild the surface" and crush "aching sorrows beneath the weight of an assumed gayety."[7] On the other hand, the humorless wife who in these stories embodies middle-class respectability, one more commodity which was becoming standardized and interchangeable in industrial America, insulates herself from the hollow pleasures of high society and directs her efforts to home and hearth.

The best-selling female writer who exemplified for Hawthorne the decline in public taste, Maria Susanna Cummins, assured her readers that, though they might not frequent the magnificent parlors of the urban "upper ten," they enjoyed a blessedness unknown to the votaries of fashion. In her novel *Mabel Vaughan* the heroine is a sensitive, religious girl who has been raised in the country. At eighteen Mabel is reunited with her wealthy family in New York. Her sister Louise is a vain coquette who ignores her husband and neglects her sons. Her brother Harry, educated in Europe, has become a reckless inebriate. Although Mabel becomes the belle of the season, she awakens to the disease of fashionable life when she sees her brother's progressive degeneration. Moreover, she receives spiritual reinforcement from a poor family, the Hopes, who inspire her by their devotion to others. Mabel decides to abandon glamor for the reformation of her brother Harry.

At this moment the bubble of worldly wealth bursts for her family. Mabel's father becomes involved in a western railroad speculation which leaves him bankrupt. Disaster strikes her sister Louise when her husband is killed in a train accident and she is left penniless. The woman of the world who has lived for vain approbation cannot rally when fortune takes away her riches. She dies from the shock. But Mabel, who has cultivated spiritual values, grows from the crisis. She goes out to the West. In a simple home on the prairie she devotes herself to comforting her father and caring for her sister's two orphaned sons. Harry joins his family and is cured of intemperance. An erring father discovers that stock is empty paper compared to the "Good Book." Free of the scramble for wealth and position, the Vaughans find a serenity that was never theirs in a New York mansion. What is more, Mabel finds true love. In the uncorrupted atmosphere of the prairie she meets a Christian gentleman dedicated to the public good. The noble-hearted couple, joined in holy matrimony, live humbly ever after, aware that "happiness is independent of ornament."[8]

Another group of books developed the theme that high society was inimical to marital fidelity. Beneath the pomp lurked vice. At a time when matrimonial ties among the poor were disintegrating and urban society losing one of its most important props for maintaining authority and discipline, popular writers allowed the allegedly dishonest connubial mores of the upper class to stand as an emblem of the city's lack of restraint. Preservation of the family became the dominant theme of the sentimental novel. Tears, earnest religiosity, and sensationalism usually meant wide sales. A case in point is the popular tearjerker of the 1850s, *Light and Darkness,* in which Mrs. Lizzie Cutler presented the tale of a long-suffering wife mismated to a reckless husband. Marion St. Julian, a model of Victorian virtue, is repelled by a pleasure-seeking society which considers her not quite comme il faut. Her husband, Julian, courted for his brilliant conversation, elegant dress, and good looks, is fascinated with the belle of the season, Florence Fulton. Forsaking the bonds of family, he runs off to Italy with the idol of society. But there retribution comes. Julian dies, and Florence kills herself. The ill-fated pair, blinded by the glitter of the beau monde, lacked the inner light which blessed the lives of simple people.

In the magazine of New York society, the *Home Journal,* editor Nathaniel Willis used the term the "Upper Ten Thousand" to describe the stylish set of Gotham that lived above Bleecker Street, kept carriages, attended Grace Church, subscribed to the opera, gave balls, and maintained both a town and country house. Writers of the popular novel left the impression that this set might have frescoed walls but were without family warmth. Their marriages were loveless matches, little more than business transactions in which a belle matched her "beauty, youth, accomplishments against a town-house, country estate, cottage at Newport and a carriage for every season of the year."[9] Mothers dragged daughters in tawdry silks to Saratoga, where they auctioned their charms to men of position: "Think of it! One of the finest houses on the Avenue; one of the best equipages in the park; servants without end—often without aim; money galore—youth and beauty all her own; and the only inconvenience a husband—he apoplectic."[10] If a family's fortune failed, a daughter was a useful commodity for staving off disaster. It mattered little, in sensational exposés of the wicked well-to-do, whether the girl wanted to marry someone she loved. She would nonetheless be bartered to a lascivious old man, in a business arrangement that saved the family from financial ruin.[11]

With such absence of feeling in choosing a mate, first families fought to marry their daughters into the aristocracy. One of the stock figures in popular fiction was the pseudo-European nobleman who readily conferred his title on an ambitious American heiress. Before long she discovered that she was wedded to an Italian barber, French valet, or home-grown ex-convict.[12] One such stereotyped literary creation appears in M. M. Huet's *Silver and Pewter*. He is Count Van Horn, a man whose only access to courts is of the criminal variety. A wealthy spinster flaunts him among her fashionable circle, who never doubt "that he [is] a Count for he [has] whiskers and moustache of the most approved pattern" (p. 79).

Sentiment had little place in the marriages of fictional upper-class characters. Living in comfort and ease, husbands and wives were strangers to each other. They might inhabit the same house, but a household that revolved around the salon provided no real emotional gratification. In the novel *To-Day* Richard Kimball portrayed a typical successful New York couple. Jacob Illingsworth, a wealthy Wall Street broker, is married to his business; his wife, a leader of *ton* in New York society, is married to fashion. After a full day in his office Jacob dines briefly with his family and then spends his leisure hours in his club to discuss more business matters. For his wife family is a cloak of respectability, but of much less interest than brilliant soirées.

Not all fashionable wives of fiction were so absorbed in the salon. Others, in more lurid stories, spent their energies in the boudoir. No longer satisfied with what mid-nineteenth-century writers considered natural sexual relations within the bonds of marriage, matrons in *Revelations of Asmodeus* and White's *Mary Staunton* dallied the daylight hours away with paramours. In George Thompson's *City Crimes* a fashionable mother and daughter, surfeited with "ordinary" adultery, copulate with blacks and commit sodomy. When their pious husband and father stands in their way, they murder him. Later, to obtain money for further sexual escapades, they plot to sell their virginal daughter and sister to a libertine.

Adultery involved only a small minority of these wealthy fictional wives, but popular literature frequently castigated sophisticated women for sacrificing "the pure happiness of domestic life" for other "heartless amusements of society." Glamorous women might appear to be more desirable than middle-class wives, but once married, many proved to be useless trinkets. Novels like Torrey's *City and Country Life* and Townsend's *The Brother Clerks* showed them so concerned about preserving their figures that they refused to nurse their children. Just as deaf to their husband's needs as to those of their infants, they often forced their spouses to live in expensive, fashionable hotels where, relieved of housework, they carried on intrigues with would-be noblemen. A character in White's *Mary Staunton* complains that husbands have to "toil and labor to gratify the vanity of . . . dolls till their souls and bodies are dry and withered as mummies" (p. 131). The urban upper-class father suffered a similarly unenviable lot. In Harriet Shubrick's *Violet* and Charles Bristed's *The Upper Ten Thousand,* he makes money for the rest of his family to spend. His holiday consists of appearing once every two weeks at a watering place, primarily to pay the bills. For his pains he suffers tyranny from his wife, disrespect from his children.

A trenchant lithograph which appeared as an illustration in a work entitled *New-York Aristocracy or Gems of Japonica-Dom* presented a pictorial image of the misery of marriage among New York's aristocracy. A wife, looking like an overdressed washerwoman, sits with her daughter in a carriage emblazoned with a coronet while two black servants stand in attendance. On the sidewalk sits her emaciated husband, plaintively looking at the family he works so hard to support. The caption tells the rest of the tale: "Mr. Fustian not being allowed to ride in his own carriage, consoles himself looking at it" (pp. 16–17).

Even in death the dashing set was shown to put style before feeling. In one satire on high society, *Cone Cut Corners,* a grieving widow, Mrs. Chesslebury, displays her bereavement by closeting herself with her milliner and dressmaker to work on a proper mourning outfit. She lays her husband to rest in "the best style," hiring the most fashionable undertaker in town. The horse carrying the hearse is dressed in a black blanket, a white neckcloth, and a plumed headdress. Social lions come to pay their respects to the gracious widow, who provides her guests with a distinguished buffet of foods and champagne. Chesslebury's daughter blames her father's inconsiderately timed demise for spoiling her honeymoon.

Friendships seemed to provide no more warmth than did family relations, at least in novels like *Oran, the Outcast* and *Our "First Families."* Innumerable social acquaintances were graced with "a mind for maneuvering, an ear for scandal, and an eye for faults." Novelists ridiculed the plutocracy for holding joyless parties that nevertheless were always *en règle.*

During a period when romanticism inspired admiration for a life in harmony with nature, fashionable artifices could be viewed only as perverse. Cosmopolitan gilding, writers often asserted, could never supply the contentment of the simple yeoman surrounded by the works of God. A poem in Talbot Greene's novel *American Nights Entertainments* contrasted the manly pursuits of the farmer with the vapid pleasures of the urban aristocrat:

Aloof from the scenes of riot, noise and strife,
Enjoys the comforts of rural life.
Him no anxiety, no fears appal;
He ne'er submits to low ambition's thrall.
. . . .
Though sometimes blunt, he always is sincere,
And what he is, is willing to appear.
Though no riches of a foreign loom
Nor costly painting decorate his room,
. . . .
Health tempers all his cups, and at his board
Reigns the cheap luxuries his fields afford.
Seen from the eyelet-holes of his retreat.
High Life appears a bubble and a cheat. [p. 185]

Hack writers, living in a period of accelerating industrial growth and the concomitant consolidation of wealth among the privileged few, often were at their florid best elegizing the glories of a country home.

Satires of high society in pulp fiction suggested that, instead of suffocating physically and emotionally in the drawing rooms of the city, people should be satisfied with the simpler society of rural America. Reinforcing this contention were the many scenes showing the urban elite holidaying in the country for several months of each year. To maintain a sense of psychic well-being, the rich apparently had to return to the land. In John Brougham's play *Life in New York,* an upper-class lady comments that during the summer "no one stays in town. I do so languish for solitude and Saratoga" (p. 11). Hardly a book concerned with the manners and mores of the urban plutocracy failed to omit episodes of the affluent whiling away the summer months in their country estate or in some fashionable watering spot.[13]

The conflict between the values of rural dwellers and members of high society was the theme of the hit play *Fashion!* produced in 1845. Its author, Anna Cora Mowatt Ritchie, pitted a pretentious New York family, the Tiffanys, against a farmer from Catteraugus, Adam Trueman. The Tiffanys live in a hothouse world that is both lonely and ludicrous. Mrs. Tiffany, a stereotype of the ignorant well-to-do, hires a French maid to teach her how to be "distingué." One of Mlle. Millinette's precepts is that "nothing is more fashionable than to keep people waiting." Mrs. Tiffany stuffs her parlor with overstuffed furniture and overstuffed people. Would-be poets invited to her salon serve as appendages to a home packed with other tasteless ornaments. As Mrs. Tiffany redoubles her attempts to keep up fashionable appearances, her desperate husband is driven to earn ever more money.

The hollowness of urban high life is contrasted with rural simplicity, exemplified by Gertrude, a country lass who is employed as governess to Mrs. Tiffany's daughter Seraphina, and by Adam Trueman, an old friend from the country. Gertrude asks sarcastically, "Do you think I could possibly prefer the ramble of the woods to a promenade on Broadway? A wreath of scented wild flowers to a bouquet of these sickly exotics? . . . Or do you imagine that I could enjoy the quiet conversation of my Geneva friends more than the edifying chit-chat of a fashionable drawing room?" (p. 37). Trueman further condemns the affectation and artificiality of the Tiffanys's existence: "The *fashion*-worship had made hypocrites of you all! I have lived in your house only three days, and I have heard more lies than were ever invented in a Presidential election! . . . Your warm heart has grown cold over your ledgers—your light spirit heavy with calculations! You have traded away your youth—your hopes— your tastes—for wealth!" (p. 23). Trueman, one of "nature's noblemen," understands that etiquette is no substitute for virtue, or fashionable clothes a replacement for pure morals.

When the Tiffany bubble bursts, the honest yeoman, Adam Trueman, is there to save the poseurs. He agrees to pay the notes the desperate Tiffany has forged, on the condition that the henpecked husband sell his house and move his family to the country. There, in the healthy surroundings of nature, the spoiled family will be able to learn economy, independence, and virtue.

Criticism of high society and celebration of rural life also constituted the theme of the epistolary novel *High Life in New York,* by best-selling author Ann Sophia Stephens. In a series of letters Jonathan Slick, a male Alice in Wonderland from Connecticut, gives a purportedly naive account of the customs of Gotham's high society, which smacks of the Whig gentry's prejudices against the vulgarity of the nouveaux riches. He is confounded by the artificiality of fashionable society. To him women in bustles look humpbacked or rachitic. The note from his city cousin announcing that she will be "at home" on Thursday evenings makes him think that she is gadding about all the other days. That a soirée is held at a much later hour than a quilting bee illustrates to him the laziness of New Yorkers. Paying an unannounced visit to a belle, he finds her skin to be yellow as saffron, her teeth in a glass, and her lovely hair lying on a chest of drawers.

The glamor of the metropolis is equally false, he finds. Distinguished men with mustaches seem to him a "tribe of ribbed nose baboons"; an "exquisite" with fine broadcloth, glistening boots, and slicked-down hair he calls a "woman in men's clothes" making "an etarnal coot of himself." Champagne to him is but a funny cider, a fork a nonsensical instrument that allows food to slide through the prongs. He soon misses "a good turkey with plenty of gravy and tatur" after finding himself ill from the "heap of tarnal cakes and sugar things" he has been forced to digest. The elegant women of the metropolis are, in his eyes, not half so pretty as the simply frocked lasses of the country, who "look as fresh and sweet as full blown roses." Slick reacts in a similar fashion to city dwellings in which "[e]very thing ... [is] as costly ... as could be" but "so proud of itself that it [can't] agree with its neighbors" (p. 43).

Mrs. Stephens's satire on the new moneyed elite coincided with a spate of contemporary books which ridiculed the members of this group for their exhibitionism, pretensions, and materialism. Writers like Huet, Arthur Townley, Azel S. Roe, and Charlotte Hilbourne depicted them as ignoramuses who accumulated splendid libraries, selected by booksellers and dusted by maids, but not read. These would-be aristocrats believed that putting livery on their servants and purchasing country seats could, in this republican country, make them genteel. "De" and "Fitz" prefixed to their names, however, could not obscure their crudeness. In the end, in the estimation of numerous writers, they were distinguished for having "more brass than brains, more malice than manhood."

In delineating the differences between the elegant upper class and rich buffoons, often modeled on Molière's *Bourgeois Gentilhomme,* many popular books revealed a sensitivity to the distinction between old and new wealth. Implicit in their criticism of a moneyed aristocracy was the conservative assumption that new social groups could not be trusted to preserve a democratic and also disciplined society. Self-made elites, cut loose from the moral restraints which bound an earlier genteel leadership, would endanger traditional values.

The remedy against flux, these authors suggested, was to keep the old ruling classes in power. Indeed, we may consider their satires on the nouveaux riches as weapons of cultural imperialism designed, even if inadvertently, to perpetuate the stratification of society. Although not expressly stated, the message was clear: scorn initiation; accept one's station in life gracefully; follow the ways of one's forebears. Thus, in what had been falsely labeled an era of social mobility, an important segment of popular literature instructed readers to know their place. In spite of the triumph of egalitarian rhetoric in Fourth of July oratory, hack writers like Cummins, Hampden, Bristed, Joseph Nunes, Eliza Henderson Otis, John Vose, and Catharine Maria Sedgwick, to name but a few, criticized men from the lower class who had realized the American dream of financial success. They tried to induce a mass audinece to feel nostalgic for an earlier day when the "right sort" of people ruled.[14]

But literature which glorified the Whig gentry sidestepped serious analysis of America's deepening class cleavages. By focusing the public's attention on a decoy—the nouveaux riches—self-appointed cultural critics sought in their popular fiction to muffle criticism of the oligarchy which was engrossing the largest share of newly generated wealth in the expanding economy of the mid-nineteenth century.

While one school of novelists longed for a golden past when virtuous men dominated municipal life, writers such as Margaret Bayard Smith, George Watterson, George Lippard, Charles Sealsfield, John Beauchamp Jones, and William Wirt Howe bowed to the common man by railing against extremes of wealth and visible social distinctions. As class lines congealed during this period and tensions rose, books aimed at a middle- and lower-class market lamented the fading Jeffersonian dream of an egalitarian society. How, they asked, could a code of equality long survive if an arrogant elite lavished upon itself baronial splendor, affecting the signs of a decadent European aristocracy—escutcheons, coronets, liveried servants, and titles of nobility purchased through the marriages of ambitious daughters? How could the common man keep his dignity if vulgar pretenders formalized a growing code of class distinctions? Would America go the way of Europe and foster a group of parasites while the masses sank deeper and deeper into misery?

Already, novelists implied, the handwriting was on the wall. The great urban centers of the nation were producing unrivaled riches and unprecedented poverty. Men of wealth, deaf to the suffering in their midst, were trying to set themselves up as a new nobility. Such upstarts were an affront to two of the most powerful forces of mid-nineteenth-century America—democracy and nationalism. Affecting the French language, wooing foreign noblemen, imitating European fashions, and rejecting a wholesome native diet, they were an insult to the Republic that made their rapid rise possible.

Novelists who lampooned fashionable society were thus a literary cadre in the Jacksonian drive against privilege. Such writers reflected the growing apprehension of economic monopoly that the popular approval of Andrew Jackson's war against the second Bank of the United States also manifested. Social reformer Lippard, who saw in Old Hickory the embodiment of the people, commented in 1845 on the new urban patrician class: "An aristocracy founded on the high deeds of dentists, tape sellers, quacks, pettifoggers, and bank directors, all jumbled together in a ridiculous mass of absurdities. . . . There is no single word of contempt, too bitter, to express my opinion of this magnificent Pretension—the Aristocracy of the Quaker City! . . . I respect the Mechanic at his bench, though his hands be rough, his face begrimed with toil, his manners uncouth and destitute of polish."[15] Thus if America were to have an aristocracy, writers of this school argued, let it not be one devoted to the new "fripperies" and "follies" of fashion but rather to old-fashioned industry and honesty.

But books written for a mass market did more than register the plaint of the public against special privilege. They also provided reassurance to the reader that the powerful snobs who rode by in their elegant equipages and fine clothes were but "an aristocracy of houses and splendid carriages, of large diamonds and small dogs." Readers could feel less threatened by the plutocracy when they discovered how ludicrous they appeared to a European familiar with genuine nobility: "Mrs. Dish, the leader of the fashionable world . . . knew how to extol the modest, silent merit of those possessed of hundreds of thousands . . . and to reject . . . the arrogance of those who could only count their fifty or twenty-five thousands. Neither rank nor political merit availed in this classification; so that at her *soirées* . . . the man of hundreds of thousands was never in danger of misapplying his *politesse* to one of the mere trumpery of fifty thousand."[16] The masses could feel less envious of a supposed enchanted circle when knowledgeable writers proclaimed that the "best society" was a colossal bore. Hard work, honesty, and an affectionate domestic circle possessed renewed dignity when books exposed the falseness of a fashionable coterie whose ticket of admission was a bulging bank account and a callousness to those who had started out as low as themselves. Although the growing affluence of American cities vexed those still left in moderate circumstances, popular fiction both articulated a growing fear and tried to soothe a festering anxiety.

6

TEARS AND CHEERS FOR THE WORKING CLASS

In the 1830s a lanky, tobacco-chewing spokesman of labor, Seth Luther, articulated a theme which was to become a leitmotif of popular urban literature. In ornamented language reminiscent of the pulp novels of the day, he contrasted the high standard of living of a nonproductive aristocracy with the privation of the producing masses: "While music floats from quivering strings through the perfumed and adorned apartments . . . of the rich, the nerves of the poor . . . are quivering with almost *dying agony,* from *excessive labor* to support this splendor"[1] (Luther's italics). If the situation were not reversed, he warned, capitalists would continue their encroachments at the expense of industrious citizens. This dread of a master class which might reduce the majority of Americans to helplessness manifested the anxiety awakened in contemporaries by the city's growing financial power. In chapter 5 we examined one side of this coin—the fulminations of popular writers against the excesses of a privileged elite; we now must turn to the other, equally important side —the response of urban authors to the condition of the working class in an era of diminishing economic opportunity.

Walt Whitman in his familiar poem "Song of Myself" paid homage to the humble occupations of urban America:

> The clean-hair'd Yankee girl works with
> her sewing machine or in the
> factory or the mill, . . .
> The floor-men are laying the floor, the
> tinners are tinning the roof,
> the masons are calling for mortar,
> In single file each shouldering his hod
> pass onward the laborers. . . .

To judge by this poem, contemporary authors in the United States at mid-century did not fear the proletarianization of the labor force. City workers, so it seemed, kept democratic vistas before themselves while they toiled. But did other writers share the poet's optimistic vision? Was Whitman's serenade part of a chorus celebrating the plebeian economic pursuits of the American metropolis, or were "men of literary taste," as Frederick Law Olmsted thought, "apt to overlook the working-classes, and to confine the records they [made] of their own times ... to the habits and fortunes of their own associates or to those ... of superior rank to themselves?"[2]

The books of the nation's literary giants during this period paint a dark urban landscape pocked by brutish slums. But while authors like Nathaniel Hawthorne, Herman Melville, and Edgar Allan Poe painted a woeful canvas of working-class districts, they did not descend into the workaday lives of their inhabitants. From on high they branded the city's commercialism for poisoning the human spirit. Repelled by the cries of fishmongers and organ grinders, they viewed the urban mass with a mixture of contempt, terror, and despair. For them, as Morton and Lucia White have shown, commercial endeavors were an emblem of man's desecration of nature, and mechanical progress augured a menacing future in which doomed American cities would share the blight of London, Liverpool, Paris, and Rome.

More prosaic books, however, display neither the metaphysical joy of the poet nor the Olympian detachment of belletristic authors; but rather the grime of proletarian occupations. A legion of hack writers peopled their books with heroes and heroines who worked as seam-stresses, mechanics, newsboys, and mill hands. Unlike the major literary talents of the period, who like Herman Melville in "The Tartarus of Maids," tended to see the working class as "rows of blank-looking girls with blank ... hands, all blankly folding blank paper," mediocre authors put faces as well as muscle on urban laborers.

While popular writers, curiously, neglected the topic of working-class life in the period 1820–40, which were years brimming over with mili-tant labor activity, between 1840 and 1870 they produced no fewer than sixty-five works of literature which took as their main theme the condition of the urban labor force. At few other times in American history have urban wage earners been as confounded by economic flux. During the decades of the forties, fifties, and sixties, a new capitalist industrial order emerged which facilitated economic growth. Small commercial entrepôts were transformed into sprawling industrial centers. Metropolitan communities mushroomed across the land, visible reminders of America's departure from a familiar agrarian way of life. As Leo Marx has pointed out in *The Machine in the Garden,* to a nation nurtured on Virgilian images of life in a fresh, green world, the city's growing manufacturing activity threatened to replace repose with noise, nature with artifice, harmony with upheaval.

Many popular writers mirrored the anxiety of those alienated by the increasing complexity of American civilization. Their scenes of urban working-class privation showed the death of the Jeffersonian dream. The independent yeoman, drawn by the mirage of easy riches, would become an exploited underling. Unable to bargain either with the proprietor or the consumer, he would perform backbreaking labor without the traditional reward of American plenty. In his *New York in Slices* the journalist George Foster counseled his readers: "...go among the naked and apparent miseries of the metropolis...and now stop your nose! for the horrible stench of the poverty, misery, starvation, crime, filth, and licentiousness that congregate in our Large City....And these are the very people, too, who do nearly all the real work of the whole City, whose brows sweat, and whose muscles ache in the toil which all ought to share" (p. 4). Such a passage may sound hyperbolic, but it expressed what contemporary investigators reported in dispassionate tone: namely, that a vast labor force earned the wages of bare survival. Crowded into cities expanding too fast to absorb them, workers labored under an ever-present cloud of salary cuts and unemployment.

In contrast to Whitman's exuberant celebration of the workman's limitless prospects in America, unheralded popular authors saw a boom-and-bust economy buffeting the labor force and nourishing urban pauperism. A theme of pulp literature was that poverty in the city defied all the old rules. Dion Boucicault in his play *The Poor of New York,* written during the panic of 1857, illustrated how a hardworking person could be reduced to beggary; unable to cultivate his own garden, he was victimized by speculators who raised the price of bread during a depression. With European immigration at a flood, novelist James Maitland showed the American worker pitted against docile foreign laborers willing to accept meager wages and to serve as strikebreakers. Indeed, even in good times the wage earner could expect dismissal when too sick or old to endure heavy work, as typified by a poor man in Benjamin Barker's *Clarilda.* George Lippard's *New York: Its Upper Ten and Lower Million* echoed John Adams's fear that urban dwellers lived in daily terror of the penury of economic depressions: "Poverty in the city is not mere want of bread; but it is the lack of the means to supply innumerable wants, created by civilization—and the lack is slow moral and physical death.... [The urban worker] year after year, and day after day, expends the very life strings of his soul, in battling against the fangs of want in keeping some roof shelter over his wife and children" (p. 284). With melancholy clarity Lippard and others delineated what confronted the impotent wage earner. Financial panics wiped out his wage increments or left him without employment. Business prosperity only brought skyrocketing prices. He could stage mammoth hunger marches and storm the flour warehouses, but, as labor historians Joseph Raybeck, John Commons, and Philip Foner have demonstrated, he could not protect his real income.

To please the popular taste for "the moistest . . . possible" material, hack writers saturated their books with the plight of two working-class groups, women and children. Such authors helped to convey the idea that women, creatures of Victorian idealization, were without protection in the urban job market. Not content to portray the actual hardships of female wage earners, they selected cases of the most brutal exploitation. If female laborers earned one-half the wages of men, popular writers portrayed their earnings as one-fourth or one-fifth.[3] If women represented a narrow range of occupations, urban authors focused almost exclusively on the sewing girl, whose poverty had already become a journalistic formula for pricking the social conscience of the middle class. Repeating charges made famous by Mathew Carey in "A Plea for the Poor" in 1831, popular writers like Charles Burdett, Timothy Shay Arthur, and Maria Buckley showed women in this glutted occupation toiling from dawn to late at night for $1.25 a week and then unable to collect their pay promptly.[4]

The cult of success and the Protestant ethos of hard work and frugality were refuted. Toiling girls, confined at work, labored and economized for naught. In novels such as Mary Denison's *Edna Etheril* and William English's *Gertrude Howard*, they lived in attic rooms without light or fire, without a decent bed or chair. Edward Zane Carroll Judson, famous under the pen name of Ned Buntline for his blood-and-thunder stories of the West, found another sort of lurid contemporary material in the poverty of the urban seamstress. Although willing to tolerate the economic exploitation of female workers who ran the presses of his newspapers, in his *Mysteries and Miseries of New York* he wrote a poem against the employers of needlewomen:

> Wan and weary—sick and cheerless,
> By a feeble taper's light,
> Sat and sang the never-tearless,
> At the dreary dead of night;
> The burden of her lay

Was work, work away
Through the night and day,
Was work, work away.

We are many in the city
Who the weary needle ply;
None to aid and few to pity
Though we sicken down and die;
But 'tis work, work away
By night and by day;
Oh 'tis work, work away
We've no time to pray.

. . . .
Hearts are breaking—souls are sinking
'Neath the heavy load they bear,
Yet live Christians never thinking
What our many sorrows are,
While we work, work away
By night and by day,
While we work, work away
With scarce time to pray! [pp. 23-24]

Such doggerel, modeled after Thomas Hood's "Song of the Shirt," fired its salvos upon the sweatshop several decades before the generation of the Gilded Age crusaded against the exploiters of women in the garment industry.

In urban novels like Arthur's *The Seamstress,* Maria Maxwell's *Ernest Grey,* and William Sikes's *One Poor Girl,* the needlewomen dared not offer grief or sickness as an excuse. Failure to turn in merchandise on time meant certain dismissal. Once a seamstress became too ill to work, her fate was hopeless. Unable to afford medical attention or to pay the rent, she wasted away; the landlord seized the mattress from her dying body.

Yet in spite of such exploitative working conditions, young women continued to migrate to the metropolis. In particular, seamstresses faced competition from country females willing to labor for five cents a shirt during the winter, when there was no farm work. According to the scenarios of Burdett's *The Elliott Family* and Judson's *The G'hals of New York,* if the urban wage earner refused this fee her alternatives were starvation or prostitution. One author asked, "Why is it not echoed up and down the long streets of the town that here, right here, where the crowds pass, such wrongs are being borne by poor white girls as scarcely live in the records of African slavery?"[5]

Equally significant, though, is what popular books failed to suggest. In eliciting sympathy for "poor white girls," such novels did not indicate that two-thirds of the workers in the needle industry were of foreign birth, with the largest percentage being Irish. Would not this more specific identification of "poor white girls" make them less suitable figures for stock heroines? Nor did popular literature suggest that the poor seamstress was anything more than a passive victim of a ruthless employer. The pulp novel never suggested that women in the clothing industry during these years were banding together in such organizations as the United Seamstress Society, the Ladies' Shoebinders, the Female Industrial Association, and the Women's Protective Union. How sympathetic could bourgeois readers be, after all, to militant lower-class women who took independent action to protect their interests?

Despite such omissions, popular writers of urban fiction did not entirely obscure the evils of a preindustrial economy. Years before muckrakers publicized the abuses of American capitalism, novels like Frank St. Clair's *Six Days in the Metropolis,* Henry Edwards's *The Belle of Central Park,* and Azel Roe's *Like and Unlike* revealed how saleswomen were gradually killed by overwork for a scanty two dollars a week. While the male store clerk typically could expect respectable status and a much higher salary, the salesgirl in the urban novel could secure employment only on terms of economic and sexual exploitation. Used by profiteering owners "to catch the roving eye of sensuality," salesgirls were hired by entrepreneurs whose greed outweighed any scruples.

Ironically, storekeepers were not the only ones to use the shopgirl to promote sales. Enterprising authors also hoped to enhance interest in their books by featuring sexually alluring saleswomen in them. Consider the example of Joseph Holt Ingraham's novel *The Beautiful Cigar Girl.* While the title might seem devoid of prurient interest, to people in the mid-nineteenth century the term "cigar girl" was filled with sexual inneundo. It was the euphemism used for the prostitutes who lined up against tobacco store windows in the business district of New York City and then serviced their customers in bedrooms in the rear of the shop. What a promising subject for writers of sensational literature, indeed, but a sales gimmick in the hands of Professor Ingraham, a minister in the Episcopal church! Backing away from the implications of his suggestive title, Ingraham recounted a moralistic tale of a poor and virtuous girl who actually sold cigars and at her post attracted the attention of an English nobleman, who honorably wedded her.

Another group of women workers pictured in popular fiction were the washerwomen, widows who worked six days a week for a pittance of fifty cents a day. In Augustine Duganne's novel *The Two Clerks* and in

Caroline Soule's short story "The Poor Washerwoman," they had to rub, pound, rinse, and starch the clothes of their rich patrons if they were to have bread to eat, no matter how needed they were by their own children.

The plight of children forced by necessity to earn their livelihood also was a subject of these sentimental novels. Abandoned by their parents, tykes entered the urban job market to sweep streets, carry luggage, shine boots, and peddle cheap wares.[6] In popular fiction the urchin newsboy or bootblack became a seedling entrepreneur who acquired at a tender age the independence and daring of the American businessman. In an age that exulted in the self-made man, novelists like Elizabeth Oakes Smith, Charles Gayler, Solon Robinson, and more than a decade later, Horatio Alger viewed the child wage earner as an urban folk hero who, without parents or home, grew into manhood by dint of his determination and perseverance. In his verbal sketches of New York life, *Peter Ploddy, and Other Oddities,* Joseph Neal pictured the ruggedness of small boys who hawked newspapers: "Tossed early into the world, the impediments which cause other men to fail, are soon surmounted in his path.... He is his own staff—his own protector.... He has no tender years.... No morning ray finds him in bed" (p. 67). Embodying the traits of the pioneer, the independent city youth survived in the urban wilderness, fortified by his boldness, industry, and self-reliance.

Unlike the seamstress and laundress, who were dependent on an economy that jeopardized virtue, the bootblack, match vendor, baggage "smasher," and newsboy could surmount their environment, acquiring the qualities of successful salesmanship that would prepare them for aggressive huckstering in adulthood. In Ingraham's novel *Jemmy Daily: or, the Little News Vendor,* the ambitious hero composes a poem to encourage the purchase of his newspapers and captures the market by his innovative salesmanship:

> A cent will take you to Japan.
> To Turkey, or the Isle of Man;
> Tell you what the Sultan's doing,
> How in Spain a war is brewing; . . .
> So come and for a penny buy
> What rich will make both you and I. [p. 42]

In spite of hunger and cold, youthful entrepreneurs like Elizabeth Smith's *The Newsboy* and Alger's *Mark, The Match Boy, Ragged Dick,* and *Ben, The Luggage Boy* were resilient, able to find joy in the "ever varied life of the streets." Whether they pitched pennies, threw dice, or stirred up a thunder of oaths and applause at a Bowery theater or concert saloon, they were a nomad fraternity, savoring the amusements of city life. In uniforms of slouched cloth caps, dilapidated, rolled-up trousers, and ill-fitting, unmatched jackets, and smoking stumps of cigars picked up from the street, they possessed a shrewdness that could not be matched by their country cousins. Indeed, though they had been denied the benefits of family and of formal education, they were experts at the art of city survival.

Not all child laborers, however, could survive so successfully, especially if they were female. Impoverished girls sent on the streets to sweep the crossings or to hawk hot corn, radishes, and matches were the city's victims. In novels like the anonymously authored *The Match Girl*, Robinson's *Hot Corn*, and Osgood Bradbury's *Female Depravity*, their brave efforts to support themselves were rewarded with the indifference of the multitude and with the beatings and cursings of their guardians if they failed to return with sufficient sums of money.

Equally pitiable was the plight of apprentices hired to replace journeymen with a cheaper source of labor. From the research of Walter Hugins in *Jacksonian Democracy and the Working Class*, we know that the term "apprentice" was already becoming outmoded by the 1820s. With the growing mechanization of production, time consumed in initiating young boys into a craft was wasted. Instead employers assigned their youthful helpers to one simple task. In this way they could train unskilled workers easily and replace them before they became entitled to journeymen's wages. The popular novelist Arthur showed how employers viewed "bound out" boys as useful hands with small stomachs. In his novels *The Seamstress* and *The Orphan Children: A Tale of Cruelty and Oppression*, young boys labored from sunrise to late at night. Subject to harsh discipline and corporal punishment, they were fed cornbread and slop and housed in filthy garrets without beds. Although employers enjoyed parental jurisdiction over these poor children, they denied them warm garments and proper shoes for winter, thereby exposing them to frostbite. Arthur, quick to highlight the grisliness of the apprenticeship system, asserted that if a master did treat his "botch" to any medical attention, his most compelling motivation was to save the expense of a funeral.

If women and children often represented the degradation of the urban labor force, the mechanic stood as the heroic embodiment of labor, a genuine producer in an economy rife with sham. For it was the man at the bench, with rough hands and an unpolished exterior, who in popular books performed the real work of America. While Hawthorne in his short story "The Artist of the Beautiful" pitted an imaginative inventor against a soulless machinist who reduced the former's dreams to clockwork, never in pulp urban novels of the mid-nineteenth century did the mechanic assume any stature less than that of hero.[7] While would-be mercantile nabobs put on aristocratic airs as they plundered the public, the honest craftsman of popular fiction enriched the nation by his toil. The literary heir of Jacksonian democracy, he was, like the farmer, a natural man steeped in the republican virtues of honesty, simplicity, and sobriety. Just as Old Hickory appealed to voters as a representative of a more simple and wholesome past, the figure of the mechanic was a literary embodiment of the common man who remained steadfast to the values of an earlier day.

Despising a life of idleness, he cherished the Protestant work ethic. More noble than the perfumed man of business and the arrogant man of law, he scorned fashionable life and found in his trade an ample avenue for creativity. His foil was the stereotyped foppish clerk who merchandised appearances while the mechanic produced the real wealth of society. A self-made man, the mechanic in popular fiction reinforced the claims of contemporary workingmen's associations that a ten-hour day would provide the craftsman with sufficient leisure to cultivate his mind. For in the pages of pulp novels like Ingraham's *Ellen Hart,* Howe's *Merchant-Mechanic,* Williams's *The Steel Safe,* and McDougall's *The Mechanic,* to name but a few, he passed his evening hours in an apprentice's library or at uplifting lectures. Practicing his humble calling, he belonged to the real aristocracy of America—the aristocracy of talent.

To be sure, the popular novel in many ways reflected the economic condition of skilled craftsmen in the building trades at mid-century. Beneficiaries of sprawling urban growth with its frenzy of construction projects, these artisans, as Norman Ware has indicated, were the most successful in creating viable unions to promote their interests. In fact, the frequency with which carpenters and masons enjoyed rags-to-riches careers in popular books suggests that contemporaries were aware that these artisans formed the elite guard of the labor movement.[8]

Except for those employed in the construction industry, however, pulp literature conveyed a hopelessly outdated image of the mechanic. In the dream factory of antebellum popular fiction, the mechanic could steadily improve his economic condition by honest toil; in the workaday world of business, even as early as the 1830s, he was a man sinking in status. As the transportation revolution expanded markets for manufactured products, the craftsman-employer shifted his allegiance from his propertyless journeymen to the merchant-capitalists who distributed his products to customers across the nation. No longer working side by side with his employees, the master mechanic became a manufacturer who relied on machinery and either reduced the wages of his journeymen or replaced them altogether with unskilled workers, assigning each to one easily learned task. As merchant-capitalists succeeded in determining the conditions of production and in breaking up the crafts, more and more workers were pressed into factory employment where they labored long hours for low wages. What emerged was a permanent proletariat that was subject to the fluctuations of the market. Increasingly the factory supplanted the small shop, and the machine the mechanic. No longer could journeymen and apprentices realistically hope to be masters of a shop. Between 1820 and 1860 the ratio of journeymen to masters tripled. By 1850 the industrious mechanic was no longer an important part of the labor force, if the condition of workers in Boston may be taken as typical of the fate of artisans in other cities.[9] With the advent of industrialization and the concomitant division of labor, then, the specialized skills of craftsmen lost their value. As David Montgomery has argued in *Beyond Equality,* the artisan became one more commodity to be bought at the lowest price. No longer could he rise from the wage-earner class.

But popular novelists, transfixed by the more fluid social conditions that predated the panic of 1819, perpetuated the myth that the craftsman of today could easily become the master of tomorrow. In the confectionery world of popular literature a dying economic order was frozen into a living reality. The novel *The Bootmaker of the Fifth Avenue* well illustrates the anachronistic versions of labor conditions that popular writers were feeding their readers. Although this book was written in 1866, a time when merchant-capitalists were dominating the shoe industry and subjecting it to increasing mechanization, the hero cobbles boots by the time-honored methods of an independent craftsman and rises from humble status to extraordinary wealth.

Given the myopia of many popular writers to the economic revolution of their day, we should not be surprised that only three novels even passingly portrayed workers organizing a strike.[10] This omission becomes more curious when we realize that 1840–70 was a time of extraordinary labor ferment—a period marked by the eruption of numerous "turnouts," including a general strike which paralyzed Chicago, the proliferation of proletarian newspapers, and the welding together of a national labor organization—to mention but a few of the energetic steps taken by workers to improve their condition at mid-century.

Yet when we consider the obvious middle-class biases of popular authors, we can readily understand why the turbulent labor outbursts of the mid-nineteenth century found no romantic representations in the popular book. Writers tended to heed the voices of the articulate spokesmen of labor rather than to scrutinize the deeds of drudges. Echoing the rhetoric of bourgeois labor leaders like Frances Wright and Robert Owen, hack novelists affirmed the dignity of labor but backed away from militant action over bread-and-butter issues. They urged idealistic philanthropic reform, not unionization; the agrarianism of George Henry Evans and Thomas Skidmore, not strikes. A case in point is the novel *New York: Its Upper Ten and Lower Million* by Lippard, who accounted himself a crusader for the oppressed producing classes. To save labor from the grip of capitalists, Lippard did not have his protagonists organize boycotts, bargain collectively, or strike, the prosaic but real weapons workingmen used in their struggle to protect themselves. Rather he purloined nebulous utopian ideas from Robert Owen, Charles Fourier, and Horace Greeley and allowed the resolution of his story to hinge upon the mechanic hero's inheriting a large fortune, which he uses to form an ideal cooperative society of craftsmen and farmers; in their free home beyond the Rockies they are to be "rescued from poverty, from wage slavery, which . . . slowly kills by the lawful operation of capital [and] labor-saving machinery." George Foster too, in his novel *Celio,* employed a similar deus ex machina to rescue the lumpenproletariat of New York City from its economic woes. Thus in the realm of popular literature cooperation in a wilderness phalanx served as a substitute for strikes. Readers frightened by the advance of the factory system could safely retain their eighteenth-century liberal idealism.

However much popular authors sought to retreat into a bygone Jeffersonian era, industrialization carried workers with it. The American economy was being transformed. Production of manufactured goods increased from $500 million in 1840 to $2 billion in 1860. During these same decades the number of businessmen engaged in manufacturing at least $500 worth of products climbed from 791,000 to 1,311,000. At no other time in the nineteenth century did the rate of industrial growth soar, in terms of value added by manufacturers, as it did during this twenty-year period. Although the era of the industrial city had not yet arrived, manufacturing grew more rapidly than either agriculture or service occupations and had become an important factor in urban growth.[11]

How did the popular novel respond to the rise of factory enterprise? How did it react to what labor historian Norman Ware found to be the degraded material well-being and status of laborers during this period? Would its vision of new mill towns prepare the reader to welcome or fear the coming of the machine age?

If, in the cheap book, urban working conditions in the old domestic economy conjured up images of unrelieved drudgery, labor in new mill towns was seen as both snare and salvation. To be sure, much of popular fiction resonated with contemporary arguments about the factory system. While some novels stressed the hardships of mill life, others acclaimed the factories for ushering in a new era of economic abundance. If some books emphasized the long hours, dangerous machinery, and poorly ventilated workrooms, others concentrated on the high pay scale, paternalism of the owners, and opportunities for social mobility. But whether books pilloried or praised factory towns, they were drawing upon data which, as Ray Ginger has indicated, varied from mill to mill and represented a jumble of contradictory evidence.

What seems most disappointing to the modern reader who wishes to discover mid-nineteenth-century views toward the development of industrial towns, however, is the almost singlemindedly prurient focus of popular urban fiction. Like tales set in the big city, factory town stories were excellent vehicles for narratives of seduction. Pulp writers like the anonymous authors of *Ellen Merton* and *Mary Bean* portrayed such towns as dangerous centers of sensuality, where girls freed from the protective eyes of parents would be beguiled into promiscuity. Exposed to the exciting pleasures of urban life, the artless country maiden would be swept from the "haunts of Industry" to the "haunts of Infamy." In particular, the town of Lowell, patterned in large part on Robert Owen's utopian experiment at New Lanark, Scotland, and a model for other factory towns in America, attracted literary notoriety primarily by virtue of its extraordinary number of independent females. Like Samuel Richardson's popular English novel *Pamela,* which dealt with the effort of a poor sewing maid to keep her purity, American books such as *A Tale of Lowell,* written under the nom de plume of Argus, and Bradbury's *Mysteries of Lowell* revolved around the question of whether mill employment was compatible with virginity. Would the farmer's daughter, smitten by "factory fever," be seduced by a man who promised her wealth without work? Would a rural maiden, bewitched by late evening balls, miss the 10 P.M. hour of admittance into her boarding house and become a bawd? Instructed by novelists in the art of seduction practiced by the dashing young clerks of Lowell, young girls could learn how to preserve their virtue and also to succeed in their factory careers.

In emphasizing the dangers of sexual degradation, many popular authors were, in effect, taking a stance that differed little from the position of management in its attempt to control the leisure time pursuits of the factory operatives. Warnings against dancing and drinking as perilous first steps along the primrose path paralleled the effort of the

Associates to steer their help away from activities which would make them less efficient on the job. Furthermore, by focusing on the sexual exploitation of the girls at the hands of roués rather than on their economic exploitation at the hands of mill owners, hack writers shifted the onus of a degraded working class from profit-oriented capitalists to the employees themselves. Implicitly they indicated that operatives who longed for material well-being were impious creatures whose susceptibility to the promise of an easy life was responsible for their reduced circumstances. Certainly, as Norman Ware has pointed out, mill hands manifested much more concern over paltry wages and taxing working conditions than over facilities for vice in the evening hours. To them the paternalism of the bosses was a thinly veiled system for destroying their independence. But popular authors who heeded the rationalizations of the Corporation also accepted the dogma of rugged individualism and thus placed the burden of success or failure on the individual worker. Like such notable contemporaries as Horace Greeley, they attributed labor's degraded status to drinking, gambling, and prostitution rather than to changing economic conditions.

Ironically, even the *Vox Populi*, publishing organ of dissident Lowell workers, printed *A Tale of Lowell*, a novel with a hackneyed plot about a factory girl ruined by her desire to enjoy the leisure activities of the respectable middle class. We can assume, then, that writers hoped to rouse the public over the plight of mill laborers by presenting stories not about the loss of economic dignity, but about the loss of a hymen to the factory foreman! Readers troubled by eroding pieties and changing economic opportunities in antebellum America could find a convenient target for their indignation in the lost virginity of the factory girl.

Equally significant is the fact that not one of the myriad books about textile towns was set in one of the numerous industrial centers of Rhode Island and the Middle Atlantic states. These mills, modeled after Samuel Slater's unabashed system of laissez-faire enterprise, were infamous for their callous indifference to the welfare of the workers and their vicious system of defrauding workers of their wages in company stores. While we would be unfair to expect novels to serve as objective histories of the labor movement, we have seen how popular writers incorporated vivid contemporary material in their attempt to appeal to a reading public that "had a . . . deep-seated suspicion of make-believe fiction" and sought books which purported to be realistic.[12] The absence of locations like Pawtucket, Fall River, and Allegheny, where working-class families were forced to send their children to the mills to maintain a bare subsistence, undoubtedly has led a literary critic like Herbert Ross Brown to conclude that sentimental hacks at mid-century fed the national mood of self-congratulation by shrouding the darker side of industrialism in optimism.

We nevertheless must take stock of several urban novels written in the 1840s and 1850s which, although ambivalent about industrialization, did reveal a depressing picture of factory life. In books like *The Factory Girl, A Tale of Lowell,* Alice Haven's *Gossips of Rivertown,* and Charlotte Hilbourne's *Effie and I,* employment in a mill was an admittance ticket into a world of deafening looms and dangerous machinery that, like "fiery fangs of the flying dragon," could clutch the clothes of a poor operative in an "angry grasp." It meant confinement in a drab and noisome room from five in the morning until seven in the evening. The vivid description of the unhealthy atmosphere of the mills found in this popular fiction was not mere vulgar sensationalism. Dispassionate observers, too, publicized the fact that New England factory operatives were required to toil longer hours than prison inmates. The erstwhile transcendentalist Orestes Brownson in the *Boston Quarterly* in 1840 lashed out against the owners of textile mills for wearing out the health of their employees. Nine years later Dr. Josiah Curtis claimed in his report *Hygiene in Massachusetts* that poor ventilation in the mills was responsible for the high rate of typhoid among female laborers.

In fact, the oppressions of the early factory system were likened to the indignities heaped upon the black slave: "And you ... from the quiet of a country village, railing bravely against southern slavery—just ... behold yonder ... factory. Yes. Have you no pity for the white men nearer to you in equality than black men who are chained in hopeless slavery to the iron wheels of yonder factories machinery? Have you no thought of the white women ... driven by want, from yonder factory to the grave or to the brothels of New York? You mourn over black children sold at the slave block—have you no tear for white children ... deprived of education, converted into mere working-machines (without one tithe of the food and comfort of the black slave), and transformed into precocious old men and women ... ?"[13] The racist implications of Lippard's prose aside, the fact remains that by 1860 the freedom of textile hands had, to a large extent, become a chimera. Forced to sign "yellow dog contracts" or face starvation, intimidated by the blacklist to submit to unfair labor practices, tyrannized to vote for company candidates, factory operatives were at the mercy of Northern "lords of the loom" and yielded to terms of employment which, according to Caroline Ware, could justly be equated with the evils of Southern slavery. Yet significantly, Southern authors of popular fiction did not exploit the theme of the degrading conditions in Northern factories as a justification for the institution of slavery. Indeed, William Grayson's long poem "The Hireling and the Slave" defended Southern slavery by contrasting it with the dehumanizing conditions of free labor in British factories, not with the terms of industrial employment in the American Northeast.

Nor can we find any significant body of popular literature devoted to exposing conditions in manufacturing establishments in the South. Certainly the debased estate of white workers in the South offered material for both plucking the heartstrings and beating the drums in the abolitionist crusade. But pulp writers neglected to reveal how poor whites, unable to compete fairly with slave labor in the factories, were forced to accept the lowest wages in the nation. One important exception, however, stands out. Rebecca Davis, in a humanitarian spirit reminiscent of Harriet Beecher Stowe's, showed how workers in the South, born into savage poverty, deprived of an education, were crushed by the factory system. In her story "Life in the Iron Mills" she re-created the flat, muddy world inhabited by factory hands. Consigned all day to a rolling mill that loosed foul smells, workers lived from infancy to death in an atmosphere that reeked with grease and smoke. In return for their tasks of manufacturing railroad iron over boiling caldrons, they were rewarded with a rat-infested cellar floor for a bed, boiled potatoes for dinner, and a drunken spree for amusement. Relegated to a living death, men were ground down by slow, heavy years of continual hot work, with no hope of escape. Their votes controlled by the mill owners, they were white slaves of callous manufacturers indifferent to their fate.

In Northern metropolitan centers as well, the development of the ready-made clothing industry and the emergence of sweatshops evoked an image in Lippard's *Nazarene* of "slave houses" where supposedly free men, women, and children were bent down with labor from sunrise to nightfall in crowded, polluted rooms that thundered with the noise of machinery. In William Wirt Sikes's novel *One Poor Girl: The Story of Thousands,* factory hands worked nine hours a day for twenty-five cents, without adequate heat and under a regime of silence. A six-cent carfare to work or a dinner of meat were unthinkable luxuries to drudges forced into employment that exposed them to consumption and an early grave.

The unsafe conditions of factory life became the subject of Elizabeth Stuart Phelps's poignant short story "The Tenth of January." In this fictionalized treatment of the collapse and conflagration of a Lawrence textile mill in 1860, a tragedy which took the lives of almost one hundred workers, Phelps showed supposedly benevolent Christians so concerned with profits that they require their employees to labor twelve hours a day in a building constructed in the interest of economy rather than of safety. If a hastily constructed mill yields large dividends, the magnates care not that the supporting pillars contain serious cracks. Indeed, their power suppresses a building inspector's report which discloses the defect. Mill hands, captives of poverty in this dingy and perilous factory, are caught in falling wreckage when heavy machinery is brought into the workroom. The lucky are crushed to death immediately; those less fortunate are entombed alive in the rubble and then killed by a fire that ravages the ruins of the building. In this story Phelps, one of the few writers of the period to employ a recent event effectively, revealed the interests of property prevailing over the welfare of humans.

Even where writers did emphasize the negative aspects of mill employment, the impression they conveyed to readers was one of a passively victimized working class. This theme makes sense when we realize that popular literature focused almost exclusively on the female portion of the factory community. How, after all, could women workers enjoy the status of what Barbara Welter has labeled "true womanhood" if they spent their days outside their destined sphere of the home? If women worthy of the readers' sympathy lacked the cardinal virtue of domesticity, they would have to possess all of the other attributes of femininity—piety, purity, and submissiveness. Thus writers of mill life wrapped female operatives in a mantle of timidity.

But such a picture did not square with the events of the epoch. When we examine the labor history of the period 1840-70, we discover that female mill hands defied the cult of true womanhood and actively participated in numerous strikes to protect their interests. When owners imposed new disciplinary regulations, cut wages, or speeded up production, they found the women in the labor force a far cry from the submissive weaklings of sentimental reading fare. Yet only a single novel, *A Book Without a Title: or Thrilling Events in the Life of Mira Dana* by Martha W. Tyler, exploited the theme of the turn-out. Significantly, the strike by the textile operatives is a failure, and the girls resolve never to labor in Lowell again. In contrast to the British Victorian industrial novel, which gingered its plots with scenes of physical confrontations between capital and labor, American factory fiction, obsessed with the struggle of girls to keep their virginity, ignored the flamboyant and often violent war that women waged to secure their economic independence.

The typical scenarios of popular urban novels conceived the interests of capital and labor to be mutually intertwined. When a depression strikes in Day Kellogg Lee's *Merrimack or Life at the Loom,* for instance, wages are cut drastically; but the foreman of the plant, who has become one of the owners, gives money from his own pocket to help girls with needy families. Although the author admits that the Corporation could have cushioned the wages of its employees with its abundant resources, he has one of the operatives praise the stewards of wealth for teaching their employees the value of hard work and savings: "We were none the worse perhaps in the long run for what we suffered; certainly not for the discipline our sufferings gave us" (p. 185). Such saccharine sentiments appear the more absurd when we examine the prescient foreboding of Henry David Thoreau: "The condition of the operatives is becoming every day more like that of the English; and it cannot be wondered at, since . . . the principal object is . . . that the corporations may be enriched."[14]

Thoreau's disturbing vision was not shared by the majority of popular writers, who repeated the conventional political wisdom of their day, praising Lowell as a foretaste of America's future. At a time when factory life was still new, it had, as Mary Noel has pointed out, even more allure than the frontier. Thus while several novelists recognized the abuses of industrial employment, a majority saw the mill, even with its dangers, as a haven that would allow the rural poor to realize the American dream. Echoing the superficial impressions of distinguished tourists like Harriet Martineau, Michel Chevalier, and Charles Dickens, who had concluded that Lowell was an alternative to the blighted factory towns of Europe, these American writers propagated the view that the New England mill town was an industrial paradise. A subtitle of one novel, "Seven Years in a Cotton Mill," suggested a common theme— namely, that factory labor need not create a permanent proletariat. Heroines move easily from bucolic village to mill town, only to make the traditional return to green fields and wild flowers. In the formula plots of books like Haven's *Gossips of Rivertown*, Ariel I. Cummings's *The Factory Girl*, Hannah E. Talcott's *Madge*, and the anonymously written *The Factory Girl*, a highly intelligent and ambitious farm girl accepts employment in a mill to provide an intellectual brother with a classical education, to present her future husband with a dowry, or to educate herself to a genteel status.

Unhappily, this picture of factory life, like the romantic but outworn one of the master mechanic, was hopelessly outdated. At the time of Charles Dickens's famous tour of Lowell in 1842—and we have only Sarah Savage's *The Factory Girl* before this time—the benevolent paternalism at Lowell had already yielded to a system of harsh discipline. Workers in the early days of Lowell enjoyed a higher standard of living than laborers in other types of employment. But by the time popular writers were setting their novels in the New England mill towns, tough professional managers were requiring factory hands to work a seventy-five-hour week for wages that had dropped below contemporary standards.

To maintain profits at a time when the price of cotton cloth was declining, the managers slashed wages and required increased productivity. As Oscar Handlin's *Boston Immigrants* and John Coolidge's *Mill and Mansion* have made clear, girls who had once labored at the undemanding task of tending two looms were now compelled to work on four. Gradually, as the pace of work was speeded up, wages cut, and hope for a ten-hour day crushed, tractable immigrants, willing to accept a system of stringent discipline, replaced independent farm girls. The town on the Merrimack, once a wonder of the Republic, had degenerated into a ruthless mechanical colossus.

But in the pages of popular books, more influenced by the reports of distinguished visitors and the homilies of the company newspaper, the Lowell *Offering,* all was well in Spindle City. The operatives, if true to the old verities of honesty, hard work, and integrity, found "Religion, Law and Love."[15] In fact, literary apologists for Lowell conveyed the impression that factory towns united the Protestant ethic with Victorian morality. They averred that the strictly regulated manufacturing centers of New England contained fewer facilities for woman's fall than the sinful commercial centers of the land. Ignoring reports of Boston's *Daily Times* that young girls were being introduced to vice because of the paucity of their wages, many novelists showed instead how in the paternalistic City of Spindles strict corporation and boarding house rules protected the operatives from ne'er-do-wells. Hilbourne, Bradbury, and a writer called Argus praised the God-fearing employers for requiring their charges to observe the Sabbath but failed to point out that such a regulation forced the girls to pay pew rents from an already meager salary. More important, they neglected to publicize the fact that the Corporation's moral prescriptions allowed foremen not only to dictate the diet and dress of employees but also to bar union activity.

In the books of Lowell's literary boosters, factory labor was an ennobling calling that allowed the poor to "gain an honorable livelihood and secure to themselves the means of cultivating their minds, thus preparing themselves for future usefulness and a happy life, whether among the spindles, in the farm-house, or in the parlour."[16] Choosing an approved method of achieving economic independence, sheltered females in novels such as Lee's *Merrimack,* Haven's *Gossips of Rivertown,* and Mansfield Walworth's *Lulu* could escape the narrow confines of country homes or the degrading shackles of an unhappy marriage. To be sure, this school of novelists offered more than company propaganda when it lauded employment opportunities for women in Lowell. Women textile workers in the antebellum period earned twice the wages of females in the domestic needle trade and, according to Horace Mann, six or seven times the salary of teachers.

If in the fiction of the period the fashionable belle became stereotyped as a useless urban woman, the factory girl who worked unassumingly amidst looms became a new heroine. Scorning the idle pleasures of urban parasites, she rose early in the morning and "[tripped] lightly to her tasks, called by the merry chiming of the factory bells."[17] She was the living proof that America could develop its industrial potential without tarnishing the character of its population. Almost a half-century after the American Society for the Encouragement of Domestic Manufacture published a report in 1817 prophesying that factories in the United States would be "seats of health and cheerfulness, where good instruction will secure the morality of the young and good regulations will promote . . . order, cleanliness and exercise of civil duties,"[18] popular authors were still proclaiming that Lowell was no Manchester and its operatives no debased proletariat. These writers emphasized that the American factory girl was a New England farmer's daughter. Her roots remained with her Jeffersonian or puritan heritage. She could live in Lowell, America's fourth largest city by 1840, and remain a rustic at heart; she could be part of the technological revolution and still return to her home in nature; she could gain material prosperity without relinquishing her Christian orthodoxy.

In the prose of popular authors optimistic about America's industrial development, manufacturing sites like Lowell became the nineteenth century's answer to Poor Richard. Such towns were conceived as a tribute to the Yankee spirit that built the nation. Founded upon the twin pillars of enterprise and morality, they were an apotheosis of the American dream. Like many novels of the period that broadcast the opportunities for success in the city, these books made the town of Lowell itself a success story, a symbol of America's industrial destiny.

But when we turn from the sugar-coated conventions of popularizers to the personal inventions of a true literary artist, we find a grim vision of the coming machine age. In Melville's short story "The Tartarus of Maids," a New England paper mill appears as "some great whited sepulchre." Unlike a mediocre gladsayer who pictured the factory girl "with the flush of health on her cheek and the light of vigor and buoyancy of spirit in the eye, contentment and tranquility in the heart," Melville portrayed his maids as "pale with work," their eyes filled with "misery," standing in rows "like so many mares haltered to the rack." Whereas in the world of tonic fiction the virtuous and intelligent operative quickly wins recognition from her superiors, in Melville's "Tartarus" the girls are stripped of individuality, their voices "banished from the spot." "Mutely and cringingly" they perform their tasks "as the slave serves the Sultan." In contrast to the blithe working-class heroines of a slick literature, who predictably ascend to their rightful station in the middle class, Melville's "sad-looking" girls cannot escape their bondage to the machine. They are caught in a mesh of "metallic necessity," an "unbudging fatality" which dehumanizes their personality as it ravages their health. Confined in stifling rooms with "poisonous particles" darting into their lungs, they resemble "condemned state prisoners [going] from the hall of judgment to their doom."[19]

The tyranny of the machine was much less apparent to manufacturers of pulp fiction than it was to Melville. The majority, who seem to have taken their cues from popular authorities like the poet John Greenleaf Whittier and the essayist Edward Everett, lauded manufacturing towns for increasing the wealth of the nation without sacrificing America's agrarian ideals. Novels such as Talcott's *Madge* and Lee's *Merrimack* argued that when hunger and desolation struck the farm, rural people could find in manufacturing centers new economic opportunities in a religious atmosphere harmonious with their country upbringing. Here victims of rural poverty could earn an independent livelihood, study in their leisure hours, and form warm human associations. At the end of their day's labor they could return to their boarding house, where they would be united with a newfound family of kind girls and a motherly landlady. Surrounded by fervent Christians, factory girls in fiction could readily find roommates with whom to share the evenings reading Holy Scripture. Curiously, however, popular writers omitted precise physical descriptions from their scenes of boarding houses. In actuality, the factory girl was herded with six or seven strangers into a small and inadequately ventilated room. She may have shared Bible-reading exercises; she more certainly shared a bed. By mid-century her communal lodgings in giant barracks overrun with vermin were hardly the sorority-house facilities pictured in pulp books. Yet with all of its shortcomings, we know from the historical investigaitons of Hannah Josephson that the boarding house was a far cry from the urban tenement and compared favorably with the prevailing conditions in lower- and middle-class homes.

The notion of the industrial town as an agency for promoting communal fellowship also cropped out in vignettes in which a textile worker discovered friendship on a farm to be a mirage compared to the warmth of human associations in a factory. In Hilbourne's celebration of Lowell, *Effie and I: or Seven Years in a Cotton Mill*, the heroine leaves the Spindle City to become a farmer's wife. When her husband proves to be a tyrant, she achieves independence by moving back to the town on the Merrimack. In a rhapsody to factory work quite different from a host of odes to rustic joy, the protagonist expresses her happiness in returning to an industrial utopia: "I was lonely, very lonely, in that strange, out of the way village. I missed my associates, the old, familiar, and kindly faces. . . . And so I came back again. And oh! how happy I did feel when . . . I . . . heard the old familiar chimes of the factory bells, booming through the air, with peal after peal of merry music. . . . Welcome smiles and kindly greetings met me on every hand; and once more my heart throbbed wildly with the hopeful anticipations of a happy future" (pp. 246–47). Just how distorted such rapture was in reality is seen in the use of bells to signify the heroine's reentry into paradise. For according to contemporary accounts, the Lowell operatives viewed the periodic chiming in belfries as a grim reminder of the Corporation's efforts to turn them into cogs of the textile machines.

Similarly, Lowell's literary boosters glossed over the realities of labor within the mill. If girls actually did bemoan the monotony of their work, novelists like Hilbourne, Talcott, and Haven blunted the edge of their plaint by asserting that tasks which felt rigorous at first soon could be performed mechanically. If operatives, in reality, often labored at night during the winter, the writer Sylvester Judd pictured them in his novel *Richard Edney* only "in the warmth, beauty, and quietness of a summer-day." If mill hands were forced to toil amidst the thunder of flying shuttles, Lee portrayed them in *Merrimack* enjoying themselves at their "jocund looms." Significantly, novels written in the mid-1850s, a period which witnessed the deterioration of labor conditions in the textile industry, were set back in the more halcyon days of the 1830s, when President Andrew Jackson, touring the Spindle City, was moved to comment, "Here are the daughters of America engaged in their toils, independent and happy."

Even the cheeriest writers who used mill towns as settings of their novels, however, at times unwittingly betrayed a more jarring picture of industrialization. For instance, in *Merrimack* Lee in one breath spoke of girls attending their tasks with light step and merry hearts and yet in another commented about operatives more "wilted" than Southern slaves. Likewise, Lee, Judd, and Talcott portrayed the mill as a cheerful environment, "an abode of enchantment [as stirring] . . . as a splendid church, or a sunny park of trees, or fine gardens" and yet inadvertently included scenes in which the health of some of the operatives broke down from confinement in the factory.[20]

Despite such unresolved ambiguities, an optimistic school of popular writers reassured the public that *"honest labor elevates rather than de-grades"* (Haven's italics).[21] A few years of employment in a mill could serve as an important step up the ladder of success. It afforded the ambitious a chance for intellectual self-improvement. In Lowell, for fifty cents a year, a lady of refined sensibilities could subscribe to a library with over seven thousand volumes. She could associate with many cultivated young women, attend lyceum lectures and concerts, and join a singing society. Although curiously silent about *The Factory Girl* and *Factory Girl's Album,* magazines which were written by operatives dissatisfied with the conditions of employment in Lowell, novelists Cummings and Day Lee lauded the opportunities enjoyed by talented girls to publish their writing in the town's highminded journal, *The Offering.* But most significant of all, work in a mill would not pose any class obstacle to marrying a professional man. For heroines in novel after novel readily moved from the workroom to a wedding chamber with suitably respectable middle-class mates.[22]

Thus an important segment of popular fiction writers welcomed the advent of manufacturing towns as a painless link between an idealized rural past and a productive new future. Imbued with the materialistic spirit of the age, they saw mechanization as a sign of progress. In a period of disturbing economic and social change, these popularizers served, in effect, as public-relations agents packaging a new product, the Industrial Revolution, in terms familiar enough to bridge the chasm between country traditions and industrial realities. To cover the harsh injustices of industrial capitalism, they threw a smoke screen of outdated myths about the ease of social mobility in the new urban economic order. They reassured the masses that it was still possible for workers to leapfrog in one generation from blue-collar status to upper middle-class affluence. No need to tinker with the nation's social fabric. Strict adherence to old-fashioned Christianity was all that was needed in the machine age to insure the continuation of economic opportunity in America.

During these same years another school of authors drew more pessimistic conclusions about the emerging industrial society, however. To these neo-Rousseaueans, man's true home lay in nature. The machine age was a threat to America's tradition of democratic egalitarianism based on an agricultural way of life. Reluctant to accept the changes wrought by their countrymen's energetic endeavors, they sought refuge in a simpler past and judged the new force of industrialism in terms of an outworn agrarian ideal.

But whether storytellers took an optimistic or pessimistic view of the Industrial Revolution, they furnished readers with only a shadow of the realities which were transforming American society. At a time when the modern industrial city was taking shape, they clung to an anachronistic Calvinistic or Jeffersonian vocabulary to describe the economic revolution which was remolding the lives of their readers.

The muddled outlook of popular writers may be attributed to their class prejudice as much as to their religious-philosophical orientation. In a torrent of books about the urban working class, not one was written by a member of the working class. Instead, middle-class authors writing for a middle-class readership, primarily of women, delivered class judgments about a class which was alien to them. They regarded working-class life as a dreary condition from which the respectable laborer could always escape.

Like their British counterparts of the social realist school of the mid-nineteenth century, American hack authors, responding to the growth of commerce and industry, often identified the city as the seat of both economic exploitation and economic opportunity. But few suggested that the worthy laborer would be condemned to remain in the proletariat. In a period when radical Republicans viewed workers as nascent capitalists and even workers themselves shared their employers' commitment to the free-enterprise system, pulp fiction reinforced the idea of class cooperation. In the ultimately harmonious metropolitan marketplace, the rich and the poor were symbiotically intertwined. In a fictional world where plutocrat and workman could change places, there was no need for class conflict.

Even those writers who exposed the hardships of the urban working class failed to deal with the real issues which confronted American laborers in an era of electrifying economic change. Many imitated instead a vogue found in British fiction. Using as a model Pierce Egan's best seller, *Life in London,* in which two protagonists explore the uncharted realm of London's diverse neighborhoods and encounter the mystifying boundaries of the city's social stratifications, writers from the United States like Judson, Duganne, and Foster examined the darker corners of the American metropolis—its brothels, criminal dens, and saloons. Their books abounded with picturesque riffraff who purportedly represented the varied lower orders of urban society. But as Peter Keating has persuasively argued in *The Working Classes in Victorian Fiction,* the romantic view which highlighted the bizarre diveristy of the city's labor force also clouded the reader's perception of the working class as a distinct social class. The divisions that did exist within American labor—income, trade, geography, ethnicity, politics, religion—were not articulated in the popular book.

Furthermore, popular American writers at mid century who preached sympathy for city wage earners, like those who propagated the myth of mobility in urban society, ignored the need for any fundamental change in the nation's economic structure. All that was needed was reform—temperance, better housing, more schools—but not revolution. Indeed, minor novelists of this stamp obscured the potential power of the urban work force and instead focused on its sufferings. Despite the symbols of strength associated with the working class—the hammer, furnace, and engine—these writers represented working men and women as passive victims to be pitied rather than as a dangerous underclass to be feared. The upper class would help the worthy poor to rise from their low estate. Workers did not need to act for themselves. Once socially aware novelists pricked the consciences of the stewards of wealth, the rich would bestow their largess upon the poor and make the relations between capital and labor harmonious.

The sanguine message of mid-nineteenth-century American literature about the working class flew in the face of reality. Fictional artisans scaled the social ramparts; real laborers found ever-diminishing economic opportunities. But novels about the inarticulate masses of the cities are less important as a mirror of social reality than as a reflection of the daydreams and aspirations of this era. They serve as a "literary witness" of a society which believed in the value of acquisitive materialism and in the ability of the individual to make his mark. The religious revivals and the public school movement of the period sought to impose a conservative Protestant discipline on urban workers who were threatening to disrupt the stability of society; these novels concerned with the condition of labor in mid-nineteenth-century American cities served as another vehicle of accommodation. In an era wrenched by economic dislocation they reassured readers that the worker who gave allegiance to Christian morality and accepted the articulated values of his betters would emerge triumphant.

7

CITIES WITH PERSONALITY

Although popular literature distorted the image of mid-nineteenth-century urban economic and social conditions, it presented a wealth of commentary on America's booming urban network, designed to instruct readers on the supposed advantages and shortcomings of different cities. Already, famous English visitors like Charles Dickens, Harriet Martineau, and Frances Trollope were capturing a portion of the book trade by descriptions of their travels to various American urban communities. Authors of pulp literature in the United States, eager to profit from the market for travelogues, gave readers of their urban confidentials and fictional stories portraits of the nation's leading cities. In a conscious effort to impose order upon something as disordered as the mid-nineteenth-century city, they caught, in colorful and easily comprehended vignettes, the quality of life in America's different metropolitan communities. For in the world of the hack writer, cities were not mere amalgams of commotion and crime, traffic and temptation; each possessed a peculiar personality. They, like people, could be identified by nicknames—there was the Empire City, Quaker City, Puritan City, Spindle City, Federal City, Crescent City, Bay City, and Queen City. And each of these places enjoyed a distinctive reputation, a unique character in novels and nonfiction exposés of the period.

Of all America's urban clusters, the one that excited the most literary interest was New York City—Gotham. It was the protean metropolis, the gateway of the immigrant, the cultural leader of the land, the emporium of the country. Its fashionable thoroughfare of Broadway, its nests of the gentry on Fifth Avenue, its tumultuous low life on the Bowery, its financial wizardry on Wall Street—all captivated the popular imagination and stimulated an outpouring of books which offered readers an inside look at the most glamorous community in the nation.

Popular books portrayed New York City as a place of youth that epitomized the opportunities of a new nation. Here, the reader was often told, enterprising men born without wealth were catapulted to fortune. A center of indomitable energy, it attracted the most industrious, shrewd, and talented from across the land. Here "fortunes [could be] made quicker and lost more easily ... than in any other place in the world." With its converging lines of railroads and steamboats, its incalculable resources, and large manufacturing enterprises, it was "the brain, heart and pulse" of America's commercial empire.[1]

While some writers decried the tireless activities of New York entrepreneurs, others, in a booster spirit, saw in the relentless commercial expansion of the Empire City a symbol of the progress of the nation. Reflecting the romantic nationalism of the age, pundits like Junius Henri Browne in *The Great Metropolis* celebrated New York City as a place of manifest destiny ordained to become "the center and sphere of all the mighty trade, the storehouse of the Nation's wealth. ... The City will be a country of itself, a nation in its strength, its resources, its ... riches" (pp. 699-700). If anything was constant about the Empire City, it was her continual growth. By 1860 the metropolitan population had already soared over one million, and New York ranked as the third-largest city in the Western world. The bursting sense of life which characterized mid-nineteenth-century America found its sharpest focus in the tumultuous expansion of Manhattan. If frontier areas muscled in on adjoining land, Gotham too aggrandized her territory with neighboring villages. Imperialistic activity was as much a part of her personality, noted William Wirt Howe and Charles Gayler, as it was of the nation.

In popular books New York was not only the commercial entrepôt of an expanding nation but the intellectual capital as well. Her press and pulpit, bar and bench, assembled talent to a degree unequaled elsewhere in the land. "Gotham ... is a city belonging to the whole civilized world. The emporium of the arts, the head-quarters of philosophy and the illustrious seat of the perfection of reason."[2] A mecca for brilliant individuals native and foreign, the Empire City stood preeminent in its intellectual and artistic leadership; distinguished orators, artists, musicians flocked from the four corners of the globe to perform for its fortunate residents. Even a visitor like Charles Dickens, who hardly can be considered a booster of New York, in his *American Notes* commended the excellence of its theaters.

The pretensions of the great city, however, made it an obvious target for sharpshooting critics. The satirist William Wirt Howe summarized in *The Pasha Papers* what he considered New York's claim to greatness. Gotham "has more trade, more wealth, more houses, more dirt, more misery, more political corruption than any other great city in the country. It is a place of very great importance—particularly self importance" (pp. 187-88). To James Fenimore Cooper, after a long residence in the great capitals of Europe, the Empire City was the "queen of business" but certainly no "queen of the world."[3]

No less awesome than the Rocky Mountains or the Plains, the Empire City seemed in Cornelius Mathews's *Puffer Hopkins* a formidable human monument, with its "multitude of houses" which "yawned like chasms and abysses" and its "breath of thousands and hundred thousands of human beings [which] crept like a black surge, along the house-tops" (p. 149). Its feverish streets suggested an ocean of scurrying creatures pouring forth in uninterrupted succession. With its "war of carts and omnibuses," its "dust and noise and evil and pollution," its jam of "masts and spars looking like the trees in some dead forest," New York was a man-made wilderness, "remorseless and irresistible as the eternal destiny of which it [was] a symbol."[4] And yet its never-ending crowds, choked-up streets, ever-varying scenes gave Gotham a grandeur in the popular book.

Above all other places in the country, the great metropolis was America's melting pot, a meeting ground of all races and nationalities. Serving as the principal gateway of European immigrants, it was the first, if temporary, home of 75 percent of foreign newcomers to the United States. To the nonfiction writer James Dabney McCabe, the surging growth of the city's "little Europes" represented one of the exhilarating mysteries of the metropolis: "The population of Manhattan Island is a mixture of all the peoples under the sun, fearfully and wonderfully jumbled together.... The resident American is always coming in contact with Spaniards, Germans, Irishmen, Frenchmen, Africans, Chinese, Japanese, Indians, Mexicans, Scotchmen, Canadians, Englishmen, Arabs, Prussians, Swedes, and Italians" (pp. 503-04). Indeed, he argued, the very heterogeneity of the metropolis created a cosmopolitan spirit of toleration that permitted every shade of religious belief and political opinion to flourish. The Gothamite, confronted on all sides with a variety of views, was a new type of person, willing to live and let live, serenely oblivious to his neighbor's cherished ideas. A sanctuary of unorthodoxy, the most populous city of the nation enjoyed the reputation of being a truly open, warm-hearted society even in the writing of Southern novelist William A. Caruthers.

In an idiom employed repeatedly by hack writers, New York was a place of "sunshine and shadow," a site "part Paradise, part Pandemonium."[5]

Embodying both the most munificent and the most depraved, it was a locale of such intensity that commentators never seemed to tire of delineating its daring pleasure seekers, ruthless sharpsters, generous benefactors, and enterprising businessmen: "Here in this powerful city can be found promiscuously intermingled whatever can displease or delight the eye, sadden or render joyous the heart, please or prove corrupting to the ear, cause the tear or excite the smile, and move to pity or upbraid to revenge."[6] If popular authors agreed about anything, it was to disagree about the quality of life in New York. It was a bifurcated giant, simultaneously a heaven and hell. Although preeminent in "secret associatoons—midnight assassins—bold robbers—old murders—dark holes—deep caverns—. . . depraved women—unparalleled cruelty—horrible suicides,"[7] it was without equal in its benevolence, vigor, and excitement. If some lithographs portrayed beggars, whores, and pickpockets, the majority depicted scenes of elegant streets, handsome parks, well-dressed people, palatial hotels, marbled department stores, heroic firemen and policemen.[8]

To Matthew Smith, writer of the near-best-seller *Sunshine and Shadow,* Gotham might be a frightening city to visit but a wonderful locale in which to live: "Order and harmony seem to come out of the confusion. Families find themselves well protected and as comfortable as in a smaller town. . . . The family who would not live in New York if you give them the best house on Fifth Avenue, after a year's residence are seldom willing to live elsewhere" (pp. 26–27). Indeed, given what Walt Whitman described as New York's "roaring, tumbling, bustling, stormy, turbulent" environment, little wonder that nonfiction commentators found few people who had spent any time in the city able to resist its charms.

While New York captivated the public imagination by its vitality, enterprise, and splendor, Boston enjoyed a reputation in the popular book as an American Athens, the intellectual center of the nation. Though she lacked the dynamism of New York, she was a citadel of quiet elegance and well-bred ease, a "literary emporium," the national seat of intelligence, talent, and tact. To Charles Dickens it was America's center of intellectual refinement, politeness, and good breeding. To James Fenimore Cooper it was the only American city with attractions comparable to European capitals. Said he, "They take the mind hard there."[9] Unlike the salons of Gotham, which glittered with vulgar display, the parlors of Boston sparkled with wit and learning. Here people interested in books rather than bonds were the leaders of society. The puritan metropolis was a serious city that amused itself with "scientific disclosures, pointed prayers, and long orations!"[10]

Notwithstanding their touted literary accomplishments, however,

Bostonians were hardly lovable in popular lore. "Over-educated and over-strained," they were depicted in Thomas Gunn's *Physiology of New York Boarding-Houses* and Eliza Otis's *Barclays of Boston* as prim, punctual, and precise. Reserved and condescending, they sneered at strangers, seeing their own city as the moral seat of the Union. Their love of learning did not compensate for their icy, narrow-minded personalities.

The ladies of Boston fared even worse at the hands of literary satirists. *Life in Town, or The Boston Spy* and Frank St. Clair's *Six Days in the Metropolis* derided them for devoting most of their time to appearing "supremely intellectual" or "interestingly sentimental" and little to dressing in good taste. In fact, so heartily had they renounced the world of the flesh that in literary lampoons they were lustreless, sallow-faced females who wore their hair in ringlets and choked from the tight laces of their corsets. They were especially peculiar when socializing with the "Men of Boston." At such times, according to Howe's *Pasha Papers,* they "employ[ed] Latin as a vehicle of narration, Greek to define the nicer shades of philosophical analysis, and Sanscrit as a channel for the flow of their emotions" (p. 181).

The city of the Puritan fathers was "queer, quaint, eccentric."

> Boston, in social arts possessive;
> Skillful in science and progressive;
> With many churches and devotions,
> And fancy works called "Yankee notions."[11]

It was a scene of "sense and no sense," where "above all things, hypocrisy and cant [bore] away the palm of popularity!" Puffed up with self-importance, caricatured in popular books like *The Pennimans,* Augustine Duganne's *Knights of the Seal,* and George Thompson's *City Crimes,* puritanical Boston built "gorgeous mansions for . . . God" and then condoned fashionable establishments of corruption.

Like Boston, Philadelphia often assumed a hypocritical personality in popular prose. Once a model of civic leadership, inspiring imitation by the rest of urban America, the City of Brotherly Love by mid-century was a conservative town which, as Sam Bass Warner has shown, failed to deal imaginatively with its widespread dislocations. Popular writers like William D. Ritner, George Lippard, Timothy Shay Arthur, to name but a few, in their scenes of gilded intrigue, riot, and economic woe intuitively grasped the failure of the city to keep pace with its physical and industrial growth.[12]

Not all popular writers, however, took such a negative view. To Mrs. Eliza Henderson Otis and Arthur Townley, Philadelphia was a more civilized place in which to live than New York. Its aristocracy was more truly refined, its pace of activity more relaxed, its streets cleaner and neater. If the city of William Penn lacked civic-mindedness, it nevertheless abounded in bourgeois reliability; if short in dynamism, it nonetheless was long in punctuality. Indeed, according to Osgood Bradbury in *Female Depravity* and Charles Barrington in *Emily,* Philadelphia enjoyed, in its quiet and ease, many of the advantages of a small town; yet it possessed the intriguing panorama of a great urban center. George G. Foster, the "carver" of New York life, presented readers in the late 1840s with a series of newspaper sketches that contrasted the personalities of these two important seaboard metropolitan centers: "The difference between New York and Philadelphia . . . is the difference between a lake and a river, the one . . . rushing, foaming, . . . roaring, . . . blinding you with its bath of spray; the other quiet yet clean and deep, . . . and there is time for the . . . peaceful sky to get its daguerreotype taken. . . . In New-York every inhabitant goes as if an invisible somebody was after him with a sharp stick; in Philadelphia we take our time. . . . [W]e do not guano humanity and put electro-galvanic wires under it."[13] Thus the inherent rivalry between New York and Philadelphia was expressed in more than the competition of its respective businessmen to gain control of the western hinterland; it also was articulated in comparisons of the two cities in popular literature, and often such books preferred the sleepy, provincial Quaker City to bustling, impudent Manhattan.

By contrast with New York and Philadelphia, Washington, D.C., appeared as a noncity in urban books of this period. A locale with "no topography—no commerce—no art—no manufactures—no physical characteristics of a city," the national capital was merely a "large lodging house for the executive, legislative and judicial representatives of the sovereign people."[14] Writers Allen Gazlay and John Tuel viewed it as a most uncomfortable home for mere mortals, what with its monotonous regularity and its plethora of marble monuments. Authors of popular books documented quite accurately the hobbledehoy appearance of Washington at mid-century. With its filthy, poorly lit streets, choked with wind and dust, it was, according to its biographer Constance Green, a physically immense, straggling, ragged national capital. Even after it had paved streets and amenities like sewers, gaslights, and omnibuses, the popular American author Alonzo F. Hill perpetuated Charles Dickens's quip that this exhaustingly spacious "City of Magnificent Distances" deserved to be dubbed a "City of Magnificent Intentions."

Although Washington as "a new capital of a New World" aspired to grandeur, many popular writers believed it hid Old World decadence behind its facade. To George Watterson, writing in 1827, its social life was a "pageant of folly," "a splendid misery [in which] the . . . feelings of the heart [were] lost amid the rude bursts of artificial joys."[15] Approximately four decades later writers entertained no higher opinion of the capital's moral merits. It was, in novels like *Ella Cameron* and nonfiction exposés like McCabe's *Behind the Scenes in Washington*, a national seat of vice and corruption, rife with debauchery and drunkenness. William Smith's novel *As It Is* ventilated the oft-heard charge that gambling had become the most popular entertainment in a place funded on the public trust. Senators and statesmen allegedly mixed freely with notorious "blacklegs" and accepted "loans" from lobbyists over the roulette table. From a guidebook written by Dr. John B. Ellis in 1869, readers learned that federal officials, using the government payroll, hired female clerks "for their youth and personal attractions" to serve as their mistresses.

Despite the prevalence of vice, Washington possessed an image of glamor in the popular book that belonged to few other places. It was a gala city, a center of frenetic social engagements for the nation's elite. "There were breakfast parties and dinner parties, day receptions and evening receptions, *matinées dansantes* and balls, suppers without women and women without suppers."[16] Certainly, no novel set in Washington seemed complete without an elaborate description of dazzling levees which brought together "the world in miniature." Accomplished people from across the land met in this "new Rome," which was open to all with talent.[17] Popular books as well as contemporary newspapers marveled at the whirl and glitter, grace and wit, which were "within the reach of any . . . intelligent, entertaining, and well-behaved" persons in the Federal City.[18]

While popular books gave only scant attention to the intermediate cities of seaboard America, they extended to them with little discrimination the familiar catalogue of mysteries and miseries. Novels like Wimpleton Wilkes's *The Mysteries of Springfield*, Frank Hazleton's *The Mysteries of Troy*, Harry Spofford's *The Mysteries of Worcester*, and the anonymously written *Life in Rochester* showed that crime, seduction, alcoholism, gambling, and mammonism infected smaller urban communities as they did the great cities. Like the fatal exposure to a glass of alcohol or one sporting bet, residence in a city, no matter what its size, could be ruinous for the weak in will.

Unlike the metropolitan centers of the North, the cities of the South were described in popular lore as languid locales of aristocratic ease and gracious nonchalance. New Orleans appeared as a fascinating, mysterious creature, both beautiful and deadly. The home of the Mardi Gras and masked balls, it was also a seat of yellow-fever epidemics that struck death to thousands during the sultry summers. A city of hospitable mansions, stately avenues, and a graceful aristocracy, it was at the same time a place of gilded gambling parlors, sensual indulgence, and midnight murders. But the most distinguishing characteristic of the Crescent City was that it clung to its sense of the past. "[Resisting] the gigantic strides of 'progressive improvement' which [had] taken such a firm hold of the American mind," it was proud of its ancient dwellings, narrow streets, and its time-begrimed roofs.[19] Its exotic population of Creole and Anglo-Saxon, Jew and Gentile, Italian and German, made it, according to Edward Durell, a meeting ground of "beauty and deformity, of vulgarity and good breeding."

In peacetime this attractive city of magnolia and myrtle offered a spectacle of wealth, taste, and art, but with the coming of the Civil War it lost its glory. Napier Bartlett in *Stories of the Crescent City* described the devastation New Orleans suffered both during the war and after. While battle raged, cannon fire gutted once-gracious homes and littered gardens with the bodies of dead and wounded men. Reconstruction brought new depredations. In place of a refined ruling class, grasping tradesmen and uneducated blacks rode to power under the mantle of patriotism, receiving appointments that allowed them to mulct the public.

Other Southern cities appeared in mid-nineteenth-century books as composite portraits of genteel infirmity and faded splendor. Charleston, unlike the Yankee metropolises whose old buildings were torn down in the name of progress, maintained the appearance of a charming English country town, free of "the smug mercantile primness of the northern cities." Its quaint structures, uniquely aristocratic and designed in a pleasant mixture of styles, and its graceful foliage, screening the decay of the city's mansions, imparted to Charleston a mellow charm.

Far different was the image of the growing cities of the West. "The metropolises of the eastern seaboard . . . represent[ed] all that was evil in old Europe; . . . the cities of the West, . . . all that was virtuous in the American experience."[20] Paeans to inland cities were not confined to the booster tracts of Daniel Drake, William Gilpin, Robert Van Horn, and Jessup Scott. A swelling chorus of novelists also saw in the burgeoning infant cities of the West the physical representation of the growing progress of the nation. Like Charles Dickens, who used Australia as a place to purge his characters of their former sins, urban novelists like Caroline Hentz and the anonymous author of *The Pennimans* cleansed their protagonists of hubris by removing them from the jaded influences of an established eastern metropolis to a fresh start in an energetic, democratic city of the West. Writers like John Beauchamp Jones, Walter

Whitmore, Mary Eastman, and H. M. Rulison conveyed the impression that cities were an integral part of the society developing in the West. They pictured Louisville and St. Louis as scenes of energetic enterprise; Chicago as a "Garden City," lively and handsome, even if its population of rats far outnumbered its human population; St. Paul as "destined to become the great city of the northwest"; Pittsburgh as a growing, busy market; San Francisco as a boom town where men could secure a fortune overnight; Cincinnati as "a vast, young city" which would someday "rival New York."[21] Towns that had been mere villages twenty-five years earlier were already envisioned in terms similar to Whitmore's description of Cincinnati in *Ella Winston:* "...the mind of man can hardly conceive the vast extent which it will someday reach, in wealth, population, grandeur and, in short, all that makes up the general character of a great and flourishing city" (p. 29). Writers of popular literature endowed the cities of the West, like their eastern counterparts, with individual personalities. Pittsburgh was already known as the Smoky City, a gloomy place shrouded with dark clouds. For those who dreaded industrialization, Pittsburgh became in John B. Jones's *Life and Adventures of a Country Merchant* and Samuel Young's *Smoky City* the symbol of the nation's scramble after wealth gone awry.

A far more attractive urban center in literary representations was Cincinnati, called by contemporaries the Queen City of the West. Celebrated for its rapid growth, this "infant Hercules" abounded with elegant architecture, beautiful pleasure grounds, and stylish people. A cosmopolitan municipality, its population included migrants from the North Atlantic states as well as newcomers from Germany and Ireland. Although the Queen City had its share of mysteries and miseries, it was "a moral city" where justice triumphed.

Another burgeoning place of plenty was St. Paul. It embodied the rapid progress of the Republic, the spirit which transformed an uncultivated region into a civilized center where "revengeful Chippeways and the insatiate Sioux" could no longer fight their bloody battles. Unlike the morally tainted seaboard cities, the Minnesota metropolis offered the magnificence of nature side by side with civilized urban life. Its residents enjoyed the opera, soirée, and festive ball as well as earthy amusements like sleigh rides, hiking, and fishing. Blessed with an exhilarating climate of pure and dry air, a romantic landscape of transparent lakes and cascading waters, a vista of rolling prairies and winding streams, St. Paul was, in the eyes of celebrants Eastman and Colonel Hankins, a paradise on earth.

In contrast to the salubrious physical and spiritual atmosphere of St. Paul, San Francisco captivated the imagination with its absence of moral restraints. A raucous boom town, it seemed to contemporaries to have sprung into existence overnight. Its wooden sheds and its streets reeking with filth and mud, combined with its population of daring young men and its scarcity of women and children, made it in the popular book America's archetypal frontier town. Animated with a spirit of reckless adventure, its inhabitants were portrayed in *Mysteries and Miseries of San Francisco,* Anna Fitch's *Bound Down,* and Hill's *John Smith's Funny Adventures* as "men on the make," who, without principle, without capital, without reputation, could rise rapidly to fortune. A boisterous meeting ground of all nations and complexions, it was a Babel on the Pacific.

Quite as important in the popular imagination as the rise of cities across the continent was the development of the perimeter of the metropolis. Technological advances in urban mass transit made possible the scattering of more prosperous metropolitan residents to outlying urban areas. By the 1840s and 1850s, as George Rogers Taylor has demonstrated, the census registered a higher rate of increase of suburban population than of residents in central cities. This demographic drift attracted comment in popular potboilers. In picturing the outskirts of the city as a retreat for busy commuters, writers paralleled the promotional campaigns of real estate speculators who were depicting the suburb as a marriage of town and country, a place that allowed people access to the wealth of the city and to the purity of a rural environment. Popular books like Robert Newell's *Avery Glibun,* P. Hamilton Myers's *The Miser's Heir,* and Henry Edwards's *The Belle of Central Park* gave the impression that purchase of suburban real estate was a sound investment. Not only would it bring skyrocketing monetary increments; it would also allow the commuter to enjoy a piece of "merrie England" away from the congestion of the city.

The reform-minded writer Edward Everett Hale in his book *Sybaris and Other Homes* envisioned bedroom communities as a means of preserving Jeffersonian principles in an urban nation. Linked by regular runs of the omnibus and railroad to the heart of the business district, the suburb would allow aspiring blue-collar workers to escape the hazards of back-street life. Urbanization was irreversible. But the suburb would permit wage earners to retain the benefits of mutual association and at the same time to enjoy nature, the independence of home ownership, and the integrity of the family. Hale summoned landowners, railroad managers, and potential settlers to cooperate in a great undertaking to plant colonies around core cities. But already by mid-century the outskirts of the city seemed a far cry from Hale's dream of an arcadia for the working class. More realistic writers like William Gilmore Simms in *The Prima Donna*, George Foster in "Philadelphia in Slices," and Margaret Smith in *A Winter in Washington* depicted the fringe of the metropolis as an area of sprawling shanties and tanneries that provided profitable investments for slumlords and tavern keepers.

The relentless march of the American populace to cities during the period 1820–70 inspired a flurry of popular books which promised to guide the uninitiated through the mazes of city life. These guides, an urban counterpart to explorers' charts of America's continental frontier, offered would-be pioneers to the city an easily comprehended map of the metropolitan wilderness. From them the reader could derive a wealth of commentary about the advantages and shortcomings of the nation's different towns.

Yet one may ask why certain cities became landmarks in the popular book. Why was the reading market flooded with images of the Empire City but not of St. Louis and Chicago? Writers apparently responded to public interest in winners. Cities shaken by exploding growth aroused the most curiosity. Equally significant is the fact that popular writers created a folklore about certain cities, not necessarily the nation's largest. For example, Boston, which had the advantage of producing cheap mass fiction, received far more attention in popular literature than Philadelphia and Baltimore, although it lagged behind them in population. Professional writers, anxious to find publishers, lived in cities with an important book printing industry and churned out stories set in locales that were at once familiar to them and intriguing to the public.

Regardless of region, size, or publishing bent, a city had to harbor sin if it aspired to push the Empire City from center stage. One sign of a city's metropolitan destiny in the popular book was its jumble of mysteries and miseries. While urban boosters bragged about their cities' transportation facilities, cultural amenities, and business opportunities, pulp writers apparently took pride in their towns' illicit activities. If New York had its "lights and shadows," Washington could boast its "fashions and follies"; if Boston was a showcase of "city crimes," Rochester was famous for its "scenes of vice and shame." Indeed, the sheer multiplication of book titles with "mysteries and miseries" attached to the names of different American cities suggests that moral ambiguity was one more, if little known, manifestation of urban rivalry. It also was an index of a city's romantic possibilities. The mysterious metropolis was the popular writer's imaginative substitute for an image of the yeoman's mystical union with the forces of nature.

Literary profiles of mysterious American cities reveal a complex ideology of urbanization in the period of the mid-nineteenth century. The same city might be regarded as a Babylon or a Jerusalem. It might reek with vice, be obsessed with money, neglect the poor, and at the same time, construct urbane institutions, generate material well-being, devote itself to the welfare of the unfortunate. Whether towns were drowning in evil or purging their doorways of the Devil, they took their cues from New York City. Popular literature left little doubt that Gotham was the nation's archetypal city. Others across the land reproduced its problems and policies.

The United States by mid-century was laced with cities from the Atlantic to the Pacific. Though these far-flung communities were remarkable for their mimicry of each other, writers of nonfiction and novels alike celebrated the diversity of the American urban experience. At a time when technology was making cities more standardized, the most important media of the day, the popular book, mythologized a nation of distinctive municipalities. No matter the homogeneity of the town—its slavish repetition of gridiron street patterns and Georgian-style buildings—in popular prose each appeared unique; no matter the similarity of a city's growing pains—its housing shortages, municipal corruption, choked-up streets—in literature written for the common man each had a singular identity. This construct of individual personality allowed the reader to penetrate the mysteries of the city. In a period of baffling urban change it demystified the metropolis. Those versed in this literature could feel less frightened of the town. From chiaroscuro portraits of the country's leading cities, a mass audience could take comfort in the thought that every city was a familiar, readily understood stock character.

8

PERSONALITIES OF THE CITY
Urban Folk Heroes and Villains

While writers of popular lore recognized that each city had its distinctive flavor, they also celebrated the intriguing individual personalities within these cities. Whether urban novelists fleshed out their books with the brawling b'hoy, insouciant hobo, effete dandy, or financial tycoon, they conveyed the impression that the city spawned an unusual variety of human species. At a time when popular taste fancied picturesque heroes and villains, the exotic personages of an urban landscape competed with ghosts in gothic castles, pirates on the high seas, and Indians in the primordial forest in captivating the imagination of the reading public.

A familiar face in city fiction was the libertine. Like the stereotyped aristocratic seducer in English novels, this American urban rogue was a fashionably dressed man sporting well-oiled locks of hair, jeweled fingers, gloved hands, and a fragrant breath kept aromatic with the liberal use of wine. Upon closer examination, his appearance was marked, when young, with a haggard complexion, bloodshot eyes, a reckless bearing; when old, with a corpulent frame, piercing eyes, thick, coarse features. But the stigmata of the sensualist were lips described as "large, projecting and of deep red approaching purple."

The rake's occupation in life was to chase "dainty morsels of virginal sweetness" and abandon them with all haste, once conquered. In a nation devoted to the work ethic, he was a wealthy do-nothing who dedicated his life to pleasure. When not seducing maidens, he dissipated a vast estate on liquor, gambling, and horse racing. He scoffed openly at the reigning morality by wrecking happy homes and mocking religion.[1] A personification of the glittering surfaces and dangerous realities of the metropolis, he was an object lesson on the emptiness of worldly vanities. Writers who wanted to conserve traditional morality in the city taught that the wages of his sin were death from drink or vengeful murder.

Urban literature abounded not only with numerous debauchers but also with many idlers. If the libertine defied the Victorian sexual code, the loafer challenged the Protestant work ethic. Removed from the manly calling of farming, he devoted his time to dressing fastidiously and dallying in liquor shops, "segar" stores, and the theater. George Lippard's *Margaret Dunbar* described an "exquisite" as "one of those mysterious, well-dressed people . . . who are mysterious because no one can tell where all those fine clothes, eye-glasses, and gold chains come from." These elegant loafers, asserted Frank St. Clair, supported their fashionable tastes by sponging on "landlords, tailors, hatters, and, in fine, all . . . so unfortunate as to regard them as patrons." The product of a tinsel civilization, they lived by their wits. Some avoided regular employment by marrying a fortune, others by swindling the hapless bumpkin, still others by serving as scouts for gambling dens. Without shame, they invited themselves to dinner, attached themselves to women like a pet dog, and toadied to the women's rich husbands.[2] According to Edward Judson in *Mysteries and Miseries of New Orleans,* every city had "a stock of these gentlemen on hand, to lead good men astray, make bad ones worse, and to bring ruin on parents by enticing young men to follow fashionable examples" (p. 28).

Not all idlers in the city were successful in achieving the high life without work. Some huddled around open fires, cooking a dinner of roasted potatoes al fresco. In popular writing city soil seemed to nurture a skid row personality—the hobo. In a society filled with competitive go-getters, the metropolis also generated a subculture of dropouts. The vagrant was voluntarily unemployed. In a milieu that offered salvation through work, he looked with horror upon a steady job; in a culture that viewed begging as an ultimate degradation, he shamelessly asked for food; in a society which prized the home, he, without embarrassment, made his lodgings a hallway, stoop, or empty wagon. Nor was he at a loss for companionship. In the numerous parks of the city he could find an entire troop of like-minded individuals who regarded happiness as a nap on a park bench with a well-filled stomach.[3]

While the fashionable wastrel and the hobo shunned work, the criminal was more than willing to take on certain jobs. Like many of his respectable counterparts in business, he defied the ethics of religion and humanity, creating new rules which allowed him to crush others in his effort to get ahead. Self-reliant, impatient with traditional restraints, an enemy of privileged classes, was he not also an embodiment of America itself at mid-century? As David Brion Davis has suggested, the fictional renegade represented the repressed aggressions of urban dwellers living in an intensely competitive environment. Readers could secretly admire such characters for their unfettered pursuit of material gratifications and, at the same time, appease their guilt by seeing the criminal punished for having satisfied forbidden desires.

Curiously enough, at a time when the press was filled with exhortations against the foreign menace, the popular imagination still conceived one of its stock cads, the gangster, as American born and bred. Despite the soaring arrest record of the Irish during this period, criminality had not yet acquired a foreign taint. Lawbreakers in mid-nineteenth-century fiction possessed Anglo-Saxon names.[4] Their selfish instincts were indigenous, not foreign.

Another typical cad in urban literature was the conniving business-man, a respectable rogue with a "Co." appended to his name. These profiteers promoted financial ventures that destroyed the fortunes of thousands. Managing to live handsomely with a minimum of labor, this breed of rascal "[made up its mind] not only that the world [owed it] a living, but that it also [owed it] champagne."[5] One representative in the novel *Cone Cut Corners* leaves his family in a quandary when he dies; no one knows quite what he owns. The life-insurance policy for his heirs is underwritten by one of his own companies, which had been dissolved after customers had paid a considerable sum for premiums. He has left his family a share in a patent for cloth made from copper wire, a large interest in an insolvent iron foundry, and interest in the Minternunny Land, Timber and Mine Co., which has neither land nor timber nor mines.

In oft-repeated literary caricatures, the financial wizards of the city were men of low birth who elbowed, squeezed, and shoved their way to prominence. An embodiment of American mobility gone awry, un-mindful of their Christian duty to others, they pursued wealth. Whether they embezzled the savings of the poor in their unsound banks, herded laborers into pestilential tenements, evicted the widow and orphan, or raised the price of bread in a depression, their sole purpose in life was to amass money. But they paid for their transgressions, at least in the pages of popular fiction. With monotonous regularity at the end of every story, they lost their ill-gotten gains while the deserving poor became rich.[6]

The figure of the pawnbroker in urban fiction vividly personified the dishonesty thought to be rampant in city life. He gloated when he stole bread from the mouths of widows and children. Charging at least 25 percent interest on merchandise left with him, he extracted the last penny from those in need. If he saw profit in receiving stolen goods, he would accept the robber's plunder; if he could furnish his home and outfit his family with goods supposedly left in his safekeeping, he cared little that nothing matched or fit; if he could obtain a treasured heirloom, he would not hesitate to pay a starving orphan in counterfeit currency. This embodiment of the grasping materialism of urban life knew the daily needs of the unfortunate yet did everything in his power to increase their distress.[7]

Another urban professional who frequently symbolized the calculated dishonesty of the metropolis was the pettifogging attorney who abounded in this era, which freely granted licenses to unqualified men. In popular literature these knaves represented the double-dealing urbanite who took advantage of his more straightforward and unschooled countrymen. Using the law as both a shield and a weapon, he cheated his clients and perjured himself in court: "No lie was too base, no treacherous deed too evil, no piece of cruelty too heartless, no fraud too disgraceful, no act of self-humiliation too groveling to cause him to shrink from its perpetration, if by committing it he could gain power."[8] Skilled in obfuscation and chicanery, he was talented at aiding the clever criminal, ineffective in defending the innocent.

One representative of this class in the urban confidential *Life in Rochester* is epitomized by his name—Mr. Grab. A rogue who knows how to go around the law and acquire other people's property, he serves a legal notice in such a way that its recipient does not realize until too late that it has been delivered. Grab makes a condolence call on a widow. When the woman leaves the room, he slips a tax notice into a package of old papers. Upon her return he delivers the package, saying, "Here are your papers." In court he can swear he has delivered the notice and at the same time make certain that the distressed woman will lose her property for failure to pay a small tax on it.

Popular books, nonetheless, did make a distinction between those who used knowledge for their own self-aggrandizement and those who used it for the service of mankind. Lawyers enjoyed a dual reputation in popular writing. If some were legal swindlers, others were defenders of the innocent. Numerous writers climaxed stories of a successful upward struggle by having the hero graduate from law school to fight for the victims of injustice.[9]

Like the legal fraternity, physicians in popular books were either angels or devils, dedicated humanitarians or repulsive quacks. In times of trouble they more than any other group observed firsthand the deplorable conditions in the slums. Although many doctors actually did refuse to tend the poor, some popular novelists undoubtedly were impressed by selfless men who ran dispensaries and clinics for the needy. In books such as Anne Royall's *The Tennessean*, Timothy Arthur's *Heiress* and *Rising in the World*, Charles Burdett's *Convict's Child*, and Mary Denison's *Edna Etheril*, the physician was a prototypic urban philanthropist who served the dying mother, the consumptive father, and the feverish child without charge.

Just as often, though, physicians were targets for resentment and satire. Popular literature registered the prevailing attitude of contemporaries who regarded the medical profession with cynicism. According to historians Richard Shryock and John Duffy, the vast majority of doctors during this period were poorly educated, self-seeking, and uncouth. State legislatures had swept away almost all regulations controlling the practice of medicine. Standards at medical schools were at a minimum and fundamental research almost nonexistent. Little wonder, then, that many popular books pictured physicians as fiends or fakers. If some doctors rescued the distressed, others just as easily created distress. In St. Clair's eyes medicine was a career that required "little moral principle, little calibre, and still less inclination, to pursue any honest calling that may require effort." To Joseph Holt Ingraham doctors were manufacturers of nostrums that were at best useless, at worst lethal. These quacks peddled pills that they claimed were "an infallible cure for the toothache—a speedy remedy for the headache—a general healer of fractures and compound sprains, and without descending into particulars, a universal and ever-lasting strengthener."[10] Unfortunately, such characters did not appear as mere figments of the pulp writer's imagination. Medical imposters were familiar figures to a public which often preferred their painless, if worthless, remedies to the "heroic" cures of the medical profession—bleeding, vomiting, and blistering.

Mass literature attacked the medical practitioner not only for vending his "Elixirs of Life" and his "Vital Fluids" but also for using his profession as a cloak for carnality and murder. Books like *Revelations of Asmodeus, Mary Beach*, Samuel Young's *Smoky City*, and Osgood Bradbury's *Ellen Grant* alleged that fashionable physicians treated ladies with nervous disabilities to intimate examinations in their bedchambers. There the doctor would arouse the patient until she became dependent upon him for a cure normally supplied by her husband. Other doctors in such fiction as Lippard's *Quaker City*, P. Hamilton Myers's *The Miser's Heir*, and Charles Averill's *The Cholera-Field* performed abortions, administered fatal medicine when paid sufficiently, or infected an entire metropolis with the plague to increase their business.

Hack authors inveighed against journalism as another profession filled with scoundrels. In criticism that often differed little from Philip Hone's classic portrayal of James Gordon Bennett as an "editorial miscreant" who deserved torture, popular writers branded the newspaper editor as a huckster who readily exchanged the ideals of his craft for a soaring circulation. Lippard described such a disreputable practitioner in *Quaker City* as "[c]rawling from the pages of his foul journal over the fairest reputations in the community;...a bravo who stabs for a dollar; a hireling, who...prowls abroad, selling his sheet to any man that will buy it, for any purpose under heaven" (p. 140). The newspaperman in other potboilers was a dangerous rabble-rouser who manipulated a malleable urban populace. Taking advantage of all that was base and mean in mankind, he pandered to the vilest elements of public taste: "He pleased the stupid men by writing everything down to their intellectual plane. He did not attempt to elevate or instruct them—that would not pay."[11] When not dragging down everything lofty, he supplied the daily reader with grisly stories of duels, suicides, and murders.[12] But worst of all, the coarse newspaperman typified by William Wirt Howe in *The Pasha Papers* was a threat to the democratic process itself. Selling his influence to the highest bidder, he attempted to inflame public opinion and affect the course of election campaigns.

While lampoons of demagogic newsmen proliferated in popular novels, nonfiction writers like James McCabe, Junius Browne, and Matthew Smith praised editors of respectable journals for their integrity, social enlightenment, and wit. In their books men like Horace Greeley, Charles A. Dana, Robert Bonner, and even James Gordon Bennett appeared as social crusaders who labored sixteen to eighteen hours a day to bring sprightly writing to the masses.

While pulp books caricatured the mercenary pursuits of many urban men, they by no means implied that venality was a masculine monopoly. Grasping women also figured among the staple characters of popular literature. One familiar personage who aroused both amusement and contempt was the flinty landlady—typically an unmotherly woman who was irascible, insolent, pretentious, and miserly. If she were not a would-be missionary dispensing unsolicited religious literature to her clientele, she appeared in equally unattractive roles as a secret drinker, slovenly housekeeper, or unwanted matchmaker. She furnished her house, even if it had the most elegant facade, with dismal bargains, and frowned over dinner at any guest presumptuous enough to fill his plate with the unappetizing-looking fare. What she denied in food, however, she granted in gossip; and whether her tenants were interested or not, she inundated her captive audience with intimate details of the lives of her boarders.[13]

But the ultimate female embodiment of evil in the urban book was the procurer. This intriguer appeared in the anonymous novel *The Three Widows*, Emma Rosewood's *The Virtuous Wife*, Bradbury's *Female Depravity*, and Lippard's *Quaker City* as a moral viper who defied the Victorian ideal of respectability and domesticity. To serve her male clientele, she posed as a concerned matronly figure, all the while plotting to turn an innocent girl into a whore. Assuming the archetypal role of the destructive old woman found in fairy tales, she represented a threat to the institutions of monogamous marriage and motherhood.

If female entrepreneurs were vile mercenaries, women forced to accept the terms of employment set by others became new folk heroines. As we have seen in chapter 6, the toiling seamstress and laundress in popular fiction elicited reader sympathy for their unprotected counterparts in the urban economy. In contrast to those woeful characters were the g'hals and b'hoys of New York celebrated by pulp authors like Judson and George Foster as well as the playwright Benjamin Baker. These workingmen and women thrived in the urban tumult. The g'hals, typically employed as laborers in pressrooms or in cap-sewing or book-folding establishments, and the b'hoys, often factory hands, butcher boys, and craftsmen, appeared as cheerful, industrious wage earners. Once the long hours of employment were over, they savored the rough-and-tumble pleasures of city life. To the Moses and Lizes of Gotham, a stroll on the Bowery, a rollick in a smoke-filled dance house, or a race up Third Avenue was adventure. No need for this unspoiled crew to indulge in effete conversazioni or lavish fêtes; they could enjoy shooting with a militia company, fighting a fire, or attending a prize fight. As free as any frontiersman, they remained in the pages of cheap publications "untamable specimens." Whether they brawled at a bar, waged war with a street gang, or ran after a fire engine, they were as tough as their hero, Old Hickory, as independent as any yeoman. An urban incarnation of Jacksonian democracy, they were America's archetypal common man and woman.

If the b'hoy and his g'hal represented heroic lower-class personalities of the city, the humanitarian became an omnipresent model of upper-class civic virtue. In contrast to the philanthropist portrayed ironically by Nathaniel Hawthorne in the *Blithedale Romance*, who sacrifices those closest to him for a visionary scheme to reform criminals, the self-constituted social workers of popular fiction unambiguously help regenerate the less fortunate. Modeled to a large extent on the elite of the city who actively engaged in humanitarian work with the not altogether altruistic purpose of protecting the rich from lawless youths, the munificent businessman of pulp literature bolstered the self-serving image urban merchants had of themselves as honorable custodians of wealth.

Who were these noble-hearted figures who played such a central role in city fiction? The collective portrait that emerges is one typified in Burdett's *Chances and Changes,* a person "princely in his charities, ... performed from the promptings of a heart overflowing with true philanthropy and Christian love.... His feelings ever alive to the sufferings of his fellow-man urged him to deeds of benevolence, ... [and] he alone, except the grateful recipients of his bounty, knew of his kindness" (pp. 18–19). He, as much as the confidence operator, was a mysterious man of the metropolis, an unsqueamish individual who confronted contagion and depravity to relieve distress. Accounts of his timely assistance to the deserving reinforced the contemporary belief that the most propitious form of relief was educational opportunity. The recipients of his welfare, once given a start with a bath, a set of clean clothing, and proper schooling, managed to improve their social status. His activities offered convincing evidence that the older ideal of the Christian community could coexist with a newer goal of the individualistic pursuit of wealth. The Christian entrepreneur's use of his riches on behalf of the needy carried the comforting message that religious values would not become infected by the growing material affluence of the city's elite.

One of the intriguing mysteries of city life was that such a profusion of personalities flourished on urban soil. In portraying the city as a carnival of unusual people, popular writers created an urban counterpart to familiar descriptions of idyllic rural landscapes. This humanscape of exotic types injected a dynamism into urban life that could not be matched in hamlets with a monotonously homogeneous population.

Literary portraits of diverse urban groups, however, were more than a flight from humdrum rural characters. By putting faces on the crowd, hack authors domesticated an unruly city scene. Their caricatures of different groups personalized the alarming anonymity of the urban masses. Ludicrous stereotypes demystified the human conundrum of urban life and reduced complex new patterns of behavior to a comprehensible social topography. Instead of vexing themselves over the changes the city was effecting in the personalities of urban dwellers, readers could smile at the sideshow of sports who made their home in the metropolis.

The cast of characters which studded urban literature was not just a comical exhibition of human eccentricity. Precisely by extending many of the stale conventions found in the sentimental novel to include stereotypical villains and heroes, writers of popular city books affirmed the triumph of traditional social values in a rapidly changing society. Recognizable devils like the upper-class rake, the heartless tycoon, and venal procurer affronted the moral order within the city by their individualistic pursuit of wealth, unredeemed by ties to a Christian community. With tiresome predictability such wickedness met its just deserts. Just as monotonously, endearingly familiar protagonists like the persecuted working-class girl, philanthropic businessman, and noble orphan found temporal bliss in the city. These easily identified characters harmonized traditional religious values with secular materialism and offered proof that the social advancement sought within the city need not conflict with the reader's ethical vision of the universe. Thus popular writers avoided a more interesting examination of contemporary urban characters for clichés which defused the potential menace of a diverse and explosive population.

9

THE UNMELTED POT
Ethnics in the City

An even more fascinating human dimension of urban life than the various personalities who made their home in the city was the diverse foreign element which gravitated to metropolitan centers. Although by the time of the Civil War immigrants accounted for only 15 percent of the total United States population, the proportion of the foreign-born in New York City was 48 percent and in western cities like Chicago, St. Louis, and Milwaukee more than 50 percent. The phenomenon of unprecedented numbers of aliens sweeping into once-homogeneous urban communities in the mid-nineteenth century gripped the public imagination. Especially in the 1840s and 1850s, as the proportion of immigrants swelled to a flood tide never before or since experienced in American history, natives agonized over the outsiders in their midst. They linked these newcomers with spiraling rates of pauperism, alcoholism, crime, disease, mob violence, and political corruption.

The stranger, a visible reminder of painful changes in urban life, was grist for the mill of popular authors. Augustine Joseph Hickey Duganne, who served for one term as a New York assemblyman on the Know-Nothing ticket, expressed the view in his novel *The Tenant-House* that the immigrant was a threat to the ideals of the Republic: "Do you seek Liberty? go not to the great cities of our republic; for in their midst you will find thousands of human beings left to become thieves and to uprear their children thieves—to sink into pauperism and make their offspring paupers. Would you discover Equality? go not to the cities, wherin [sic] wallow men and women in ignorance and filth . . . and osing the equality of their humanity, in the disorder of brutish instincts"

(p. 292). Clearly, Duganne was not alone in his fear that cities were being infected by turbulent newcomers who could poison American democracy. A whole school of pulp novelists joined the antiforeign crusade led by nativists like the orthodox minister Lyman Beecher and the inventor of the telegraph, Samuel F. B. Morse. These writers popularized the idea that the great urban centers were hotbeds of discontent swarming with ignorant and impoverished immigrants who would undermine the stability of American society.

As the invasion of Catholic immigrants to America's cities mounted in the 1840s, antiforeign sentiment and hostility to the Catholic church became one. Nativists, convinced that the Church was conspiring to take over the Mississippi Valley, singled out the Jesuits as atheistic supermen, free of the restraints that bound the rest of society. Edward Zane Carroll Judson in *The G'hals of New York* underscored this view. He accused this alien organization of seeking "to spread unfailing nets, to ... destroy all who stood in the way of the ... remorseless order ... [and to use for its purposes] sworn, superstitious colleagues ... trained ... in all the blind, treacherous, narrow-minded sentiments of the Jesuit creed" (p. 49). This novelist, who spent a year in prison for his part in fomenting the anti-British Astor Place Riot of 1849, tried to persuade his readers that from the great metropolitan centers of the nation a relentlessly immoral order was plotting the destruction of American democracy. Already, he asserted, the Society of Jesus had "planted its seeds in all the large cities of the United States ... and these seeds ... [were] daily producing fruits, as well in converts as in money" (p. 125). With a treasury supposedly groaning in weight from the contributions of parishoners least able to afford such lavish donations, the Church was using its enormous financial power to gain control of the United States. Moreover, he alleged, the Catholic religion had political muscle. With a credulous flock ready to obey Rome, it could secure the election of ambitious politicians sensitive to the desires of the papacy.

Unless Americans awoke to the danger in their midst, William Earle Binder in his novels *Viola* and *Madelon Hawley* warned, the Church, using a vast network of spies and veiling its activities in secrecy, would overturn the liberal laws of the nation, abolish free speech, terminate elections, and impose the pope and inquisition on the Republic. It would allow the Empire City to serve as the springboard of its operations for implanting religious authoritarianism in the New World. In George Lippard's *New York: Its Upper Ten and Lower Million*, a fictional legate of the Church, doubtlessly modeled on the papal nuncio Monsignor Gaetano Bedini, reveals the plot of Rome to gain control over the American Republic: "It is our true policy, then, to absorb and rule the

Republic of the North. To make our Church the secret spring of its Government; to gradually and without exciting suspicion, mold every one of its institutions to our own purposes; to control the education of the people, and bend the elective franchise to our will. . . . And this must be done by making New York the center of our system. . . . From New York we will control the Republic" (p. 68). Such an accusation was a familiar scare tactic but a credible one to nativists still incensed by Bedini's attempt in 1853 to restore authority to the hierarchy from lay trustees in Philadelphia and Buffalo as well as by Bishop Hughes's earlier battle in New York City to abolish Bible reading in the schools and to obtain public funding for Catholic parochial schools.

While writers like Judson, Lippard, and Binder depicted the city as the target of a foreign church which aimed to subvert the institutions of the Republic, other novelists viewed the metropolis as a festering bed of nativism which could destroy the ideal of a pluralistic society. It was the spawning ground of a "Protestant crusade" which aimed to crush America's long tradition of toleration. Irish boys in an urban community, warned John T. Roddan in the novel *John O'Brien,* were in danger of being wrenched from their Church. Whether they attended public school with godless classmates who cursed and played hooky, went to public meetings where they heard sermons against the pope, or were bound out to masters who forbade them to practice their faith, Catholic children were subject to the persecutions inflicted by a Protestant establishment located in America's cities.

As the nativist crusade gained momentum in the 1840s and 1850s, pulp writers viewed earlier incidents of violence against Catholics in both Boston and Philadelphia through the lens of their own parti pris. To the Reverend John T. Roddan, conservative priest and editor of the Catholic journal *The Pilot,* the burning of the Ursuline Convent in Boston in 1834 was the work of ignorant men, eager to throw religious statues into the flames and to enrich themselves with the treasures of a religious sanctuary. But to the Know-Nothing author Justin Jones, whose other books betray an unquestioning acceptance of Protestant orthodoxy, this deed was more than an act of vandalism. In his novel *The Nun of St. Ursula,* based on a widely circulated but unfounded rumor, the instigators of the mob action are two highminded Americans who want to rescue a young girl held prisoner in an "unholy place." When they incite ruffians to pillage and arson, they are, according to Jones, lighting a torch of liberty on the anniversary date of the St. Bartholomew's Day Massacre.

Just as the Catholic press of Boston used the destruction of the

Ursuline Convent to sear the conscience of Americans who believed in fair play, so the Catholic press utilized the burning of St. Michael's Church in Philadelphia in 1844 to shame the citizens of the City of Brotherly Love into toleration of the foreigner. In *Bickerton; or The Immigrant's Daughter* Charles James Cannon presents a hypocritical "model" city where the rich congratulate themselves on their holiness, oblivious to the immigrants huddled in shanties. The immigrants drain the swamps and construct the streets of the growing city but are rewarded with the contempt of natives, who view them a dangerous rabble ready to over-turn their fair city. The Irish become the victims of the society of "Thugs and Hindostan," who meet in secret to stop the foreigners from getting control of the country. With the help of "the reverend clergy . . . who were constantly preaching . . . the danger to which the State was ex-posed from the encroachments of the Church," the society's members launch a crusade "to protect the Public Pot from the felonious intents of the foreigners" (p. 83). To goad the Irish into fighting, the Protestants hire criminals to parade through "little Dublin" with placards reading "Americans to rule America," "The Bible is the best School Book," "No Foreign Domination." A riot breaks out, and a military force is summoned against the Irish. Still unsatisfied, natives tear down a Catholic church and set it ablaze. Respectable citizens react to this violence by voting the Thugs into office.

This same nativist outburst figured in the novel *The Nazarene* by George Lippard, founder of the Brotherhood of the Union, an organi-zation dedicated to promoting fellowship and equality in the United States. In the story a clandestine organization, the Holy Protestant League, meets in deep vaults to wipe out the "Anti-Christ of Rome." Under the guise of purifying Christianity, clergymen and a bank director foment an anti-immigrant political platform and hire cutthroats to riot against the Irish. Disguised as priests, these gangsters urge the Hibernians to use violence, and thereby furnish native Americans with an excuse for attacking Catholic churches.

Just as bigoted clergymen and politicians in popular fiction tried to separate the immigrant from his religion, so others schemed to take his purse. Popular exposés like James McCabe's *Secrets of the Great City,* George Foster's *New York in Slices,* and Thomas Gunn's *Physiology of New York Boarding-Houses* accurately recorded the frauds perpe-trated on newly arrived foreigners and thereby gave a new forum for airing charges found in the daily press. They showed how, upon land-ing in his newly adopted home, the immigrant was greeted in his native tongue by a host of friendly compatriots who offered to take his money and purchase for him a railroad ticket at a price lower than

that available at the official landing depot or to lead him to an economical boarding house. As a result, he would find himself in a strange
country without money. The newfound friend vanished, once the
immigrant had parted with the purchase price. The boarding house to
which he was sent would turn out to be a vile hole "overrun from
basement to garret with cockroaches, fleas, bedbugs, wharf-rats, and
every other sort of vermin." Yet for such quarters he would be
charged rates that would soon pauperize him.

The immigrant girl from a foreign shore suffered all the dangers to
which the farmer's daughter was exposed. Popular novels showed her
a target of runners for houses of prostitution. Upon noticing a pretty,
bewildered girl, a scout would offer to find her inexpensive lodgings.
Here the landlord treated the innocent with friendship until she had
spent all her money. He would then allow her to meet her daily charges
by parting with little articles of clothing. When she was drained of all
resources, he gave her a choice—walk naked on the streets or work for
him.

Although by 1855 New York City had enacted legislation to protect
immigrants from runners, the novelist Peter McCorry ignored secular
measures for helping newcomers and instead affirmed the power of
religion for shielding the foreigner from danger. In his novel *The Lost
Rosary; or, Our Irish Girls,* Mary and Ailey O'Donnell, fresh arrivals
from the Emerald Isle, are met at the port of New York by a woman
who offers to take them to a comfortable boarding house. They are
disturbed when upon their arrival at Paddy Farren's establishment they
see rough-looking men congregating around the house, consuming
liquor, and exchanging vile oaths. Perceiving that they have been
brought to a trap, they decide to leave that very evening. When they
move to different lodgings in which a picture of the Virgin Mary is
displayed, they know that they have found safety. Soon they are adopted
by truly helpful compatriots, secure honest employment, and are reunited with their childhood sweethearts. The author reassured his readers
that the "genuinely true hearted Irish girl" would be able to build a
new life in the American city. "Her virtue is a wall of adamant,
supported by the Sacraments of the Church which are as effectual here
as elsewhere" (p. vi).

That the Irish figured as such an important element in the fiction
of the period is hardly surprising. Of all the immigrants who spilled onto
America's shores between 1820 and 1870, by far the largest ethnic influx
came from Ireland. Carl Wittke in *The Irish in America* has pointed
out that the Celts, unprepared by their circumscribed rural backgrounds
to cope with the harsh environment into which they were thrust, arrived

in United States cities impoverished and uneducated. They crammed into the older commercial portions of the city, where they starved in tottering hovels. Grog shops infested their neighborhoods. Searching for escape from their dingy homes, they found conviviality in the saloons, where ward heelers recruited them into machine politics.

Popular writers did little to educate their audience to the problems the Irish faced in a new land. They deplored Irish violence but disregarded the wage cuts and strikebreaking practices which triggered those riots; they scorned the neglect of Irish children but ignored the exclusion from profitable urban occupations which forced Irishmen to find work on canal and railroad projects away from their families; they branded the Irish as lazy but remained silent about their menial labor leveling the city's streets, digging sewers, and building docks; they denounced them for their propensity for crime but failed to look beyond the sea to their homeland, which was remarkably law abiding. In short, pulp authors repeated the ethnic slurs which were part of the common coinage of the day and typically portrayed the Celt as a man wearing a ragged coat, his nose bleeding and waving a shillalah.

As the Irish overflowed into the city's almshouses, hospitals, and prisons, urban writers devoted more attention to them than to any other foreign group. Stereotyped as dirty, alcoholic ruffians who tortured the English language with their comical brogue, they were reviled with the labels hurled at minority groups in many periods of American history. A. L. Stimson, Lucius Sargeant, and Anne Royall pictured migrants from the Emerald Isle as a group with an aversion to soap and a proclivity for breeding an army of unruly children. They were spendthrifts who had no shame about living on relief or selling their brooms for a dram of drink. When not depicted beating their wives, they crowded the reformatories of the cities. At a time when the Irish were the most visible element involved in riots, Edward Dixon, Elizabeth Smith, D. Corcoran, and many others labeled them as a group born with "an ingrained propensity" which pulled them "within the vortex of rowdyism as mysteriously and, withal, as irresistibly as the magnetic principle draws the needle of the pole" and as swaggering ruffians who enjoyed standing in barrooms to deliver speeches on the rights of the "payple" while brandishing their fists at those who disagreed with their views.[1]

While the influx of the Irish was still relatively small, a popular book, *The Life of Paddy O'Flarrity*, promised Celtic immigrants that if they conformed to Yankee traits of "industry, sobriety, prudence, and attention," someday an Irishman could be president of the United States. But once they became a force in urban politics, popular literature differed little from respectable journals like the *New York Times* and the *Chicago Tribune* in their depictions of the Irish as noisy drunkards and religious fanatics who were tainting the American democratic process by their unholy alliance with political machines. The immigrant group the quickest to make its influence felt, the Celts were, in the eyes of many pulp writers, a subversive element which sought to overthrow the Republic and replace it with tyranny. Even when serving in law-enforcement agencies, they were, in novels like William Ritner's *Great Original and Entrancing Romance* and George Thompson's *Brazen Star,* bullies who came "howling with hunger" from a distant shore "to feed and fatten upon Yankee abundance." As nativist anger flared in the 1840s and 1850s, the Irish became the scapegoat for everything that was going awry in America.

Unlike the American self-made man, the Hibernian who achieved success was viewed as a "small-potato patrician" who could not shed the vulgarity of his peasant past. In *New York Aristocracy* an author with the pseudonym Joseph lampooned Irish immigrants who were trying to rise into high society: "Was ever an Irishman or woman, ever mistaken for anything else than what they were? Amidst a thousand tongues, how clear and sharp, and unmistakable breaks in that rattling brogue" (pp. 92–93). Quick to enrich themselves by entering ward politics, they supposedly viewed honesty as a virtue that paid poorly. Having moved as fast as corruption could carry them from shanty to brownstone, their attainment of a city mansion, a new name, and fancy clothes could never, in the opinion of critical popular writers, hide their ludicrous lineage.

Like the stage Irishman who had already taken his place as a character favorite by the mid 1850s, the Celt, with his spirited speech and dress of shabby gentility, was a familiar figure used for comic relief in the popular book. The "paddies," puffed up with blarney, rarely enunciated dialogue that was not punctuated with predictable invocations of God or the Devil. The daughters of Erin often appeared equally ridiculous. Invariably possessing the name of Biddy, they worked, when they did not drink, as maids and washerwomen, "cleaning the cities of America." Judson, Henry Dexter, and Hannah Farnham Lee lumped them together as slatterns with rough exteriors and tender hearts, and used their picturesque patois—"sure as I know," "faith it's more thin I can ate," "poor little craythur," "don't spake of the stirabout"—to provide an element of farce in overwrought prose.

Just as critics branded the Irish as mercurial, raucous, dirty, and improvident, their defenders pegged other stereotypical adjectives on them—vivacious, loyal, gregarious, and generous. But whether books condemned or praised the Hibernians, they reserved much more sympathy for the women than for the men.[2] Literature geared toward a mass market could look with sympathy upon the more tractable immigrant females, who were not competing for the goods of American society, but feared an assertive male minority that was entering Eastern cities in droves and increasingly becoming rivals for economic and political power.

The Germans, who by 1860 represented 31 percent of the foreign-born population in the United States, did not arouse the same antagonism in popular prose as did the Irish. They were less likely than the Celts to congregate in cities. Urban pulp books, mirroring the comical stereotypes of the vaudeville stage, contrasted the unreliable, rowdy Irishman with the stolid, phlegmatic German. Books like G. M. Wharton's *New Orleans Sketch Book,* Margaret Smith's *What Is Gentility?* and Gunn's *Physiology of New York Boarding-Houses* pictured the Rhinelander as "the Dray horse of mankind," whose national traits corresponded to the puritan ethic of hard work and thrift. A migrant group which usually arrived in America with capital, skills, and middle-class morality, they were accepted as robust, industrious, good-humored people who participated in the national dream of economic mobility. Although the Germans made an important contribution to the development of American socialism, popular writers, far from portraying them as radicals, depicted them as a mindless but jovial "tribe without malice" who brought musical taverns, not Marx, to the city. If urban books ridiculed them for bloating themselves with food and beer, at least such behavior was harmless; if writers laughed at their boisterousness in beer gardens, they acknowledged that their gemütlichkeit at Sunday celebrations was an improvement over the former somberness of Sabbaths in the city.

The virtues of the Germans paled in the popular books when they lived in a city in concentrated numbers. In Cincinnati, where they comprised 47 percent of the population in 1850, they were regarded as a clannish group who created Teutonic "ghettos" complete with their own schools, churches, breweries, hotels, newspapers, and theaters. In language that smacked of nativist aspersions on the Germans in mid-western cities in the 1850s, H. M. Rulison's *Mock Marriage,* set in the Queen City, declared, "[O]ne would think he was treading the streets of a German city, so Germanic is everything in that quarter." Thus, once the Rhinelanders became a sizable minority in an American municipality, pulp authors viewed their thrift as stinginess, their joviality as vulgarity, their industriousness as dollar worship.

Although in the census of 1850 Italians represented only 0.17 percent of the total immigrant population in the United States, they received disproportionate attention in popular urban books. Identified with poverty, brutality, and crime, they were stereotyped by James McCabe and Junius Browne as a criminal underclass, "indolent, sensual and reckless of the future." Repeating the smears of Protestant philanthropists who saw them as outcasts of city life, pulp writers ridiculed them for their penchant for garlic, monkeys, and musical instruments. Despite the fact that Italians listed in the *Directory of New York City* represented a wide variety of occupations and professions, in the popular lore reflected in Solon Robinson's *Hot Corn*, Alger's *Rough and Ready*, and Wharton's *New Orleans Sketch Book* they eked out a subsistence living as ragpickers and organ grinders, torturing city residents with their monotonous music. A group which during this period remained unassimilated and apolitical, they were portrayed in Duganne's *Tenant-House* and William Simms's *Prima Donna* as hot-tempered fanatics who found the use of the stiletto as "natural as eating macaroni."

The Chinese were an even rarer, more exotic breed, not appearing often in popular literature. When they did, they inhabited the slums of the city. Scorned as "Fee-fa-fums," they appeared in *The Mysteries and Miseries of San Francisco* and Alonzo Hill's *John Smith's Funny Adventures* as small yellow pagans, "filthy and ugly as toads." McCabe and Gunn alleged that they defiled the white bloodstream by their bigamous unions with Irish women and polluted the atmosphere with the smell of their strange cooking and omnipresent opium. In spite of their unstinting washing, ironing, and cleaning, they were reviled by an Anglo-Saxon society that regarded all nonwhites as natural inferiors.

Another foreign element that must have fascinated the reader, judging by the large number of references to so few people, were the Jews, successful émigrés who were the only group to have been urbanized before coming to the United States. Personifying the greed of the American city, they were caricatured in popular prose as aggressive, vulgar, avaricious, and dishonest, Shylocks trading on human misery as slumlords, moneylenders, and manufacturers of cheap clothes. Even when engaged in a respectable calling such as opening a store in the West, John Beauchamp Jones in *The Adventures of a Country Merchant* censured them for driving Christians out of business by their price-slashing policies. Despite the prominence of second-generation Jews in the learned professions, in popular books like Judson's *Rose Seymour* and Thompson's *Outlaw* as well as in John Brougham's drama *The Lottery of Life* they were capable of any base activity for the sake of money. Duganne, Edward Durell, Winter Summerton, and many other writers pictured them kidnapping Africans, selling liquor and guns to

Indians, conniving with thieves, purchasing infected rags from yellow-fever victims to resell at 100-percent profit, and speculating in coffins, hoping to reap a large reward should an epidemic ravish a city.[3]

Popular literature accurately recorded the prominence of Jews in the garment industry. This livelihood made the Jews a foil for the poor sewing girl who worked from sunrise to sunset in their businesses only to be defrauded of her wages. These girls were a particularly suitable group for underscoring the brutality of Jews since they were impotent workers. In William Wirt Sikes's *One Poor Girl* an Israelite, Sly Isaac, lures poor girls with an advertisement promising "Good wages! Prompt pay!" Of girls who appear, he demands two dollars security. When seamstresses return the shirts, he condemns their work and keeps their money. The schemes used by "greasy, hooked-nose" Hebrews to swindle desperate girls rivaled the wiles of libertines to steal their virtue. But what readers would never have found in this anti-Semitic literature was that Jews who specialized in manufacturing "slop clothing" in New York City were paying higher wages than the Yankee elite who dominated the Boston garment trade.

Popular literature focused almost exclusively on the Jews of New York City, a miniscule part of Gotham's population but the most important and influential Jewish community in the United States. Never would the reader have gathered from descriptions of this community just how heterogeneous it was. Instead of differentiating Sephardim from Ashkenazim, the immigrant from the native, the rich from the poor, the learned from the ignorant, pulp books lumped together all the "Children of Abraham." They were noisy, first-generation immigrants from Germany who spoke with a thick Yiddish accent, lived on the Lower East Side, and singlemindedly dedicated themselves to trade. Despite the fact that by 1860 many secular Jews had moved uptown into neighborhoods scattered throughout the metropolis, according to Matthew Hale Smith, as soon as they sought lodgings on a city block all others fled. Too different in social customs to be tolerable to Christians, even in a milieu as varied as the city, they remained, in popular prose, noisy "ghetto" dwellers who were the scourge of respectable urbanites.

In popular books like Summerton's *Will He Find Her?* and Myers's *The Miser's Heir* as well as in Foster's *New York by Gas-Light,* the composite portrait of Jewish men was of repulsive, "spider-like" creatures with a diabolical expression in their eyes; of women, as beautiful temptresses, "lovely as a dream of olden story" and as fecund "as cats or Irish women." Writers and their audience were inclined to see the male of a detested minority as a threat to their manhood; the female, as an object of sexual lust. If Jewish men could be dismissed as rascals who devoted their lives to making money, the women could be viewed as femmes fatales upon whom a repressed Victorian society could project its sexual longings. Popular books in this period depicted Jewish women as exotic beauties prone to use their allure to cheat the Anglo-Saxon community. In Marie Hankin's *Women of New York* they were wily peddlers who wheedled the unsuspecting into buying worthless trinkets; in Bayard Taylor's *John Godfrey's Fortunes* others were aggressive social climbers seeking matrimonial alliances with the Protestant upper class in order to promote the rise of their own relatives into high society.

In spite of manifold ethnic slurs, the Jews frequently appeared as a colorful group who preserved their traditional religious values in a disruptive urban environment. If they cajoled and cheated to earn their daily bread, they did not expend their fortune on riotous living. If they lusted after wealth, they never begged on the streets. No matter how tirelessly they labored in factory or store, they found time to keep up their religious observances. Although they concealed the defects in the merchandise they peddled, they were openhanded in giving alms to the poor. If the women were enticing, they also were remarkably faithful. Thus popular literature, like other forums of the day, regarded the Jew as what Charles Rosenberg has called "a venturesome conservative, an individualistic traditionalist. To reject him completely was to reject much that was American."[4]

Yet the Jew appears nowhere as hero in these popular novels. Prejudice was too great. Although he personified America's success story—the restless migrant who by dint of his industry and perserverance made his own fortune—he was still too strange, too much the infidel to become the literary model for ambitious youths who dreamed of finding riches in the city. The very qualities admirable in the native self-made man, the Horatio Alger hero, aroused contempt when this figure was a Jew. The thrift of Ragged Dick degenerated into avarice in the Hebrew; the cleverness of the Yankee "man on the make" was perfidy in the Israelite garment manufacturer. The old rules did not win for Jews the plaudits they earned for Protestant Americans struggling to succeed. In popular books the Protestant merchants of Water Street were models of business integrity; the Hebrew immigrants with less capital who traded in the slums of Chatham Street, examples of commercial duplicity. The Jew fitted too easily the role of melodramatic villain—the grasping landlord, the heartless moneylender, the pitiless capitalist. In a country obsessed with getting ahead, he became a symbol of materialistic ambition. Readers of antiurban, anti-Semitic fiction could project their own longings for gain onto a foreign people, purging their own guilt by displacing it onto a strange group who were outsiders to the Christian community. All the chicanery of the city slicker, all the machinations of the metropolitan marketplace, could be embodied in the pagan Jew, the man who connived for profit and gloated over the misfortune of others.

Even more distinctive than the foreign immigrant in popular urban fiction were the free blacks, who lent a picturesqueness to the American city. As Leon Litwack has demonstrated, by the 1830s blacks in Northern cities already faced as much hostility and segregation as Southern blacks. Subject to a system of economic exclusion, social ostracism, and political proscription that knew no Mason-Dixon Line, they lived in an environment characterized by violence, poverty, and social disorder. Relegated to service occupations and to the lowest-paid menial labor, Negroes were even more despised than the most detested white aliens. Considered an inferior, ignorant, licentious race, they were required to use segregated schools, hospitals, prisons, church facilities, and cemeteries.

Although by 1860 blacks constituted no more than one to three percent of the population in major cities, they nevertheless intrigued the popular imagination. Hack writers reinforced the racial caricatures found in contemporary minstrel shows, Northern classrooms, and abolitionist literature. Stripped of individuality, the blacks were either savages in their capacity for evil or childlike clowns in their acts of kindness. Cheap books like Lippard's *Quaker City,* Charley Bowline's *The Iron Tomb,* and the anonymous *Life of Paddy O'Flarrity* portrayed repulsive sable-faced servants with a "hideous grin," "thick lips," "woolly" hair, and rolling white eyes. "[A]s ugly as the devil himself" and "enough to scare anyone," declared Judson in *The G'hals of New York,* the very sight of them could make a white man feel as if a host of lizards were crawling over him. Those who acted as though they had an equal right to walk on the streets were, in the view of Robert Bird, "insolent black Republicans," too readily tolerated by a submissive Caucasian community which also allowed pigs the run of the city's thoroughfares. Heroic, then, in the eyes of George Foster, was the city b'hoy who improved his firing aim by using black buttocks as a target.

The mid-nineteenth-century popular book affirmed the notion that blacks should know their place. They stood apart from the rest of humanity. Creatures of instinct, they allegedly savored cruelty and desired "not so much to kill as to observe the blood of a victim fall drop by drop, as to note the convulsive look of death, as to hear the last throttling rattle in the throat of the dying."[5] When able to secure legitimate employment, they appeared in books like Charles Swan's *Minny*

Lawson, D. Corcoran's *Pickings from the Portfolio of the New-Orleans "Picayune,"* and J. Wimpleton Wilkes's *Mysteries of Springfield* as chimney sweeps, bootblacks, house servants, and pinboys in bowling alleys. But their typical occupations in sensational novels like *Mary Beach,* Thompson's *City Crimes,* Duganne's *Tenant-House,* and Lippard's *New York* were as bodyguards in assignation houses, doormen to gambling hells, and chefs who divested the snatched bodies of corpses of their fleshy remains. When not drunkards, thieves, and rapists, they were overseers at abortions or seducers of poor blond girls and degenerate upper-class wantons. Living in garbage-strewn slums and ravaged by disease and constant violence, they lay drunkenly on the stoops, cavorted about the streets partially nude, or frothed at the mouth as they battled in the gutters like wildcats. Some, manumitted by well-wishing masters, wandered the great cities unprotected from vice and crime. Others fell prey to Southern kidnappers, who hunted them in Northern cities to sell into slavery in the South.[6]

Denied any psychological complexity, the Negro personae of ante-bellum popular books were as ludicrous in their goodness as they were in their evil. Childlike adults, they assumed the role of noble savages, possessing earthy common sense and kind hearts. When not evoking fear, they were "step-and-fetch-it" comical characters, who were called "boy" even when old men. In fact, so compliant were they in their own debasement that they were without hostility even when white patrons addressed them, "Hey, darky." Quaking in their shoes and rolling their goggle eyes in fear, "half-witted African Gumbos" reached a summit of satisfaction when given a "mess of pig's feet" as a meal. The Afro-American was absurd not only in his behavior; his conversation as well provided comic relief. When not trying to use big words which he never pronounced correctly, he emitted sentences like "Samson hab a white heart in his black bosom. . . . Bress de Lord, dat put sense in de Nigger's head."[7]

The black woman appeared in mid-nineteenth-century popular urban books as a ludicrous creature whose skin was "as black as soot" and whose teeth "shone amid the darkness."[8] Any white man seen accompanying her on a public street became an object of derision or mob abuse. In Justin Jones's *The Belle of Boston* a white man, tricked into kissing a veiled "Ethiopian," finds his hair standing on end when he discovers that the grotesque creature whom he has touched intimately is a black woman. A white character in Oliver Bolokitten's *A Sojourn in the City of Amalgamation* finds his stomach in rebellion after he has sexual relations with a black woman. When the man vomits, the author concludes that his stomach knows more than his mind.

But whether male or female, culprit or victim, black urban dwellers were viewed by popular authors as savages unfit for city life. Curiously absent from this literature, which exploited other colorful events of contemporary urban society, were any vignettes of the numerous race riots in which blacks were massacred by whites, including the great draft riot of 1863 in New York City. Even at a time of antislavery agitation, pulp writers never portrayed blacks as dark-skinned Americans capable of fighting for equal rights under their own leadership. Rather, books such as Justin Jones's *Big Dick* and Judson's *Ella Adams* typecast them as "noble mulattos" or immigrants from a South American country who needed the guidance of Caucasians in the fight against slavery. Thus Negroes, who were restricted in almost every phase of their existence in mid-nineteenth-century America, found in popular urban books no freer scope for their actions. Bound down by crude caricatures that persisted in mass media entertainment through the middle of the twentieth century, the Afro-American was humiliated in a literature which mirrored the assumptions of a racist society.

As the United States experienced its first massive wave of foreign immigration, popular writers explored the human hieroglyph of the city. Hardly an urban book appeared at mid-century which did not include the strange figure of the foreigner. These characters might appear as quaint figures who added local color to the urban scene or as ruthless villains who made the city a menacing place. But whether funny or frightening, the alien injected a necessaary element of excitement into popular literature. At a time when national life was becoming increasingly mechanized and regimented, he loomed as a symbol of nonconformity.

The image of the foreigner plotting to destroy American democracy doubtlessly stoked the flames of nativist resentment and contributed to the ethnic conflagrations which erupted in numerous cities during the mid-nineteenth century. But only a minority of pulp writers described the foreign-born engaging in diabolical conspiracies. Most portrayed him performing mundane occupations; his was an incidental but intrinsic role in the urban scene. Like Walt Whitman's more renowned celebration of "each one singing his" in the metropolis, the assortment of immigrant workers included as an essential part of city life in mid-nineteenth-century urban literature educated readers to recognize the growing complexity and heterogeneity of American society.

Even though the literary figure of the immigrant was an imaginative response to the increasing diversity of American cities, popular authors so caricatured minority groups that they blunted any serious understanding of a mosaic urban populace. Theirs was a view of the hybrid city from the gutter. But the extravaganza of grotesque non-Anglo-Saxon types who populated the literature of the common man helped to defuse a potential menace. Instead of agonizing over the changing ethnic composition of the metropolis, readers could nourish their own self-esteem at the expense of immigrant clowns. Pent-up fear could be released through laughter. Thus scurrilous descriptions of the foreign-born were more than a literary counterpart of the ethnic tensions which flared in mid-nineteenth-century American cities; they were also a safety valve for social tensions.

10

THE PAGEANTRY OF CITY LIFE

The city of popular literature was living theater. With a cast of thousands and an endlessly shifting repertoire—part pageant, part side-show, part melodrama—it was a place where the world was still young, where heroes and heroines found adventure. As industrial technology diminished the conviviality of rural life, eliminating the companionship of the spinning room and celebrations for the harvest, many pulp authors delighted in a community with teeming streets, unusual entertainments, bursting shops. Though they recognized the city's iniquities, they were more impressed with its fun.

Like Charles Dickens, who reveled in London's vigor and animation, cultural amenities and opulence, these writers trumpeted the excitement of the American city. They depicted it as a locale of unrivaled human vitality representing all classes, all interests, all nationalities: "Saints and sinners, mendicants and millionaires, priests and poets, courtesans and chiffoniers, burglars and bootblacks, move side by side in the multiform throng."[1] A community where all of life was intensified, it seemed to enlarge the mind, sharpen the faculties, and quicken the wit. "Everybody likes to be in a crowd; perceives [its] electric influence, . . . thinks better and brighter and faster, talks quicker and shrewder, feels more acutely, enjoys more keenly."[2] The outward splendor, gaiety, and animation of the metropolis, according to many writers, intoxicated the spirit; and even those weary with the whirl soon found in the roar a necessary exhilaration.

Epitomizing the youth, vigor, and opportunity of the nation, the city was America's genie in a bottle, promising what was difficult, extraordinary, fabulous, impossible. Even a critic of urban society like the prolific popular writer of city exposés, George G. Foster, had to admit that "only in a large city, where some hundreds of thousands combine[d] their various powers" could "the human mind . . . effectively stamp itself on every thing by which it [was] surrounded."[3] It provided the natural arena for those with ambition and daring to test their strength.

For those outside the enchanted circle of urban life, the city was a place of processions, blazing lights, glare and glitter, fun and noise. In contrast to the disillusioned hero of Herman Melville's novel *Pierre,* who felt "bitter and sad" at the prospect of coming to the city, a youth in Charles Gayler's potboiler *Out of the Streets* was ecstatic when about to enter this land of magic. To this prototypical character of popular fiction the metropolis exuded a mysterious hum that "fell like music on his ears, and in the thought that he should be there, all his sadness vanished, and when the bell rang out warning to be off . . . he could scarcely refrain from shouting out his joy and delight."[4]

As portrayed in popular prose, the festivity of the metropolis made it a magnet for those seeking fun. At holiday times its inhabitants became linked in ties of fellowship reminiscent of those in any country hamlet. Children caroling through the streets brought a mood of Christmas jubilance not easily available to those on an isolated farm. On New Year's Day in Gotham people visited friends and neighbors, and could even enter the homes of strangers. No sea of anonymity or alienation, the urban population in novels like Robert St. Clar's *The Metropolis* and Osgood Bradbury's *Female Depravity* wished each other well, and those who were financially comfortable opened their homes, offering to a tide of guests magnificent tables of delicacies and wines. Elegant ladies welcomed all visitors and pressed the free-flowing bottles upon their guests. Mrs. Lydia Maria Child, cookbook author and editor of the *National Anti-Slavery Standard,* commented in her highly popular book *Letters from New York* on the practices of New Year's Day: "Every woman, that *is* 'anybody,' stays at home, dressed in her best, and by her side is a table covered with cakes, preserves, wines, oysters, hot coffee, etc.; and as every gentlemen is honour bound to call on every lady, . . . the amount of eating and drinking . . . must of course be very considerable" (p. 87).

New Year's Day was but a token of the opportunities for sociability in the city. Readers who examined John Bell Bouton's *Round the Block* could take heart in the realization that an urban block was a microcosm of the communal spirit that wove neighbors together in villages across the land. One of the characters in the novel, justifying a New Year's call to the home of a neighbor whom he does not formally know, finds an appropriate reason for the visit: "Here is a block full of people. Their houses are joined together, . . . all the way round. . . . If a fire breaks out in the block, it may be all burned down together. If the measles makes its appearance on the block, it probably runs through it. Is there not therefore, a community of dangers among us; and if of dangers, why not of pleasures? Why should not inhabitants of a block be regarded as a distinct settlement, or tribe whose members owe kindness . . . to each other before the rest of the world?" (pp. 19-20). In this novel, which anticipated Emile Durkheim's insight that greater population density promotes greater human intimacy, the city block became the true hero of the tale, a unique home for those impatient with the constraints of tradition-bound rural society.

Despite the fact that the old, informal patterns of neighborhood life were disintegrating under the impact of high rates of population turnover in the mid-nineteenth-century city, novels depicted residents of different urban districts enjoying a strong sense of community ties. Like any aboriginal tribe, the characters in popular books such as John T. Roddan's *John O'Brien*, William Sikes's *One Poor Girl*, and Augustine Duganne's *The Tenant-House* considered their territory special and flaunted their loyalty by engaging in rivalries with those from other wards. Even a fire department became a local campground, a shrine of sorts, for adolescent youths who could prove their mettle by battling the outsiders, the fire brigade of another neighborhood.

While the city offered conviviality and "the contagion of numbers," it did not impose conformity. According to celebrants of town life, the urbanite enjoyed a freedom from meddlers that would be the envy of overly scrutinized village folk. "The right to do 'as you d--n please' . . . is nowhere so universally recognized, or less curbed by authority" as in the great metropolitan centers of the nation.[5] The city resident could dwell in a mansion or in a garret, dine elegantly or not at all, get up early or late, live in the latest mode or scorn the fashions of the day, with no small town busybodies to gossip or interfere. Where but in the great urban communities did one have a chance to escape the ties of the patriarchal family and still find companionship? Where else could a whole geographical area be turned into a bohemia? The city welcomed innovation. If it lacked the traditional ties to a particular community, it created new types of social solidarity through its clubs. Whether one enjoyed billiards, boating, or books, the cities provided voluntary associations for sharing mutual interests to a nation of "frantic joiners."

In the world of the popular book the magic of the city was manifest in both its open community activities and its exclusive social gatherings. Readers weighed down by the numbing routine of domestic and business chores found in fictional scenes of urban balls an American counterpart to the tales of the *Arabian Nights*. They could delight in a "panorama . . .

of elegant men and beautiful women richly and variously attired," in scenes of "starlight and flowers," where "pearls and diamonds flashed in a blaze of innumerable chandeliers." They could be transported through the printed page into galas with carefree laughter. They could regale themselves with the "gorgeous confusion" of "feathers sway[ing] to and fro, ... [of] snowy clouds of lace float[ing] past ... in a ... brilliant chaos, changing and shifting like the colors in a kaleidoscope."[6]

The pleasure of observing beautiful women was in no way confined to the select circle invited to the revelries of the oligarchy. The city teemed with an intriguing variety of females—exquisitely dressed French women, cold and stately New England beauties, voluptuous Italians "undulating like waves in the bay of Venice," and cherry-cheeked descendants of the Knickerbockers, "placid, cool and joyous."[7] Nowhere else, it would seem from popular books, could such dresses and bonnets, shawls and jewelry, be seen. Compared to the predictable, calico-frocked country lass, the sight of a city belle was, in the estimation of many urban wags, one of the titillating attractions of town life.

That urban women delighted the eye is hardly surprising. Nowhere else but in the city, it would seem from pulp literature, was such an abundance of elegant goods available. In marbled palaces of trade customers could buy what would satisfy the most demanding taste and the most commanding purse. Visitors in popular books marveled at shops like Stewart's, Lord & Taylor's, and Arnold Constable's, which cascaded with luxuries unattainable in village stores. In the inexhaustible market of the metropolis anything could be had—whether it was the best fruit, the finest flowers, a Newfoundland dog, a Shetland pony, a good milch cow, or a secondhand carriage. And even if one were constricted by a tight budget, the city was a bargain bazaar for those who knew where to shop.[8]

Descriptions of urban hotels also revealed a world of wonder to readers who sought in their leisure hours a passport into a universe of physical splendor. These public palaces, as Daniel Boorstin has pointed out, created for a democracy an open door into a realm which had formerly belonged only to kings and noblemen. Books such as Eliza Potter's *A Hairdresser's Experience in High Life,* Costard Sly's *Sayings and Doings at the Tremont House,* Joseph Holt Ingraham's *Alice May,* and the anonymously written *Isabella Gray* described hostelries like the Tremont House of Boston, the Astor House of New York, and the St. Charles of New Orleans, where liveried footmen carried out the slightest wish of the guest.

In addition to offering glamorous hotels, the city afforded its citizens an opportunity for elegant dining. Urban literature reveled in scenes of sumptuous feasts available in city restaurants. No place in America offered the culinary delights of Delmonico's. Bayard Taylor in *John Godfrey's Fortunes* described a typical dinner there. In a room resplendent with fragrant tropical flowers, cut glass, and silver service, the discriminating diner could sample oysters and Chablis, turtle soup and iced punch, fish and sherry and glasses of Cliquot and Rüesheimer, *côtelettes en papillotes, riz de veau* accompanied with a particular pea which only grew in Arras, and a '34 Lafitte procured from the lower part of the hill. Those who dined less expensively could still taste a wide assortment of desserts and liqueurs at Taylor's sumptuous ice cream palace in New York City. Over and over, popular guidebooks like Junius Henri Browne's *The Great Metropolis* and George Foster's *Fifteen Minutes Around New York* apprised the reader that no one could enjoy the basic human requirement of food like the city dweller. Farmers, unable to afford the products of their own gardens, stripped the countryside of its harvests to provision the people of the metropolis, who paid liberally for gustatory satisfaction.

Nor was it to be imagined that the brick and mortar of the city shut out the urbanite from the pleasures of nature. Like Whitman's New York, which coexisted with the surrounding forest, and Hawthorne's Boston, which sheltered gardens luxuriant with foliage and birds, the city of popular literature had its arcadian charms. Pulp books portrayed the urban resident attending the theater at night and refreshing himself in a public park during the day. If the man with a hoe could feast his eyes on a rushing stream, the New Yorker could enjoy views of his magnificent bay and the dancing waters of the Croton Reservoir. If the tiller of the soil could enjoy the sight of cows and sheep nestling in his fields, the city dweller could regale himself with an exotic assortment of wildlife at his zoological parks. Country folk who congratulated themselves on the beauty of their landscape soon learned from urban books that the New Yorker found in Central Park a panorama of grottos and rambling hills and a forest of greenery. Nor was bucolic quiet a monopoly of the farmer. The urbanite could escape to a sylvan retreat in the cemeteries of the city.[9] Clearly, the pastoral facilities within the metropolis gave town dwellers a bridge to their rural past.

The beauties of a winter cityscape were another pleasure of urban life. Popular books like Maria Susanna Cummins's *Mabel Vaughan* and Charles Bristed's *The Upper Ten Thousand* portrayed the city when it was garbed in white as an exquisite montage of laughing people swathed in furs and colorful costumes. A heavy snow on Broadway created a wonderland of buildings which looked like "iced over . . . big holiday cakes." Although a farmhouse blanketed in snow was a familiar image of rustic charm, how could that compare to a winter scene where gaily painted sleighs glided through the thoroughfares of a metropolis?

Just as the city often enhanced nature, it also created a man-made world of taste and refinement. Ever since the passage of the Land Act of 1785, agricultural life had become associated with large, scattered holdings that meant solitude for the farmer. As cities grew in number, the historian Arthur M. Schlesinger, Sr., has argued in *The Rise of the City*, the tiller of the soil came to feel increasingly cut off from an exciting community that hovered over the horizon. Although he might enjoy county fairs, picnics, and hunting expeditions, his diversions paled before the brilliant pastimes of the city. Situated on a lonely farm, he came to crave the dazzling shops, the bustling crowd, the carefree life of a beckoning town. "In the city were to be found the best schools, the best churches, the best newspapers, and virtually all the bookstores, libraries, art galleries, museums, theaters and opera houses" (p. 80).

This fact was not lost upon the supposedly antiurban Nathaniel Hawthorne. In his *Blithedale Romance* Miles Coverdale, who has moved to the country from Boston, chides himself for having left his "pleasant bachelor-parlor" filled with books and periodicals as well as urban amenities like reading-rooms, picture galleries, and walks "along the cheery pavement, with . . . the brisk throb of human life" for the "toil and moil amidst the accumulations of a barn-yard" (pp. 49–50).

Popular books, too, confirmed that civilization and the city were one. They realistically depicted the gravitational pull of towns on the most intelligent. A country lad in Azel S. Roe's novel *Like and Unlike* articulated the attraction the metropolis held for him: "I can plainly see that for many reasons the city has advantages for one in my circumstances— and indeed, for any young man. There is more to stimulate him to activity . . . more persons above him, whom he is bound to respect, and their manners are more courteous and reserved. And there is a better choice of society" (pp. 244–45). While few contemporaries writing in media other than popular books were willing to concede the civilizing influence that the city brought to bear on the development of human personality, pulp novelist Adam Badeau in the *Vagabond* acknowledged that in no village could one find the graceful, elegant people, accomplished in the arts, knowledgeable about literature, informed about politics that one so easily encountered in the much-abused city. Acting as a "grand intellectual focus of the country," the great urban centers housed theaters, art galleries, and music academies as well as newspapers, amateur clubs, and facilities for private artistic performances.[10] They provided schools for the poor and were themselves open schools. Their numerous subscription libraries, night schools, and public lectures gave people access to knowledge. Their streets, studded with windows displaying books, paintings, and engravings, brought education to the masses.[11] Even their squalor could inspire the imagination, as scenes of faraway arcadia could not. From the streets of the city, predicted urban novelist Sikes, would come America's Hogarths, artists fascinated by haunts of poverty and vice.

Nor were the amusements of the metropolis confined to the intellectual elite. If high society found pleasure in art galleries and in boxes at the opera, the common man could enjoy minstrel halls, concert saloons, and dance houses. In the inexhaustible storehouse of urban wonders, the immigrant could enjoy oyster stew mixed with raucous music at Tony Pastor's, could watch specialized ethnic stage presentations, the freaks and animals at Barnum's, and theatrical spectacles at the Bowery Theatre; the salacious "tableaux vivants," performed by unclad "model artistes"; the "Plug Ugly," scenes of stabbing, throat-cutting, and tomahawking at the Pit Theatre; and rat combats at Kit Burns. The object of the latter entertainment was to wager which canine could devour the most rodents in a given number of minutes. To cap the evening's gore, spectators could watch a fight between two huge bulldogs.[12]

The city spilled over with a vitality that could never be found in a quiet country nook. With its gaudy concert saloons, bowling alleys, billiard parlors, ornate "temples of Bacchus," gambling dens, and tawdry houses of prostitution, the city offered possibilities for all kinds of enjoyment. Along its streets sauntered fashionable exquisites and fluttering belles. Wherever one looked, there were sights to delight the eye and quicken the pulse. German bands swelled the air with melody while parades of fire companies, marching in military gait, filled the streets with pageantry. A stroll along Broadway, suggested Browne, could provide a pleasure unknown to country villagers confined to a much-too-familiar Main Street. For Broadway pulsated, throbbed with a feverish intensity. "A walk through [it was] like a voyage round the Globe" (p. 339). Even James Fenimore Cooper, not the observer most enamored of America's cities, considered Broadway to "safely challenge competition with most . . . promenades of the old world." A promenade on the Bowery furnished another kind of fascination. The plump and noisy "birds" of the Bowery, in all their extravagant plumage, brought a gaiety on Saturday night that could not belong to those isolated in the quiet country. How could the farmer's tranquility compare to Christy's 'garden, the bursting shops, the "crack" ice-cream saloons, and theater with a fifteen-cent admission price? The Bowery with its swaggering b'hoys and gaudy g'hals, its noise and tumult, vibrated with an excitement, a variety of life that, in the estimation of George Foster, made it as much as any freeholder's farm the home of a great social democracy.

So replete were many popular books with this pageantry that they helped to create a collective fantasy of the city as a national gateway to abundance and pleasure. A man who has lived all his life in a small town expresses his delight with the city in Day Kellogg Lee's novel *The Master-Builder:* "I shall never get used to the roar of these streets, nor see an end of all the city wonders. But do not imagine from this, that I am home-sick. Far from it....I like the excitement ... and hope I may not get so used to it as ever to meet it with indifference" (p. 311). Such a paean sounds curiously like a nineteenth-century commercial for city life. Like many pro-urban popular books of the period, fiction of this sort persuaded a mass audience to see the commotion of the city, not as an annoyance, but rather as stimulus to creative energy. It coaxed the disgruntled in farm and village across the land to view the city as an escape from monotonous drudgery. The writer Allen Gazlay in his book *The Races of Mankind* summarized compelling motives for urban migration: "greater facilities in the pursuit of wealth; a more intimate enjoyment of social intercourse . . . ; intelligence, amusements, the arts, commerce, among which fashions, taste, and the pomp and vanity of display, are not the least exciting" (p. 214). Thus an important segment of popular literature paralleled the tracts of urban boosters who viewed cities as repositories of culture and artifacts of progress. True to Aristotle's dictum, it taught a mobile population that "men come together in the city in order to live; they remain there in order to live the good life."

11

THE AMERICAN DREAM FULFILLED
The Urban Cornucopia

For a generation captivated by the myth of the self-made man, the urban novel of the mid-nineteenth century provided compelling reasons to migrate to the metropolis. Nourishing the dreams of countless urban youths that they too could find vast fortunes on the urban frontier, it trumpeted the triumph of the disinherited who became inherited. Many a city novel was a modern Cinderella tale promising that people of worth would be discovered in as unlikely an environment as the far-flung, mysterious, and crowded American metropolis. No ruthless engine of human destruction, the city was often pictured as a place filled with kindly benefactors who served as talent scouts to ferret out deserving youths and reward them with fame and fortune. Like the prophets of the self-made man, a corps of popular urban writers promulgated the notion that a harvest of opportunity could be reaped by the ambitious, not on the much publicized western frontier, but rather within easily accessible East Coast cities.

That contemporaries allowed hack authors to fuel such unrealistic hopes tells us more about the social aspirations of the epoch than about the chances for economic advancement during this era. For most Americans the myth of mobility had become a mental reflex. They accepted as dogma the idea that in a society which valued honest labor, material abundance was open to all. A new popular genre of the 1840s, the Who's Who of Wealth, held out the promise that men of low origins were scaling class walls and enjoying financial affluence. Political oratory reinforced the idea that the nation's statesmen came from humble origins. As social stratification hardened in the mid-nineteenth century, the media enshrined the credo that America was a land of opportunity.

Repeated hymns to the self-made man suggest that contemporaries were far from relaxed about the ease of mobility in their society. We may reasonably deduce that one of the functions of popular culture in this period was to obfuscate the bitter realities of entrenched wealth in the cities and to make people tolerate growing economic inequities.

Thus, although we know from the historical research of Edward Pessen, Peter Knights, and Stuart Blumin that downward mobility was more frequent than success in the antebellum years, in the blithe world of popular urban literature fortune smiled most dependably on protagonists who were imbued with the Protestant ethic. Those guided by the mundane virtues of honesty, industry, and thrift invariably prospered, while profligates plunged into a never-never land of poverty. No matter how penniless a lad might be, he did not long remain friendless in urban fiction. In a setting that threw together people from all walks of life, a poor but worthy youth would meet a wealthy person who would pave his way to fortune.

In a classic novel of this genre, *Out of the Streets,* Charles Gayler expressed the unarticulated dreams of a generation that longed for the victory of the common man over would-be aristocrats. The hero, Harry Wright, born in the Tombs of a starving mother, raised in an orphanage on Blackwell's Island, left on the streets of the city to earn a livelihood blacking boots, lives and thrives in New York. Like any Horatio Alger character, he grows up industrious, honest, and studious. Left to the buffetings of a supposedly cold, cruel world, he finds that life in Gotham is neither cold nor cruel. He is continually adopted by kind city people.

Like others in innumerable stories, this hero earns his livelihood at a humble calling. But a lucky accident providentially delivers the bootblack from poverty. While plying his trade in one of the municipal parks, Harry sees a mad dog about to tear a young girl to pieces. Undaunted, he rushes to the rescue. The lovely child he saves, Agnes, has a rich, kind father who insists on taking the valiant ragamuffin to his mansion. Mr. Loxley, overwhelmed with gratitude, determines to give the city waif a gentleman's education.

Several years later Harry returns, a polished man. He wins the heart of an heiress who prefers him to the simpering, dissolute rich. To cap his joys, he finds his long-lost father and inherits a fortune. Uncowed by the difficulties that have beset his path, unwarped by the privations of his early years, this fatherless and motherless boy develops all the heroic traits of a pioneer. Generous, honest, bold, and determined, he has come, not out of some legendary forest, but out of the streets of the city to realize the American dream of success. Certainly, the secular notion of advancement through aggressiveness, shrewdness, and competitiveness—characteristics prominent in nineteenth-century businessmen who forged financial empires—is curiously absent in this hero whose credo is riveted to conservative Protestant values.

The plots of popular fiction also corroborated the Jacksonian ethos of the common man triumphing over a privileged elite. Despite the fact that wealth tended to remain in the hands of the same families in the second quarter of the nineteenth century, popular novelists broadcast to the public the notion that limitless opportunities awaited the ambitious in the great urban communities of the nation. Joseph Scoville's novel *Clarence Bolton* provides a paradigm of this school of literature. The hero is the orphaned son of a poor carpenter. In the protective atmosphere of the Empire City, Clarence is discovered by a scion of the Knickerbocker aristocracy, who provides him with funds to attend Columbia College. After graduating at the head of his class, Clarence accepts employment in the countinghouse of a prosperous merchant and labors diligently to secure a commercial education. As fortune continues to smile, he gains a partnership in a mercantile firm and learns from a Mr. Lee how to grow rich by steady habits. He gains wealth beyond his most optimistic expectations, is elected to Congress, and wins fame as a statesman. As if this were not enough, this son of working-class parents marries a beautiful, wealthy girl and lives happily ever after in a mansion. Obviously no victim of social stratification, in the vast but not lonely city of New York Clarence finds friends, family, fame, and fortune. Thus the typical urban success novel implied to a generation drawn to the city that, even without the advantages of inherited position, an energetic and honest man could advance economically by simply adhering to old-fashioned country morality.

Stories such as *Out of the Streets* and *Clarence Bolton,* which are typical of scores of narratives, might seem at first blush to be literary manifestations of an egalitarian age hailing the self-made man. However, in light of the authors' careers and the prevailing economic conditions, the books appear rather to constitute a strategy for promoting satisfaction with the status quo. Like the vast majority of novelists who wrote for the masses during the mid-nineteenth century, Gayler and Scoville enjoyed the security of a middle-class upbringing that was a far cry from the impoverished origins of their heroes. Nor did these writers commence their professional lives at profitless proletarian occupations. In addition to earning an income as a novelist and playwright, Gayler worked as a lawyer and campaign writer for the Whig candidate, Henry Clay. Joseph Scoville, who also harnassed his literary talents to contemporary political debate, served as a campaign biographer of the spokesman of the planter aristocracy, John Calhoun. Indeed, Scoville in many respects personally embodied the conservative New York–cotton axis, combining promotional efforts on behalf of the slavocracy candidate with his five-volume chronicle of New York's mercantile elite, *The Old Merchants of New York*. Secondly, as we have seen, rags-to-riches stories promoted by urban novelists like Gayler and Scoville clashed with the harsh economic realities of the day. But precisely by camouflaging the ever-shrinking opportunities for economic mobility in the nation, this conservative school of authors provided a palliative for those who wanted to believe that success was still open to all.

Such stories, however, were more than a sop. They also served as a strategy for social control. By reinforcing the notion that the rich deserved their wealth, they tried to deflect the poor from radical action. For their tacit message assured readers that, even if society was static, the talented nevertheless would rise. The ruling classes could be trusted to aid the ascent of the common man. Like the merchant princes of the day who were involved in numerous philanthropic causes, fictional businessmen like Mr. Loxley and Mr. Lee helped the less fortunate.

The heroes, Harry and Clarence, in their pursuit of old-fashioned honor and respectability also embodied a conservative ideal. Having assimilated in college the values of the established social order, they eventually discover their genteel lineage or become linked with the aristocracy by ties of marriage. Their new wealth need never tarnish their characters. For, as John Cawelti has pointed out in *Apostles of the Self-Made Man*, novels of this ilk reconciled traditional Christian virtue with the newly emerging goals of an urban-based business society.

The conservative thrust of urban success stories is apparent also in the rules didactic authors offered to aspiring go-getters. Mirroring the dos and don'ts of nonfiction success manuals, they provided a long list of vices that would spell financial ruin for would-be millionaires, as well as an easily comprehended score of virtues that would swing open the gates to economic plenty. Let us consider three stories—Charles Burdett's *Three Percent a Month,* Emerson Bennett's *Alfred Morland,* and Azel S. Roe's *Looking Around*—which illustrate how popular literature accommodated the tensions of a newly emerging business society to traditional moral values. In each, the hero learns to resist quick riches and devote himself to hard work and plain living. George Arnold, the model urban man of *Three Percent a Month,* commences his career as a clerk at "nothing a year" and works himself up to become head of one of the most reputable firms in New York City, amassing a fortune by dint of indefatigable industry, determination, and unswerving integrity. Alfred Morland, guided by his father's legacy of a Bible and a coin with the inscription "Do Right," returns a purse holding $5,000 which he finds on the street. The owner rewards him with a job. Alfred, like many a faithful clerk rewarded by a responsible master in success manuals, becomes devoted to the interest of his employer and eventually is elevated to a partnership in the prosperous firm. Similarly, William Randolph Herbert, the hero of *Looking Around,* learns from his mentor, a clergyman, the importance of industry, thrift, patience, and deference to one's employer. These exemplary traits help him to advance steadily and win the heart of the boss's daughter.

From these stories the reader would hardly glean that family lineage and capital accumulated from a previous generation were the most important ingredients in success. Unlike the real buccaneers of industry, who were unsqueamish in using cutthroat methods to forge shipping, oil, and mining empires, the tepid heroes of these novels become rich in old-fashioned mercantile pursuits. Their generous feelings rather than shrewd calculations allow them to get ahead.

The key ingredient in their success, however, is not their commitment to Christian morality and Poor Richard ethics but rather their inexplicable luck. Some deus ex machina—a lost wallet, drowning child, runaway horse—launches them on the road to wealth, and without it, presumably, their talents would remain undiscovered. But as John Cawelti has pointed out, authors who resorted so frequently to literary legerdemain obviously did not understand the forces at work in their own day which were allowing a few men to carve out spectacular fortunes. Their reliance on accident to rescue the hero from poverty betrays their doubts about the opportunities for advancement in American society. Instead of examining the institutional structure of merchant-capitalism, they spun improbable yarns of ordinary people mastering economic forces over which they in fact exercised little control. In lieu of enlightening readers on the problems they faced in an economically expanding industrial society, they reassured them that the nation could pursue secular wealth without forfeiting spiritual salvation.

In the 1860s, however, a new school of popular writers emerged which relinquished the old formula of hard work and perseverance at a commercial endeavor as the linchpin of success. Presumably influenced by the legendary careers of financiers like Daniel Drew and Jay Gould, who had built enormous fortunes from clever speculations, these authors sought to reconcile quick riches with personal integrity. Their protagonists regard business as a school for building character and display a strong sense of responsibility. But they succeed less because of hard work than because of fortunate investments. One hero's musings encapsulate a leitmotif that ran through these novels: "On a sudden I am lifted from a position which was wretched . . . to wealth, station, and honorable reputation: to more than this—to a life of happiness and bliss."[1] In Richard B. Kimball's *Henry Powers* the hero's speculation in the gold market allows him to clear $250,000. In Thomas Picton's *The Bootmaker of the Fifth Avenue,* a banker purchases stock in an oil field for his neighbor, a cobbler. The humble craftsman amasses $100,000 overnight. In Ralph Keeler's *Gloverson and His Silent Partners,* a German nobleman befriends a homely cashier and leaves him a legacy of stock in a gold mine which becomes worth a fortune. Stories of this kind left the impression that men with few prospects could, by living in the city, be brought into contact with clever people who would aid their economic advancement.

What was true of the great metropolitan centers of the nation also was true of life in western cities, and popular lore promised a life of abundance and adventure to enterprising merchants who set up shop in the flourishing towns of the Plains. In his celebration of the booster spirit which built the burgeoning cities of the West, John Beauchamp Jones in *The Life and Adventures of a Country Merchant* told of Nap Wax and Jack Handy, two aspiring country merchants who leave Kentucky to find their fortune in a new city of Missouri. Personifications of Daniel Boorstin's town-building entrepreneurs, they discover in the Missouri city handsome opportunities for the energetic businessman of steady habits and forthright character. The prescient hero, Nap, stakes his money on the speculative community of Venice, a village which consists of nothing more than three houses, and wins an appointment as registrar of a federal land office in this paper hamlet. Returning from a purchasing trip in the East, he is astounded by the changes a few short months have wrought in the city he has founded and virtually owns: "The sounds of hammers were heard in all directions. Trees had been felled, bushes cleared off, and houses were springing up on all the lots he had given away or sold. . . . A spirit of speculation and improvement was rife and there had been such an increase in population . . . that Nap declared he felt like a stranger, although standing on his own premises" (p. 336). The speculative spirit of the age, its identification of frontier town building with national improvement, found expression in this novel, which lauded the western shopkeeper not only for establishing the basis for his own individual fortune but also for promoting national greatness. By opening a "magazine of supplies" where the "settlements [were] few and far between," the country merchant was furnishing what historian Richard Wade called a spearhead for the migration of Americans across the continent.

In another novel, *The Spanglers and Tinglers,* Jones proclaimed the advantages of relocating in the boom town of San Francisco. Clerks, he asserted, earned salaries ten times higher than the going rate in the East; shopkeepers sold at quadrupled prices merchandise that was gathering dust in eastern stores; and real estate developers who built shanties to house the stream of migrants pouring into California made spectacular profits.

Whether men sought their fortunes in the East or the West, the city had, in fiction, a most bridgeable social structure that the industrious could cross. In contrast to the tribal intermarriage patterns which Edward Pessen has shown to have predominated among the rich during this era, popular urban books pictured the metropolis as an open city where class prejudices never would bar a worthy working man's path to the wife of his choice. In Osgood Bradbury's novel *Jane Clark* an industrious mason plies his craft until the strange mesh of city life brings him into contact with a wealthy young woman. Ida Mellen prefers George Stedman to the fashionable dandies who pursue her. To her, class is no barrier in selecting a mate. In a ringing affirmation of the cult of the common man, the heiress says, "I consider the mechanic and the laboring portion of the people quite above the others. It is they who are the producers and make the wealth of the country" (p. 72). Ida marries the honest mechanic and lives happily ever after.

Other authors, presumably influenced by the example of a few lucky men like William Dodge, who secured his fortune by marrying into the Phelps family, also propagated the myth that the rich frequently moved out of their own narrow circle in selecting marriage partners. In his gothic romance *The Daguerreotype Miniature,* Augustine J. H. Duganne told of an unemployed lad who falls in love with a miniature portrait displayed in a shop window. Several days later Arthur sees this same lovely creature in danger of being trampled to death by her runaway horses. With no thoughts of his own safety Arthur hurls his body in front of the wild animals and saves Rose's life. The rich girl, eternally grateful to her protector, consents to marry him.

Regardless of the fact that the rich chose marriage partners who were their social equals, hack authors held out the possibility to Sleeping Beauties in farms and villages across the land that in the cities resided some Prince Charming who would discover them. No matter if a fair maiden were but a salesgirl in a cigar store. In the metropolis of Joseph Ingraham's *The Beautiful Cigar Girl,* where people from all walks of life mingled, she would become the sought-after wife of an English nobleman. It counted for little, in the fictional wish-dreams of Henry Morford's *Days of Shoddy,* if a young lady were but a penniless struggling teacher.

A millionaire would marry her. She could be a lowly "flygirl" on a city newspaper, but that job in the novel *The Match Girl* would bring her in contact with the editor-in-chief, who would fall in love with her on sight and ask her to become his wife. She could be the daughter of a humble watchmaker in Arthur's *Rising in the World* or of a convicted forger in Ingraham's *Ellen Hart,* but, illustrating the spirit of Jackson egalitarianism, a successful urban physician would wed her. In fact, in the city, where rich and poor lived side by side, inability to pay the rent provided an opportunity for meeting a wealthy next-door neighbor who might proffer both the payment for the landlord and an offer of marriage.[2] Thus, although the acquisition of wealth, whether through a career or marriage, was characterized by stability rather than fluidity in mid-nineteenth-century America, popular books conveyed the encouraging news that the dynamic city was filled with chances and changes that created continual opportunities for those of low estate.

Mid-nineteenth-century popular novelists, reflecting the optimism of a generation that did not associate the city with giant corporations, placed their protagonists in an urban economy that permitted individual enterprise to succeed. Unlike the latter-day heroes of Theodore Dreiser and Frank Norris, who were caught in a web of impersonal financial forces which drove them to despair and suicide, the typical personae of an earlier literature imposed their will upon the urban economic order. Happily anchored in traditional ties of family sentiment and Christian ethics, they did not become victims of a ruthless competitive system. They could make money and still go through the eye of the needle. They could explore new frontiers of commercial and social activity and at the same time achieve Christian grace.

In stark contrast to the pessimistic post–Civil War literature, which emphasized the impotence of virtue in the face of relentless financial forces, these novels presented the race for riches in the city as an honorable search by the talented for status in an open, humane society. The city was no Hobbesian state of brutish egocentricity. In the overwhelming majority of popular urban books written during 1820–70, principled men could scramble after wealth without becoming obsessed with greed; they could search for economic security without forfeiting old-time religion. Novelists expropriated the readers' long-established moralistic assumptions and welded them to the pursuit of material abundance in the metropolis. While the rise of industrial-capitalism and the exploding growth of cities were undermining traditional notions of piety, these writers, by accommodating worldly success to Bible morality, domesticated people's apprehensions of the unknown.

Darwinian social critics had not yet popularized the image of the economy as a savage battleground; urban popular fiction was still able to reinforce the sanguine tenets of classical economics. In the ultimately harmonious universe of the metropolitan marketplace, the fate of the rich and poor were symbiotically intertwined. While it would await a later period for captains of industry to justify their millions with the Gospel of Wealth doctrine, an important segment of antebellum pulp literature projected an image of the urban rich as stewards of wealth, whose affluence was an outer sign of divine grace. These paternalistic custodians of property cared little about the profit motive or self-indulgence; they wanted money to help others. Imbued with a sense of noblesse oblige, they sought worthy people among the impoverished to elevate to a higher sphere. No need for revolution, strikes, even grumbling among the urban poor. The reader, living in an era when charity was carried on by private subscription, was assured implicitly that no drastic overhauling of the welfare system was necessary. Those who had merit would be scouted by the rich and permitted to enter their magic circle.

While the worthy poor made it in the sunny world of popular fiction, such was not the case in the foreboding universe of Herman Melville. His short story "Bartleby the Scrivener" mocks the cult of success. The protagonist, employed in a Wall Street office where workers are name-less, is the only character dignified with a name and thus an identity. Motionless, forlorn, and friendless, he is a pallid copyist in a smug business society "deficient in . . . 'life.'" In an alienating environment, isolated from the sight of his employer, with a "dead brick wall" his view upon the world, he is a fixture deprived of any purpose save to carry out a mechanical task. But unlike the complacent heroes of popular literature who devote themselves to their employer's interests, Bartleby achieves humanity precisely by answering his boss' orders with the refrain, "I prefer not to." Dismissed for his persistent if polite defiance, he continues to challenge the authority of his employer by re-maining glued to the office. He refuses to mask his alienation by getting caught up in the meaningless activities of the throng behind which "misery hides aloof." In contrast to the enterprising go-getters of pulp literature who find fortune and true love, Bartleby goes nowhere. He sleeps, eats, and dresses in a solitary office. When his employer tells him he must leave, he repeats, "I prefer not to." In desperation his boss has him hauled to the Tombs. There he again rebels, choosing death to hollow charity. In so doing he jeers at the piety of philanthropists and forces a self-satisfied employer to see how the scrivener is a true copyist of the deadening world of work.

But presentiments about the sterility of commercial endeavors did not shake popular authors who equated the pursuit of wealth with the pursuit of God. That they retained such a Panglossian view in an era of shrinking economic opportunities suggests that their tales were a narcotic which served the interests of an established oligarchy. By offering the masses a world of happy endings in which the stout of heart triumphed over every obstacle, they helped to blunt the reader's anxieties about his own meager advancement in society; by garbing their improbable plots with realistic detail, they lulled a mass audience into daydreaming that conservative religious ideas were the best insurance for material success.

Although such stories are a murky reflection of social conditions in American cities during the period 1820–70, they mirror the social myths of a society anxious to reconcile its aspirations with cruel realities. Writers who spun yarns about the common man making it in the metropolis confirmed the out-of-towner's predisposition that nowhere but in the city were chances so good for finding fortune, intellectual stimulation, and an upwardly mobile matrimonial alliance.

But success tales did more than manufacture dreams for the disinherited. By galvanizing potential migrants to realize their aspirations for a life of plenty in the burgeoning cities of the nation, they buttressed the desire of urban entrepreneurs to lure battalions of laborers and consumers townward. If urban readers took the conservative message of these stories seriously, they would be as the elite wished—tractable and hardworking. Having learned from a myriad of books ranging from Ingraham's *Harry Harefoot* to Horatio Alger's *Ragged Dick* that success would reward God-fearing, temperate employees who started humbly and served their masters loyally, they might accept their station in life. Confronted with disturbing economic, social, and demographic dislocations, they might learn to appreciate the values of discipline, order, and caution. Thus popular writers who made success seem accessible to the multitude in the city taught that the cornucopia of urban life offered security, stability, and respectability.

12

"AS A CITY UPON A HILL"
Moral Opportunities of Urban Life

If economic and social mobility represented what could be achieved in the metropolis, the elimination of human want represented what yet had to be accomplished in the mid-nineteenth-century city. Persistent indigency, after all, was supposed to be abnormal in America. But slums were metastasizing. In unprecedented numbers the disinherited were scampering into America's cities, bringing in their wake vice, crime, and drunkenness. As violence swept once-respectable neighborhoods, citizens with position and property shuddered at the prospect of social upheaval. No longer were the lower orders of society docile. Instead a slum population was engulfing urban communities in chaos.

By 1820 the well-to-do in United States cities joined a galaxy of quasi-religious philanthropic societies aimed at uplifting the masses from their degeneracy. In an era of weak, inadequately financed municipal government, the public-spirited rich became involved in charitable voluntary associations. Assured of their ability to guide others, they castigated the poor for their idleness, extravagance, and alcoholism and preached to them the values of industry, thrift, and temperance. Convinced that their wealth was a badge of personal merit and of God's favor, they regarded themselves as their "brother's keeper," men who did not work for themselves alone but, as Christ had wished, for the comfort of the unfortunate. The Bible, they felt, would purge the indigent of their vices. Amelioration of social ills would inculcate a respect for law and order in the flotsam of the slums. Evangelical Protestantism would muffle social protest and safeguard society from revolution. The elite of mid-nineteenth-century cities served as what the evangelical minister

Lyman Beecher called a "moral militia," keeping their communities godly and stable.[1]

Indeed, the rise of evangelical religion in the period 1820–60 made reform a moral duty. Americans thirsted to perform "good works" which would eradicate social evils and put humanity in a state of grace. They agitated for the freedom of the slave, the liberation of women, the humane treatment of the blind and insane. They sought to unmanacle the drunkard from his dependency on Devil Rum, to free the workman from his debasement by sweatshop employers, to cleanse the world from the carnage of war. And in the cities the stewards of public morality wanted to purify the urban environment of the scourges of filth, intemperance, idleness, and indigency. City missionaries proclaimed the brotherhood of man and publicized the notion that urban society must be restructured through the Gospels. Evangelical clergymen scolded organized churches for catering to the rich while neglecting the poor.

Typical of the philanthropic impulse of the period was the exhortation of the minister Peter Stryker, who urged his parishioners to learn what life was like in the "lower depths" of the metropolis: "Hear that cry of distress. Look down into those lower depths of poverty. See that array of men, women, and children, all members of the human family, freezing, starving, filthy, helpless. As they sink into the deep mire, they stretch out their hands and plead to you for help."[2] Although Stryker clearly recoiled from the "pagans" of the slums, his admonition rings with the confidence of an era which assumed the perfectability of man and the ability of the human will to transform evil into good.

This spirit of militant Christianity was not confined to the well-publicized activities of the urban mission church or the voluntary enterprises of the New York Association for Improving the Condition of the Poor (NYAICP), the Children's Aid Society (CAS), the Young Men's Christian Association (YMCA), and the industrial training school movement. It also permeated the world of popular literature. In contrast to the belletristic novels of this period, which were unconcerned with social issues, pulp books served as an important arm of the reform movement. They sought to accomplish for the human wreckage of urban life what Mrs. Stowe was achieving for the victims of Southern slavery. They would arouse the conscience of America to the need for urban reform. By allowing the public to see the lowest strata of urban society, they would involve the comfortable middle class in the urgent task of imposing discipline on the outcasts of the slums.

Clearly, then, the generation of Jacob Riis was not the first to muckrake the slum. As Roy Lubove has persuasively argued in his work on the NYAICP, middle-class Americans of the antebellum period were taking a "morbid fascination in gazing at the depths of filth and depravity to which humans could sink."[3] In a period brimming over with crusades for the betterment of humanity, books addressed to highminded reform appealed to readers. For example, the writer Edward Zane Carroll Judson followed a well-trodden path in moving from sea adventures to sociological investigations of the rookeries of the metropolis. Judson, with an eye for writing what would win popularity, abandoned high jinks with pirates for philanthropic battles against the cankers of urban life. His *Mysteries and Miseries of New York* enjoyed four printings and eventually sold 100,000 copies. Hoping to capitalize further on a surefire formula, he wrote two sequels to this popular novel.

Judson was but one of many writers who presented the city as a place which offered the Christian a heroic challenge. Numerous authors, as short on literary originality as they were long on religious enthusiasm, repeated in easily digestible form the charges of physicians, ministers, and journalists who had penetrated the filthy, disease-ridden districts of the city. Their lurid verbal snapshots showed the slums in luxuriant detail. Usually such areas were racially integrated neighborhoods with crooked, narrow streets crammed with filthy, rickety houses that landlords did not bother to repair. When the drains were not broken, tenants had to lug their own water from a hydrant and climb with it up staircases ready to collapse. No matter how tottering the building or damp the cellar, it swarmed with hordes of shivering, starving creatures.[4]

Capitalizing on the old saw that truth is often stranger than fiction, popular writers like Osgood Bradbury, Charles Burdett, and Edward Everett Hale, to name but a few, took their readers on vicarious slumming tours of the "urban wilderness" and allowed them to enter the rooms of the poor. Most typically, these apartments were ten-by-fifteen-foot holes shared by hordes of people who slept on straw, under tables, and on chests. A rickety table and a few decrepit chairs completed the furnishings of such a room. Though gloomy and unventilated, the lodgings of the tenants were kept bolted to prevent burglaries by the thieving inhabitants of the building.

The tenement, in many popular books, became a symbol of city life—a place located in the midst of civilization yet fearsome. It was a living tomb for the indigent—a dwelling where floors were thick with mud, ceilings grimy with furnace smoke, and windows stuffed with rags to keep out the freezing air. For those lowest in the urban social structure, even this was luxury. For them, dark subterranean cellars had to serve as homes shared with worms and rats.[5]

In a land of plenty the lack of decent food for the urban masses did not go unchronicled in popular literature. Polluted milk was one appalling item. Disease among herds was common. Often urban dairies were located next to distilleries, and owners could save money by feeding their cattle swill. Slum dwellers, especially, were customers of the resulting product. The journalist George G. Foster in his novel *Celio* took up the campaign launched in the 1840s by Robert M. Hartley, founder of the NYAICP, to curb production of swill milk. He charged that "the milk-man [labeled] his cart 'Pure Orange County Milk' and from it [supplied consumers] with the disgusting, unwholesome, poisonous drainings of the distillery" (p. 67). Eventually, the struggle of concerned citizens like Foster for sanitary conditions in New York City's dairy industry bore fruit when regulatory legislation was enacted in 1862. Other writers, like Ann Sophia Stephens in *The Old Homestead,* tried to shock the public with descriptions of the poor fainting upon the streets from pro-longed starvation. Lest the reader remain unmoved, more lurid novelists like Judson in *The Mysteries and Miseries of New York* included scenes of living cadavers swallowing meat raw and gulping down onions with the skin still on.

No tour of the slums was complete without a visit to the Five Points of New York City. A reservoir of crime, disease, and vice, it stood as a symbol of the problems of urban poverty. The neighborhood gained international notoriety when Charles Dickens, accompanied by two policemen, visited it in 1842 and recorded his impression of it as a district which matched in overcrowding, filth, and debauchery London's vilest areas of St. Giles and Seven Dials. Numerous American bush league writers like Burdett, John D. Vose, and Robert Greeley, anxious to mine a vein already tapped by the popular English author, provided readers with grisly descriptions of this ninth circle of the urban hell. Located within sight of America's most aristocratic avenue, Broadway, this neighborhood was nonetheless a "city within a city" that only the most intrepid would dare to enter. According to George Foster in *New York by Gas-Light,* it was "a sight to make the blood slowly congeal and the heart to . . . cease its beatings. Here, whence these streets diverge in dark and endless paths whose steps take hold on hell—here is the very type and physical resemblance in fact, of hell itself" (p. 52). In this "factory of crime" residents more frightening than pirates on the high seas and more savage than Indians in the forest lived as a class apart, governed by their own values. Half-nude, drunk, and disfigured with disease, they congregated in bars and dancing houses while their ragged, vermin-infested children ran unprotected through the streets.

Among the attractions of this neighborhood was the Old Brewery, a hostelry of sorts for the mid-nineteenth-century New York poor, who, for the price of twenty-five cents a night, could share a room with victims of smallpox and with desperados who would commit murder if they thought a roommate had any money. The most notorious tenement in America, its floors were jammed with men, women, and children of all races, who commonly indulged in miscegenation and incest. In what Charles Dickens aptly called the attraction of repulsion, novelists like Judson and Winter Summerton kindled the imagination of readers with graphic scenes of people sleeping ten to each dirty bed, huddling under old coffee bags, and devouring a few crusts of bread in a daily battle with hunger.

Yet if the Five Points was a loathsome blot upon the city above ground, it was even more disgusting below ground. In Charles Averill's novel *The Secrets of the Twin Cities* and George Thompson's shocker, *City Crimes,* it hid subterranean refuges for monstrous criminals. Here, where no policeman dared to enter, dangerous outcasts swarmed in gloomy caves under the very heart of the city. Here human beasts, living in their own underground city, ate the refuse from the connecting sewers, sat on heaps of excrement, and copulated with their own children.

At a time when the poor were steadily multiplying and displaying little success in improving their status, popular literature conveyed the impression that panhandling was becoming a well-established urban practice. The writer John Neal in *True Womanhood,* struck by the glut of paupers in New York, considered their condition to be "worse than the beggars of London, or the Lazzaroni of Naples. . . . And this in New York! . . . The city swarming with police, and the people rioting in self-indulgence, while others in their midst were literally starving to death" (p. 167). On the other hand, the supposedly antiurban Herman Melville declared in his novel *Redburn* that in contrast to the "almost endless vistas" of poverty in British cities, "New York was a civilised and enlightened town," notable for its absence of beggars.

Melville notwithstanding, many civic-minded individuals shared Neal's disgust with the visibly dependent poor in America's cities. By the 1820s philanthropists, convinced that the lower classes were responsible for the mounting urban disorder, abandoned their earlier acceptance of the indigent as an element which required the succor of more fortunate Christians, for a harsher, less costly moral exhortation. As the historian David Rothman has made clear, charity began with upbraiding slum dwellers for their vices. Pulp writers, in their frequent depictions of the needy as idle, improvident drunkards, buttressed this contemporary bourgeois fear of pauperism. They felt sympathy for the "worthy poor" who had been financially reduced by economic fluctuations beyond their control, but as taxpayers they manifested a more strident contempt for loafers who lived on handouts. Sprinkled into their self-righteous call to the comfortable to rout poverty from the community were admonitions against indiscriminate almsgiving. Like their counterparts, the articulate spokesmen of charitable organizations, they saw a permanent class of dependents as a threat to the work ethic and to a stable social order.

Like the NYAICP, which was launched in 1843 to eliminate welfare cheating, popular urban authors wanted their readers to be aware of the tricks dissemblers used to make relief a racket. William B. English in his novel *Gertrude Howard* (1843) warned would-be benefactors that "unscientific" charity allowed miscreants to avoid work and to cultivate vice: "It is too often the case, that the well meaning philanthropist, by his indiscriminate charities, does incalculable mischief to the morals of those whom he would assist, and great injury to the public. . . . It is the duty of our charitable societies, while they distribute alms to the worthy and virtuous poor, to discountenance in every way in their power, beggary as a most serious evil to the morals of the people" (p. 9). To emphasize this point, many novelists wove vivid incidents into their plots, all aimed at educating their readers to deceptive panhandling practices. Julia Wright in *Our Chatham Street Uncle* showed how beggars hobbled on one leg while the other, perfectly sound, was tied in a concealed position; William Hammond revealed in *Robert Severne* how guttersnipes pled with "green coveys" for money to care for a sick mother only to spend it on drink, the vice contemporaries considered a root cause of poverty.

Filching scenes from Charles Dickens's popular novel *Oliver Twist,* American urban authors created their own versions of Fagin, a repulsive character who kidnapped children in order to acquire a pliable staff to train in the craft of begging and stealing. In novels like the anonymously authored *Oran, The Outcast,* terrified youngsters told strangers fabricated stories of distress to obtain funds that would keep their masters well supplied with rum. The depravity of the professional beggar did not end here. One pauper in P. H. Skinner's *The Little Ragged Ten Thousand* stole infants from hungry, weak mothers and then appeared on the streets with tin cup and starving child. To increase her day's earnings, she stuck pins into the baby, a practice which elicted anguished screams that melted the hearts and opened the purses of the passing throng.

But the poor in the pages of popular prose were, for the most part, sympathetic types consigned to unbearable conditions through little fault of their own. Their natural foil was the rapacious slumlord, who made huge profits from their misery. Callous to the hardships of his tenants, he was portrayed in Judson's *The G'hals of New York* and

Thompson's *City Crimes* as a grasping type, ready to evict the widow and orphan if the rent were not paid. Even if a starving woman had just given birth, she and her newborn babe would be thrown onto the streets, an inevitable sentence to death, when the rental money was not delivered on time. *"To make, to take, to grasp, to grind, to bind, to hoard, to heap, to keep"* were words engraved on the hearts of the landlord class.[6] Deaf to tears and callous to handwringing, the slumlord in popular books like Buckley's *Amanda Willson* and Joseph Scoville's *Clarence Bolton* usually mixed meanness with lewdness. He would excuse a woman from paying the rent if she surrendered to his lust. Thus this familiar figure of melodramatic lore effectively personified both the greed and lechery of the merciless city. He also served, as Carroll Smith Rosenberg has argued, as a new scapegoat. Genteel Protestants could exonerate themselves from the cancerous spread of tenements by focusing their rage on a recognizable individual who frequently was a foreigner. Curiously absent from this literature, which frequently intertwined realistic details of the current urban scene, was identification of William Astor and Trinity Church, twin pillars of the Protestant establishment, as notorious examples of tenement profiteers.

Often this stock villain appeared too comfortable in his mansion to disturb his equanimity with scenes of the ugly slum. Instead, he would send the rent collector to do the dirty work. In popular books like Catharine Maria Sedgwick's *Married or Single?* and Augustine J. H. Duganne's *Knights of the Seal,* such men served as spies for their sub-human masters, keeping watch to make sure that a starving tenant did not pawn furniture which stood as security for the rent. Duganne's portrait of the typical tenement agent was of a man "without one kindly feeling in his heart," who would "tear the bed from under the dying, pluck the shroud from the corpse" in order to obtain the landlord's dues (p. 76).

With such cold-hearted urban profiteers, how successful was the Christian portion of the community in succoring the destitute? The overwhelming impression conveyed by popular fiction at mid-century was that, despite its brigades of materialists, the city teemed with men of God who battled the Devil to save endangered souls for Christ. If St. Peter found his mission in the conversion of the Roman heathen, modern apostles were bringing the word of God to the savages of the American city. In novels crowded with do-gooders, the reader could well believe that saints walked along city streets, dedicating their lives to the relief of the forlorn.

The notions of most novelists who depicted humanitarian efforts on behalf of the urban poor, however, stretched little further than the prevailing assumptions of voluntarism. The problem of poverty, suggested writers like Burdett, Bradbury, and I. Anderson Smith, could be eradicated by the individual philanthropist, who in fairytale fashion transformed a char child into a prince or princess. For in scores of books, once the private welfare investigator determined that a slum dweller belonged to that class known as the worthy poor, he imposed his values on an otherwise dangerous underclass. By simply giving clean clothes, a bath, and an education to a deserving beggar, the bourgeois benefactors invariably succeeded in eradicating a major malfunctioning of urban society.

A case in point is Maria Susanna Cummins's penny dreadful *The Lamplighter,* which sold 100,000 copies within the first ten years of its publication and was translated into several languages. It recorded the fate of poor Gerty, an orphan kicked by her cruel guardian onto the streets of Boston at eight years of age. However, in the benevolent city many Christians become the little girl's benefactors. At first a kind lamplighter, Truman Flint, takes her to live with him. When he dies, Emily Graham, a wealthy, blind young lady becomes a sister to Gerty and persuades her father to allow the orphan to live in their mansion. Gerty later attends a fine school and trains to become a teacher. But her true mission in life becomes serving as a lamplighter, a dedicated Christian who brightens the spirits of others. Taken from the darkness of the slums, she blooms into a beautiful woman devoted to helping others. The ameliorative belief that philanthropy could bring about human perfectibility thus found expression in the urban novel.

Implicit in this novel, as in many others, was the message that religion was a prerequisite for rising in the world. In converting Gerty to militant Christianity, her benefactors have secured both her eternal salvation and worldly success. In a period of disintegrating social control, a popular book like *The Lamplighter* taught that the rehabilitation of the individual through religion would solve the problems of the urban environment. No need to restructure the economic order. Hard work and morality would regenerate the poor.

The conservative thrust of this prototypical novel is seen in more than its assumption that evangelism was a panacea for social problems. It is also visible in its use of the benevolent rich as heroes and heroines. Such a device uncritically reinforced the self-serving and self-propagated view of the urban elite—namely, that it was the most fit to lead society because it ruled America righteously. In this sense religiously oriented writers served as cultural imperialists for the powerful and wealthy men who controlled the nation's municipalities; their message was unmistakable: the affluent were robust Christians best equipped to uproot the blight of the city.

Despite the fact that the poor were assuming the status of a proletariat caste in antebellum cities, mid-nineteenth-century hack writers refused to recognize the perpetuation of poverty among the population of the slums. No matter how deprived a person might be, through the timely intervention of a charitable individual he could become a respectable middle-class citizen. In an anonymously written potboiler, *Old Haun,* the heroine, Anna Hervey, is introduced to the reader as an impoverished tyke who has to part with her family's last heirloom. Although she is cheated by the hideous pawnbroker, Old Haun, she finds a friend in a humanitarian physician, Dr. Foster. When Anna is orphaned, he takes her to live with him. Soon he suspects that his adopted daughter has been the victim of a scheme to defraud her of a large inheritance. His unflagging efforts to uncover the plot succeed, and Anna becomes an heiress.

Anna is not the only waif delivered from poverty in this novel. New York City becomes the land of opportunity for a poor Irish lad, Mich Lynch, who had been Anna's protector in the slums. Given an education by a benevolent attorney, he fulfills the hopes of his benefactor and becomes a successful barrister. When he earns an enormous fortune by dint of his own efforts, he proposes marriage to his long-loved childhood friend, Anna, and the happy pair, given the chance to develop their potential, carry on the great urban tradition of philanthropy, alleviating destitution among the unfortunate immigrants of Gotham.

Just as Anna and Mich devote their lives to aiding victims of poverty, so numerous fictional representatives of the wealthy class prove their moral worth by opening their doors to the poor. In Greeley's *Violet* an angel of mercy brings an alcoholic outcast of the Old Brewery and his starving daughter to live in her respectable home. In Hammond's *Robert Severne* the hero does not punish a young delinquent who has cheated him of a large sum of money. Instead he reaches out to save this flotsam of the slums and provides her with new surroundings where she can be instructed in morality and showered with kindness. In the drama of this period as in the novel, the rich try to rescue the poor from degradation. When a wealthy woman in Augustine Daly's *Under the Gaslight* sees a six-year-old girl attempting to snatch her purse, she takes her to her mansion and raises the child in luxury, telling her fashionable friends that the former juvenile delinquent is her own niece.

The poor as well as the rich kept the doors of their homes open to the destitute in popular literature. In Julia Wright's religiously inspired novel *The Corner Stall,* a humble pieman realizes from his Bible classes that it is his duty to rescue a young thief named Ratty from the debasement of his life along the wharves. By his concerned attention he transforms a would-be criminal into a useful citizen. In James Maitland's *The Watchman* a poor nighttime guardian of the peace discovers an abandoned orphan. As a good Christian he cannot harden his heart to a deprived child. Although it will mean great sacrifice, he brings the filthy, unschooled urchin to live in his own home and introduces him to the values that will mean a life of future success. Even impoverished seamstresses in William Sikes's *One Poor Girl* bring a starving girl to their boarding house and offer to share their scanty fare and very bed with someone more miserable than they. Thus many popular books judged the materialism of the city to pale before its "noble trait of generosity," "beautiful sacrifice," and "great heart." Contemporaries writing outside the media of urban confidentials and novels also came to believe by mid-century that the city, with its combination of resources and talent, could do more to eradicate poverty than could the rural village.

With such bestowals of philanthropy, the poor were depicted as grateful and meek. Despite the fact that at mid-century the needy were demanding welfare as a right and threatening violence if their demands were not met, in the pages of popular novels one does not encounter impoverished, angry militants protesting the paucity of their dole. Rather the indigent went onto the streets, shamefacedly seeking relief from the more fortunate members of the community. Pitifully they prayed in thanksgiving for the angel sent by God who had delivered them from starvation. The surliness and class consciousness of the mid-nineteenth-century poor are conspicuously absent from the pabulum world of hack fiction.

The power of religion to redress the wrongs in the city is seen in more than cloying scenarios which featured a victim of urban blight rehabilitated by the good deeds of a Christian activist. It is also manifest in numerous stories which portrayed the city as the most challenging place in which people with religious convictions could live. Here missionaries could open Sunday schools and convert the neglected slum dwellers to Christianity. Here they could bring the Bible to the intemperate and teach charity to the grasping. Here they could break down the barriers of human isolation and create a caring, compassionate community.[7] For in religiously oriented popular fiction the city dweller was as susceptible to the ardor of a Great Awakening as was the rural inhabitant. In John Neal's *True Womanhood* Wall Street businessmen and workers alike jam into lunch-hour camp meetings to hear preachers rail at them for their greed and callousness to the poor.

While novelists like Neal, Elizabeth Stuart Phelps, and Cara Belmont believed that religion would cleanse urban dwellers of their sins, other writers focused on the more pragmatic goal of using institutional means to purify the city. They conveyed the impression that the city was as yet bereft of adequate communal weapons for waging a war on poverty. According to popular authors like Burdett, Stephens, Joseph Holt Ingraham, and Charles Gayler, municipal care for the poor consisted of shipping unfortunates to the watch house, where they received a free fire and cot, or to prison, where policemen charged men fainting upon the streets from starvation with drunkenness and vagrancy. The luckier were assigned to the poorhouse, a place so overcrowded that, even here, many could find no refuge. In such circumstances the city fathers provided paupers with twenty-five cents a week as a form of outdoor relief. Moreover, lest the poor become welfare loafers, applicants for relief were obliged to report once a week to the almshouse. Here the commissioner could review each case while thousands filled the room, pushing and shoving to receive their quarter-dollar dole. Even if a poor person were critically ill, the law required police officers to bring him to the almshouse to be properly registered before he was allowed to die in a charity hospital.

For those not mortally afflicted with sickness, treatment in a municipal hospital like Bellevue was, according to Stephens, a fairly certain condemnation to death. In her novel *The Old Homestead* clerks ignorant of medicine assigned patients to wards compartmentalized according to particular diseases. Instead of receiving medical attention from the resident physician, charity parients were placed under the care of political appointees who packed the ill into infested rooms and, when all the available bed space was filled, forced them to lie on floors. Those who received medical treatment were most often attended by students without experience and without the advice of a superior. The nursing staff was gruesome. The municipality assigned female prisoners to the task of nursing charity cases. In a grisly scene reminiscent of Charles Brockden Brown's portrait of drunken, evil nurses in *Arthur Mervyn*, Stephens fueled the indignation of her readers with a description of nursing attendants robbing the dead and stealing stimulants meant to serve as an essential medicine for victims of typhus: "... these were the persons provided by a law of New York City for the sick poor—these fierce women, reeling to and fro like fiends ... making sport of pain, joking about coffins—laughing with drunken glee over the death throes they had witnessed. These were the nurses a great, rich city gave to its poor—merciful economy—sweet, beautiful humanity!" (p. 199). Nor were Stephens's allegations made of whole cloth. A report issued by a physician in 1847 denounced the Bellevue administration for consigning over one hundred patients to sleeping quarters on the floor. Another report circulated in 1848 blasted this institution for allowing alcoholic wantons to serve as nurses.

Not all popular writers, however, took such a negative view of municipal welfare services. Others credited New York City with providing numerous free facilities for its unfortunates. In contrast to Stephens's portrait of Bellevue as a charnel house, A. L. Stimson and George C. Foster pictured the Charity Hospital of New York as "an oasis" where patients without means were treated with "untiring care, the most admirable discipline, the most conscientious discharge of duty."[8] Although Stephens and Gayler chided New York City for its niggardly treatment of adult unfortunates, they lauded Gotham for its generous institutional care of impoverished orphans. Singling out the juvenile asylums on Blackwell's Island and on Randall's Island as models of paternalistic concern and discipline, they showed how removal of abandoned youths to a sylvan setting saved them from gutter life.

Notwithstanding these seedling government efforts at public assistance, more had to be done. The writer Allen W. Gazlay argued that unless more energetic collective measures were adopted to eradicate urban poverty society would be fighting a large-scale war without arms: "No consideration arising from . . . the effects of a dense, badly educated population, can for a moment arrest the growth of cities; yet one can scarcely forbear the contemplation of a period when that growth will . . . [demand] laws and regulations of a character entirely different, if not much more stringent than are now demanded" (pp. 222–23). As the hope for an immediate millennium faded by the 1850s, those committed to ameliorating the lot of the unfortunate grudgingly realized that poverty was not merely a question of intemperance and immorality. They directed their efforts to impersonal, secular means of helping the indigent—job placement, public health, summer camps for poor children.

The first item on their agenda, however, was the destruction of the slums. By the 1850s the tenement had replaced alcoholism as the primary explanation of urban ills. In the wake of the cholera epidemics of 1849 and 1857, urbanites blamed the mounting disorders of city life on the slums. These enclaves of human despair embodied all those traits the bourgeoisie found most abhorrent—filth, lawlessness, disease, lewdness. Philanthropic societies, supported by middle-class people of strong religious convictions, conducted detailed surveys of tenement conditions and proposed concrete measures for state action to improve housing and public health. Newspapers, too, kept up a barrage of criticism of slumlords and demanded reforms. In 1852 the *Daily Times* described vermin-infested, congested houses owned by profiteers and clamored for government intervention. How, after all, could reformers teach the poor thrift, hard work, and temperance in the morally corrosive atmosphere of these rookeries? How could society protect itself against crime, prostitution, and pauperism while large numbers of human beings were housed in an environment which bred vice?

The tenement defied the tenets of Christian morality. This knowledge, which had been shared by a relatively small number of charitably minded individuals who had made their own excursions into the homes of the poor in the 1830s and 1840s, became common coin in the decade between 1856 and 1866 when agitation for tenement-house regulation reached flood force. Indeed, missionary organizations like the NYAICP, the CAS, the Female Moral Reform Society, and the Five Points House of Industry were not alone in their efforts to pressure the government into legislating stringent tenement-house regulation. A group of popular authors, using the medium of fiction to campaign for decent living quarters for the poor, urged those interested in saving souls not to build more churches or tract societies but rather to tear down the swarming nests of human misery in their midst.

In 1857 a committee appointed by the New York State legislature published a report on tenement conditions in New York City and Brooklyn, excoriating landlords for constructing houses which were "the parent of constant disorders and the nursery of increasing vices."[9] Chairman of this committee was the author of melodramatic tales, Augustine Joseph Hickey Duganne. Disillusioned by the failure of the legislature to act upon his group's recommendations, he wrote the novel *The Tenant-House* to arouse the conscience of urbanites to the "blot on civilization" in their midst, the noisome tenements of New York City.

Like many public-spirited citizens of this period who had shifted the thrust of their reforming activities from purging the poor of their licentiousness to the pragmatic goal of purifying the environment of the city, this master of the purple flourish attempted to inspire sympathy for children born in the slums. If education could provide a light to illuminate the spirits of idiots and the blind, why, he asked, could not zealous efforts on behalf of poor children allow them to blossom even in the "great wilderness of city life"? Youngsters surrounded by filth, exposed to vice, unless weaned from the evil of their environment would continue to corrupt future generations. For in his eyes, vicious habits acquired in the nursery of the slums were not some Calvinistic mark of Cain; rather they were "habits almost inseparable from the condition of life out of which no helping hand seeks to rescue them ... which never can be ... eradicated until that blot upon civilization is removed ...

—the crowded, reeking, pestiferous tenant houses of the poor" (pp. 219-20). With the moral fervor of a gospel meeting, this popular book held the promise that model housing legislation and infant schools could both rescue the poor and save a comfortable middle class from urban disorder and crime.

The concern of Duganne with children raised in the slums was a sentiment shared by many reformers. Contemporaries were sorely aware of the need to engineer a new environment which would save abandoned youths. In 1850 George Matsell, Chief of Police of New York City, complained of the growing number of vagrant and vicious children who swarmed in the streets of the city: "Children are growing up in ignorance and profligacy, only destined to a life of misery, shame, and crime, and ultimately to a felon's death. Their numbers are almost incredible, and . . . the degraded and disgusting practices of these almost infants in the schools of vice, prostitution and rowdyism, would certainly be beyond belief."[10] The rate of juvenile delinquency was soaring. As John Hawes has pointed out, urban life often led to the breakup of families and forced youngsters to survive without parental protection. Few youths who migrated to the city in search of better economic opportunities maintained ties to the church of their childhood. Reformers predicted chaos unless the poor were trained in civic responsibilities and social conformity. Youthful offenses, they believed, could be prevented by the inculcation of stern morality and encouragement of hard work. To weld different ethnic groups and economic classes into a disciplined community, the state extended the system of common schools. To teach youths a proper regard for American social values, a new sugar-coated literature instructed youngsters on their moral development. Literature for adults, too, aimed to instill in parents an appreciation of strict child-rearing practices. For instance, the educator Horace Mann urged people to read pious books like Catharine Sedgwick's *Home*, which depicted tender but firm parents and unquestioningly obedient children. And to recruit the middle class into the crusade to save unfortunate children, novelists spun moist yarns about unwanted vagabonds whose earliest memories were of drunkenness and brutality. In canvases crowded with ragpickers, street sweepers, and vendors of matches, urban writers evoked the reader's dread of a future in which thousands would be cast adrift in great cities to fend for themselves at a tender age.

In taking up the cause of disadvantaged youths, pulp novelists not only cluttered their books with scenes of destitute orphans starving, begging, blacking boots, and sleeping in abandoned buildings, but also provided their audience with statistics that would awaken them to the need for immediate action. In contrast to novels which emphasized the religious duty to eliminate urban destitution, several works written in the 1850s supplied the reading public with facts and figures, the new weapons philanthropists relied upon for battling poverty. The novelist Elizabeth Oakes Smith in *The Newsboy,* a sensational romance which sold several thousand copies, repeated an allegation of a New York City police report in 1852 that in Gotham alone "10,000 children, amid a Christian community, [had] neither home nor protectors, neither parent nor guide, but [went] up and down its thoroughfares, with ... none to lead them by the hand" (p. 459). Robert Greeley in *Violet* charged that, of these youthful vagrants, 2,000 were girls already proficient as thieves; and that of 16,000 criminals arrested in one year, one-quarter were under twenty-one years of age. Militant action would have to replace a nonchalant laissez faire if the city were to be cleansed of its vile breeding grounds of vice. Society, instead of building prisons to contain the human refuse of urban life, ought to redirect its efforts, eliminating the causes of crime.

In the period 1840–70 no fewer than thirty-nine books appeared which took as their main theme the rescue of neglected urban youngsters. This flurry of literary propaganda becomes understandable when we recognize that urban reform was animated not only by evangelism but also by a new and important spirit of secularism. From their pulpits ministers like Horace Bushnell, William Ellery Channing, and Theodore Parker in the mid-1840s assailed the traditional assumption that children were born into sin. The child's nature was plastic. Nurture in youth was the most crucial factor in character formation. With proper training volatile youngsters, the dregs of urban civilization, could be cured of deviancy, and society safeguarded from crime and anarchy.

The Reverend Mr. Pease, an early welfare leader, became the hero in Solon Robinson's near best-selling novel *Hot Corn,* which in a spirit of reform revealed the degrading horrors to which New York's slum children were exposed—begging, stealing, alcoholism, and prostitution. Pease, working at the Five Points Mission, a Methodist charity, realized that one could not correct the immoral conditions in the squalid districts of the city by simply offering Bibles and tracts to its inhabitants. Instead he built a prototype settlement house modeled on London's "ragged schools," which became one of the "wonders of New York piety." Concerned that the galloping increase of relief cases would saddle the city with a permanent pauper class, Pease pioneered in establishing an industrial training school on the site of the Old Brewery. There he taught the ragamuffins of New York how to earn their own living. In the novel he extends a merciful hand to a vicious Irish urchin, Wild Maggie, domesticating her by kind words and useful work. In a mood of moral uplift, typical of the naiveté of the period, the author implied that a coarse child, given a chance to discover the pleasure of industry over idle vice, would reject slum habits; that besotted adults, inspired by those who sought their spiritual regeneration, would take the pledge. In short, Robinson promised a big return for a small investment: "If those who would reform the vicious, knew the power of love and kind words towards the poor fallen creatures who abound in our city and how much stronger they are than prison bars . . . , we should soon see the spirit of reformation hovering over us like the guardian angel sent to save a city that should . . . contain only five righteous persons" (p. 386). In seeking to subdue the "vicious" element of the slum population, we may assume that Robinson quite deliberately made his wild child Irish. Like many other popular authors, he shared the prejudices of the Protestant urban mission movement: the hordes of newly arrived Catholic immigrants were a riotous element that had to be tamed into meekness by learning a menial trade and love of the Lord.

No matter how villainous a child of the slums seemed to be, in the popular books he could be saved. He was, after all, only an unfortunate victim of an unhealthy environment. Simply change his surroundings and a social transformation would take place. Smutty Tom, the thieving protagonist of George Thompson's *The Locket,* finds in robbery one of the few means for keeping his skeletal frame alive. A youngster who must find shelter on the cold streets of New York with no one to care for him, he battles for survival. Illiterate and ignorant of the difference between right and wrong, he prefers stealing to begging. While committing a burglary, he is apprehended by the man whose house he has invaded. But handsome, wealthy Walter De Lacey realizes that the young thief is not responsible for his illegal career. Taking pity on this child, he becomes his patron saint. A bath, a new suit of clothes, and affection quickly convert a juvenile delinquent. Through association with refined people Tom corrects his grammar, polishes his manners, and becomes honest. Smutty Tom metamorphosed into Tom De Lacey, a bona fide gentleman, has been given the chance to develop himself and to fulfill the philanthropic dream.

Thompson's well-intentioned but naive ideas were the stock-in-trade of contemporary authors who wished to instill a stern Protestant morality in the youth of the city. Apparently oblivious of the way in which poor immigrants were resisting the efforts of pious humanitarians to bring them within the Protestant fold, they heaped accolades upon institutional agencies devoted to safeguarding the spiritual and social well-being of young males. Matthew Hale Smith in his confidential

Sunshine and Shadow in New York acclaimed the YMCA not only for protecting uprooted rural youths from intemperance and immorality but also for providing them with wholesome associates and inspiring evangelical work. Horatio Alger in *Ben* publicized the admirable work of the Newsboys' Lodging House, which furnished urchins with a bed for six cents a night and instructed them in cleanliness and morality.

In addition to taking up the cause of impoverished youths in the city, urban writers sought to salvage the fallen women. Like the Female Moral Reform Society founded in 1830 to end sexual transgressions, novelists realized that virginity in the cities could best be safeguarded by providing friendless women with decent homes and jobs. Their books abounded with heroes and heroines who scoured the metropolis to conserve public morality. A case in point is the novel *Up Broadway* by Eleanor Ames, in which the heroine, Mrs. Kirk, bestows her mite on a streetwalker. She learns that the strumpet has been trapped into her occupation by a false marriage which left her with a starving child.

Mrs. Kirk determines to save the wronged woman. Reflecting a new awareness that many of the so-called degenerates of urban life were really victims of forces beyond their control, the charitable Mrs. Kirk provides the fallen Magdalene with food, coal, and enough money to purchase furniture. What is more, she makes it possible for her to renounce sin by finding for her respectable, remunerative employment. The city becomes, in this typical novel of the period, a challenging field for missionary work, offering rich women self-employment in helping the less fortunate.

A similarly successful reconstruction of a fallen woman served as the theme of *John Norton's Conflict*. The hero, filled with compassion for the poor, becomes a benefactor to a sensitive lad and his mother, an alcoholic prostitute who has been forced into her ignoble trade by her maternal determination to feed her starving son. Norton, outraged to see a good woman brought so low, moves the grateful mother to Staten Island, away from her coarse associates, and provides her with a business selling fruit at the Fulton Street market. Without any backsliding, the one-time wanton becomes respectable. Popular authors implied that if blacks could be redeemed from the shattering effects of slavery, why could not city slaves, sold on the flesh market of a depraved metropolis, also be redeemed by timely reformist action. If drunkards could renounce drink, why could not the female victims of urban poverty also be regenerated?

Indeed, one of the important themes that emerged from numerous books was that the "city [shone] far in the future . . . as the hope of our world."[11] Like the rest of the nation, it was undergoing continual improvement. The playwright John Brougham in 1856 allowed a character in *Life in New York* to express civic pride in what he regarded as the improved moral tone of New York City: "[T]hanks to the increasing intelligence and growing self-respect of the people, the many dens of iniquity with which the city was at one time overrun, and which the unthinking kept alive by injudicious visits, are to be seen no more: or, if they are visible, it is only to the doomed and degraded class by which they are sustained." If the concerted effort of enterprising Americans was bringing progress to the prairies in the form of turnpikes, canals, and railroads, the activity of energetic philanthropists was conquering urban poverty. Already by the 1860s the notorious Five Points was no longer an incubator of vice. Christian missionaries had torn down the infamous Old Brewery and replaced it with a mission station, the House of Industry, where numberless urchins learned the Bible and a craft. Elegant ladies in novels like Neal's *True Womanhood* and Sikes's *One Poor Girl* were bringing ragpickers, beggars, and thieves to the Wilson Industrial School to teach them a useful trade.

Despite the criticism of the city which we examined in chapters 2 and 3, many popular books indicated that the metropolis neither had a monopoly on evil nor was itself incontrovertibly evil: "The character of [the] city is not depreciated, for although it confessedly contains its proportion of hardened criminals and unblushing vice, yet its established character for virtue, religious sentiment, moral practice and efficient benevolence of its inhabitants, is indisputable and undoubted."[12] If popular writers showed urban communities inhabited by sharpers, they also pictured the countryside not without its slanderers, spongers, and schemers. Sin resided in the human heart and knew no geographical boundaries. In fact, urban novels often coupled references to metropolitan corruption with instances of small town wickedness. If the city was cluttered with saloons, did not many a hamlet harbor the ubiquitous tavern? If municipal communities were tainted by the presence of gambling casinos, was not the entire country involved in rash speculative adventures? If urban cads plotted the ruin of innocent country girls, did not many a seduced and abandoned rural lass migrate to the city as a refuge from disgrace? If city belles were auctioned on the flesh market of the metropolis to the highest bidder, did not many village maidens move to town precisely to capture a rich husband?

Examination of popular mid-nineteenth-century urban literature reveals an image of the city not only as a place of mystery and misery but also of mission. It appeared, as Lucia and Morton White have only half-correctly argued, as a locale of "heartless commercialism, miserable poverty, crime and sin, smoke and noise," but not as a center of "personal defeat, icy intellectualism, . . . and loneliness."[13] The very cankers of the city were a goad for humanitarian activity. While the heroes of James Fenimore Cooper's and Mark Twain's universe sought personal and metaphysical redemption outside of society, the personae of books written for a mass market molded the city in the image of the Gospels.

Popular literature held out the hope that the city offered its residents an opportunity to build a New Jerusalem in America. As Day Kellogg Lee suggested in the novel *The Master-Builder,* out of the darkness, strife, and chaos of the metropolis would come a holy city peopled with Christians who labored for the perfection of mankind. Certainly urban literature of the mid-nineteenth century resonated with a theme rooted in the founding of the nation itself—the creation of a "city upon a hill." To the Puritans who came to America, the city represented the highest worldly expression of man's desire to establish God's kingdom on earth. And despite the assertions of scholars that the United States has been burdened by an antiurban tradition, scrutiny of literary sources written for the common man reveals that, more than two centuries after the founding of the Massachusetts Bay Colony, writers of popular books still regarded the city as the highest moral artifact of a civilized society: "The highest name of society, the highest type of social perfection . . . is a pure and enlightened city, and [St.] John took the city as a figure to describe the highest state of perfection and peace on earth. . . . How happily selected, therefore, was the symbol of a city, whose inhabitants are all enlightened and pure, whose gates stand open day and night . . . and whose houses are warmed by the ardors of love."[14] Thus popular writers at mid-century buttressed the urban mission movement. Like the Reverend Richard Storrs, Jr., who exhorted his congregation to "preach [CHRIST] IN THE CITIES for nowhere else is the need of this greater, . . . and from no other points on earth will the influence of it extend so widely,"[15] they depicted the city as a place of social experimentation directed to the regeneration of humanity. Imbued with the optimistic romanticism of the age, they registered a democratic belief in man's ability to change his institutions and improve his condition.

13

CONCLUSION

The turbulent years of urban growth between 1820 and 1870 stimulated the imagination of popular writers and prompted an avalanche of books which promised to initiate readers into the mysteries of urban life. These books, though a far cry from mimetic realism, document the transformation of burgeoning cities from small commercial entrepôts into sprawling industrial centers. A barometer of the emerging patterns of metropolitan life, they record the cosmopolitan environment of antebellum municipalities which jumbled together various classes, nationalities, and races into neighborhoods crammed with both residential and business structures. In bold verbal brush strokes these books convey the restlessness of urban society at mid-century, the inexorable uptown movement of the population, and the scattering of the poor from center-city slums to outer residential wards in the geographically expanded city.

With an extraordinary color and excitement which anticipate our own tabloids, they reproduce the social decay which lurked behind the facade of urban wealth; of an economy that allowed the rich to become richer and the poor, poorer; of a society which permitted merchant potentates to enjoy unprecedented opulence while forcing those dependent on them to live in highly visible poverty. Representative titles of their exposés—*New York: Its Upper Ten and Lower Million; Silver and Pewter: A Tale of High and Low Life in New York; Big Dick . . . A Romance of High and Low Life in Boston*—articulate the concern of contemporary Americans over the deepening class cleavages in the cities.

If, as the French scholar Marc Bloch has noted, the function of the historian is to follow the traces of human life wherever they may be found and inject into his analysis the living quality of the past, then the works of popular writers become vivid contemporary sources for reading the daydreams, fears, and aspirations of an earlier generation vexed by cities which were skidding out of control. With a liveliness and pungency that often has been suppressed by historians concerned with academic objectivity and quantitative accuracy, they, to a remarkable extent, corroborate the model of the mid-nineteenth-century city developed by recent scholarship. Quite luridly and graphically they register the shock waves of a community invaded by hordes of newcomers, buffeted by riot, assaulted by criminals. In cameos which reveal the poverty, vice, violence, disease, and political corruption of an atomized, divisive society, they provide a unique record of the unstable, volatile city at mid-century.

A significant body of popular writers in the 1840s and 1850s responded to this mounting disorder by exhorting readers to beware of worldly vanities and pleasures. Failing to understand the economic forces unleashed by accelerated industrial growth, they grasped at sentimental clichés. Lacking insight into root causes, they so mingled fact with fiction as to blur the reader's vision of fundamental problems beleaguering the rapidly changing metropolis. In place of serious analysis of social issues, they reaffirmed the prevailing doctrine of laissez-faire individualism and urged a mass audience to embrace Christian virtues as armor against the satanic traps of the town. These accommodative novels sought to impose a conservative Protestant morality on people living in communities plunged in disorder. They implied that if enough individuals were undeviating in their personal rectitude they had the power to restore quiet and harmony to unsettled cities.

Other writers, however, increasingly came to see that the urban milieu itself was in need of reconstruction: policies which served the old "walking" city were no longer adequate for the expanded metropolis. Consequently, during the fifties and sixties an important strain that developed in much popular literature was a plea for secular reform of the city. Didactic authors vividly revealed the plight of the city's unfortunates and attempted to arouse the middle class to battle against metropolitan ills. Addressing themselves to a wide-ranging reform impulse that was part and parcel of the antebellum humanitarian crusade, they called for an improvement in the working conditions of female and child laborers, for temperance legislation, amelioration of the penal system, purification of municipal government, tenement-house regulation, and toleration of the immigrant.

The vitality of the urban frontier not only generated exhortations against self-indulgence and pleas for reform but also advertised the opportunities for self-fulfillment available in mushrooming cities. In title pages that suggested the alluring dynamism of the metropolis—*Chances and Changes; The Lottery of Life: A Story of New York; Jemmy Daily . . . A Tale of Youthful Struggles and The Triumph of Truth and Virtue over Vice and Falsehood*—pulp writers added a specific urban dimension to a folklore which pictured America as the land of opportunity. In cliff-hangers which always turned out well in the end, the rugged individualist, fortified by a passion for industry and frugality, found both spiritual and temporal redemption in the city.

During this era when millions poured into America's expanding urban network in the hope of improving their economic status, popular literature thus fed the national dream of self-advancement through hard work. It created a collective myth of the city as a place where the stalwart could hold fast to agrarian righteousness while at the same time pursuing material abundance. If we accept the postulate that myths exert an important affective power on people's lives, then we can see how popular urban books contributed to the unprecedented flight of the populace to cities. By denying the reality of diminishing opportunities for social mobility in the city, this fiction whetted the appetite for urban life of those who no longer wished to till the soil. By dangling the prize of fortune before the minds of those who hungered for prosperity, the popular book was an ideological magnet which pulled people cityward.

Fluff literature of the mid-nineteenth century did more than buoy the hopes of those predisposed to relocating in cities. It gave them easily comprehended logistics for avoiding failure in the city and thereby hastened the psychological assimilation of immigrants from a rural to an urban society. In the stock formulas of this prose heroes and heroines enjoyed a sober happiness. Riches did not corrode their self-reliance, thrift, or respect for property. Indeed, the city allowed them to harmonize acquisitiveness with conventional morality, economic mobility with Christian virtue. No need, then, for an aspiring yeoman to forsake the familiar precepts of his forebears. The comfortable, time-encrusted norms of the farm still appeared as a relevant guide for a new life in the town. Commitment to traditional ethical values was the popular writer's ransom for success in the city.

In veiling the clash of two cultures with tired pieties, urban literature helped to quiet social tensions. It taught disappointed newcomers that patience, loyalty, and humility eventually would secure them their just deserts both in this world (even be it urban) and the next. It coached those who yearned for material bounty to steel themselves against the vice of greed. It instructed those lured by the bright lights of the town to think less of their pleasures and more of pleasing their betters. In this sense, popular books tried to maintain a cultural consensus in the United States in an epoch of economic upheaval and social dislocation.

Curiously, during this fifty-year period of simmering urban change and unrest, the popular book remained essentially unchanged. Formula potboilers, compounded of familiar elements, unflinchingly repeated the same plots and value system. They communicated the Zeitgeist of an essentially optimistic age that believed in the power of the individual to make his mark in this world. In powerfully suggestive images which dovetailed with the reveries of the inarticulate, they etched an urban landscape pocked with moral crevices yet dominated by vistas of economic, social, and intellectual plenty.

Both novels and nonfictional confidentials evoked a tempestuous urban civilization where life could be more intensely lived. Though the metropolis was a place of mysteries and miseries, in the end it was a stage for miracles. Though plagued with fires, crime, a polluted environment, appalling poverty, it met these challenges heroically. Already by 1870, the reader of popular books learned, the city could pride itself on its new uniformed metropolitan police and fire departments, communal efforts to relieve economic distress, expanded educational, associational, and amusement facilities, and even its more wholesome moral tone.

Thus popular literature, filled with numerous ambiguities that revealed both the lights and shadows of the urban world, nevertheless broadcast the lure of city life. Saturating the reader with a flood of happy endings, it carried the encouraging news that the city was part of God's kingdom and that those imbued with the discipline of Calvinistic morality could reach a state of grace in a terrain that contained both good and evil.

Such optimistic but archaic ideas about the city may have given Americans faith that they could adjust to the nation's first urban explosion, but they could not be of service for long. A faith built on outdated religious precepts was inadequate for coming to grips with the problems of the modern industrial city. Tales which spelled out obsolete rules for safe conduct in the city gave the reader of popular literature a pseudo preparation for urban life. Such books were little more than placebos which may have temporarily allayed the public's anxieties about unwanted changes in the nature of American society but furnished it with no viable intellectual construct for coping with the realities of the unruly metropolis. At a juncture in American history when the nation most needed a full-fledged collective commitment to meet the urban crisis, naive stories about the individual city dweller rising above the obstacles in his path encouraged contemporaries to cling to a doomed, fragmented piecemeal approach to municipal problems. Thus mid-nineteenth-century popular books, in failing to come to terms with the city, paved the way for the despondent, disillusioned urban literature of a later era.

NOTES

1: INTRODUCTION

1. Taylor, "The Beginnings of Mass Transportation in Urban America," pp. 31–52.
2. Still, *Urban America*, p. 76.
3. Park, *The City*, p. 1.
4. Hall and Whannel, *The Popular Arts*, p. 66.
5. Holbrook, "Life and Times of Ned Buntline," p. 604; Noel, *Villains Galore*, p. 18.
6. DeVoto in Lingelback (ed.), *Approaches to American Social History*, p. 48.
7. Waples, Berelson, and Bradshaw, *What Reading Does To People*, pp. 66–67.
8. Quoted in Hart, *The Popular Book*, p. 86.
9. Shove, *Cheap Book Production in the United States*, pp. vi–vii.
10. Mott, *Golden Multitudes*, pp. 77–79, 143, 148.
11. Schlesinger, "Social History in American Literature," pp. 143–44.
12. Bode, *The Anatomy of American Popular Culture, 1840–1861*, p. 111; Wolff and Fox in Dyos and Wolff (eds.), *The Victorian City*, II, 559.

2: HAZARDS OF CITY LIFE

1. For example, see descriptions in Dixon, p. 206; Mary Howe, p. 156; Sarah Hale, pp. 10, 14, 16, 28, 35, 37, 79, 85, 88; McCabe, *Secrets of the Great City*, pp. 208–21; Gunn, pp. 17–20, 49–57, 298–99.
2. S. Hale, pp. 104–22; Foster, *Fifteen Minutes Around New York*, p. 92.
3. Ibid., pp. 98, 100.
4. Gunn, pp. 31–39, 230–31.
5. Dickens, *American Notes*, p. 83; Still, *Mirror for Gotham*, pp. 98, 173.
6. For representative samples see G. Foster, *Celio*, p. 115; Poe, *Doings of Gotham*, p. 31; Alger, *Rough and Ready*, pp. 26–27; Morford, *Shoulder-Straps*, p. 103; Stephens, *The Old Homestead*, p. 27; Judson, *Three Years After*, p. 29; Sikes, p. 249.

7.   See descriptions in Taylor, *John Godfrey's Fortunes*, p. 179; Bird, I, 119. Paulding, *Chronicles on the City of Gotham*, p. 85; Nichols, p. 20.

8.   See *Mysteries and Miseries of San Francisco*, pp. 54–56, 69; Thompson, *City Crimes*, p. 10; Burdett, *Convict's Child*, p. 242; *Mysteries of New York*, p. 64; Thompson, *Gay Girls of New-York*, p. 14; Duganne, *Two Clerks*, pp. 15–18; G. Foster, *Celio*, pp. 15–20; Wilkes, pp. 11–12.

9.   Thompson, *Life . . . of Bristol Bill*, pp. 35–36.

10.   See examples in Burdett, *Convict's Child*, p. 19; Ingraham, *Ellen Hart*, p. 3; Stephens, *Fashion and Famine*, p. 228; Averill, *Secrets of the Twin Cities*, pp. 9–10; Thompson, *Life . . . of Bristol Bill*, p. 37; Thompson, *City Crimes*, p. 95; Vose, *Seven Nights in Gotham*, p. 87; Bird, I, 121–22.

11.   Asbury, *The Gangs of New York*, pp. 105, 112.

12.   For descriptions of teenage gang violence see Roddan, pp. 49–50; Foster, "Philadelphia in Slices," p. 35; Hampden, pp. 58–61; Huet, p. 53; Ingraham, *Alice May*, pp. 40–42; *Mysteries of Philadelphia*, pp. 65–66; Duganne, *Tenant-House*, pp. 254–57; Ritner, p. 73.

13.   Duganne, *Tenant-House*, pp. 255–56.

14.   For some representative examples see Swan, p. 106; Thompson, *City Crimes*, p. 42; Baldwin, pp. 6, 13; Burdett, *The Gambler*, pp. 15, 35, 38, 72; Thompson, *Life . . . of Bristol Bill*, p. 49; Williams, *Steel Safe*, p. 15.

15.   Good samples can be found in Alger, *Ragged Dick*, pp. 103, 128, 191; Stephens, *Old Homestead*, pp. 25–26, 36, 54–55; Maitland; Burdett, *Lilla Hart*, Bouton, p. 315; Alger, *Fame and Fortune*, pp. 160–61; Burdett, *The Gambler*, pp. 13, 82, 93, 96; Whitmore, p. 52.

16.   Gould, *John Doe and Richard Roe*, pp. 255–56.

17.   Bouton, p. 467.

18.   Dickens, *American Notes*, p. 80.

19.   For examples of novels that exploited this particular sensational aspect of urban life see Solon Robinson, p. 29; Burnham, p. 85; Rulison, p. 43; Cooper, *Home As Found*, p. 106; Duganne, *Tenant-House*, pp. 459–79.

20.   Gayler, pp. 96–97.

21.   S. Robinson, pp. 29–30.

22.   For examples of works which employed this stock figure see Ritner, pp. 49, 59, 71, 84; Montaigne, pp. 94–95; Foster, *New York in Slices*, pp. 48–49; Johnson, p. 7; Judson, *Charley Bray*, p. 27.

23.   Roe, *To Love and To be Loved*, p. 59.

3: THE CITY UNDERGROUND

1.   For contemporary popular analyses of why girls drifted into prostitution see Judson, *G'hals*, p. 147; Rulison, p. 54; S. Robinson, p. 34; Browne, pp. 434–44.

2.   S. Robinson, pp. 203–04.

3.   Foster, *New York by Gas-Light*, p. 17.

4.   For sample descriptions of urban dance halls see ibid., p. 52; John Robinson, p. 15; Thompson, *Venus in Boston*, pp. 24–25; Jones, *Big Dick*, pp. 12–16; Lippard, *Nazarene*, pp. 141–42; Vose, *Seven Nights in Gotham*, p. 83; Foster, "Philadelphia in Slices," p. 45; Summerton, pp. 10–14; McCabe, *Secrets of the Great City*, pp. 308–21, 410; Matthew H. Smith, pp. 435–45, 631–34.

5.   For representative books on the dangers of gambling in the city see Foster, *New York in Slices*, pp. 26–27; Rulison, p. 41; Judson, *Three Years After*, pp. 42–47; Williams, *Gay Life*, pp. 36–39; Nichols, pp. 29–30; Fitch, pp. 43–46; W. R. Smith, pp. 114–15; Thompson, *Mysteries . . . of Philadelphia*, pp. 22–24; Wilkes, pp. 16–17; Foster, *New York by Gas-Light*, pp. 39–43; Judson, *Mysteries . . . of New York*, pp. 120–24; *Mysteries of Philadelphia*, p. 73; Nick Bigelow, p. 42; *The*

Victims of Gaming, pp. 14–15, 168; Burdett, *The Gambler,* pp. 116–27, 166–72; M. H. Smith, pp. 394–404; *Ella Cameron,* pp. 21–22; Ellis, p. 400.

6.   For representative examples, see Bradbury, *The Belle of the Bowery,* pp. 4–7; Ingraham, *Jemmy Daily,* pp. 13, 20; Abbott, *Cone Cut Corners,* pp. 234, 246–47; S. Robinson, pp. 66–73, 89–92, 115–16; Skinner, pp. 114–15; Bradbury, *Old Distiller,* p. 26; *Orphan Seamstress,* pp. 29–30; *Easy Nat,* p. 27; Foster, *New York in Slices,* p. 96; Adams, p. 47; *History of the Bottle,* pp. 3, 8; Townsend, p. 111; Wright, *Corner Stall,* pp. 200–21.

7.   For examples of fashionable alcoholic dissipation, see Sikes, pp. 231–32; Foster, *New York in Slices,* p. 92; Buchanan, p. 55; Jones, *Belle of Boston,* p. 20; Jones, *Tom, Dick and Harry,* pp. 30–32.

8.   For representative books which employed this standard scenario see Shortfellow, p. 57; Vose, *Seven Nights in Gotham,* p. 126; Wright, *Our Chatham Street Uncle,* p. 159; Smith, *What Is Gentility?,* pp. 7–8, 11; Ingraham, *Miseries of New York,* p. 11; Lamas, pp. 4–32; *Price of a Glass of Brandy,* pp. 11–23; Bradbury, *Belle of the Bowery,* pp. 4–6; Burdett, *Convict's Child,* p. 36; Burnham, pp. 39, 48, 56; Hentz, pp. 26–37; *History of the Bottle,* pp. 3–32.

4: SWEET CHEATS OF THE METROPOLIS

1.   Joseph, p. 51.
2.   Hawthorne, *Blithedale Romance,* pp. 178–79.
3.   Three typical novels which elaborate this theme are Sedgwick, *Poor Rich Man,* Asa Greene, and Greeley.
4.   For books which adumbrated the techniques of business duplicity see Curtis, *Trumps,* p. 88; Foster, *New York in Slices,* p. 34; *Herbert Tracy,* pp. 36, 51; Asmodeus, p. 55; Foster, *Celio,* p. 67.
5.   Abbott, *Matthew Caraby,* pp. 131–32.
6.   *Revelations of Asmodeus,* p. 9.
7.   Morford, *Days of Shoddy,* pp. 173–74.
8.   Ibid., pp. 321–22.

5: THAT OH-SO-WICKED HIGH SOCIETY

1.   For representative examples see Talbot Greene, p. 14; Potter; English, p. 17; Stephens, *Fashion and Famine,* pp. 234–40; Franklin, p. 7; Lasselle, *Annie Grayson,* p. 127; Maxwell, pp. 169–70; Thompson, *Harry Glindon,* pp. 44–45; Kimball, *To-Day,* p. 283; Brisée, p. 6.
2.   See descriptions in Coolidge, pp. 55–59; *Florence De Lacey,* pp. 18, 50; Vose, *Fresh Leaves;* Ritchie, *Fortune Hunter,* p. 7; Benedict, *My Daughter Elinor,* p. 211.
3.   Examples of such descriptions can be found in Torrey, pp. 15, 183; Scoville, pp. 78–79; Abbott, *Cone Cut Corners,* p. 99; *Squints Through An Opera Glass,* pp. 2–3, 14–15; English, p. 5; Rulison; Averill, *Secrets of the Twin Cities,* pp. 11–12; Thompson, *Mysteries . . . of Philadelphia,* p. 17; Bristed; Shubrick, pp. 20, 24; Cooke, p. 51; *Oran, The Outcast,* p. 20; Dexter, pp. 88–90; Buchanan, p. 10; *Revelations of Asmodeus,* pp. 17–18; Ritchie, *Fortune Hunter,* p. 11.
4.   Descriptions of the city belle can be found in Gayler, pp. 23–24; M. Hankins, pp. 18–19; Bristed, p. 6; Shubrick, p. 24; Arthur, *Bell Martin,* p. 4; Cooper, *Home As Found,* p. 64; John Jones, *Spanglers and Tinglers,* p. 90; Vose, *Fresh Leaves,* pp. 46, 52, 72; Lasselle, *Annie Grayson,* p. 36; Hentz, p. 116.
5.   Bouton, p. 59.
6.   Quoted in Pattee, *The Feminine Fifties,* p. 110.
7.   Cummins, *Mabel Vaughan,* p. 156.

8.   For six representative examples of novels which reiterated this theme that the "fashion of this world . . . 'passeth away,'" while Christianity would provide genuine satisfactions see Alden; White; Torrey; Watterson; Smith, *Winter in Washington,* Mrs. T. Smith.

9.   Cummins, *Mabel Vaughan,* p. 208.

10.   Webb, p. 42.

11.   For representative examples of this theme see Gayler, pp. 53–54; Bouton, pp. 328–50; Bradbury, *Ellen,* p. 57; Joseph, pp. 145–46; Thompson, *City Crimes,* p. 156; Eastman, pp. 275–76; Lippard, *New York,* p. 46; Lippard, *Life of a Man of the World,* p. 35; *Startling Confessions of Eleanor Burton.*

12.   For representative samples see Jones, *Big Dick,* p. 69; Bowline, pp. 9–10; Ritchie, *Fashion!,* p. 20; Nunes; Rulison, pp. 28, 37–38; Torrey, p. 181.

13.   For examples see Newell, p. 46; Cummins, *Mabel Vaughan,* p. 270; Roe, *Like and Unlike,* p. 273; Hampden, pp. 345–46; Kimball, *Henry Powers,* pp. 105–17; Curtis, *Trumps,* p. 106; Joseph, pp. 145–46; Morford, *Shoulder-Straps,* pp. 157–58; Bristed, pp. 80–203; Penn, pp. 22–26; Sealsfield, pp. 152–75.

14.   For a representative sampling, see Cummins, *Mabel Vaughan;* Hampden; Bristed; *Helen Leeson;* Joseph; Nunes; Otis; Sedgwick, *Married or Single?;* Stephens, *High Life;* Vose, *Fresh Leaves;* Townley; Hilbourne, *Modern Aristocracy;* Cooper, *Home As Found;* Curtis, *Potiphar Papers;* Schemil.

15.   Lippard, *Quaker City,* pp. 155–56.

16.   Sealsfield, p. 181.

6: THE WORKING CLASS

1.   Quoted in Dulles, *Labor in America,* p. 68.

2.   Olmsted, *A Journey to the Seaboard States,* pp. 214–15.

3.   Compare Foster, *New York Naked,* pp. 139, 141 with historians of the labor movement such as P. Foner, *History of the Labor Movement,* p. 341 and Ernst, *Immigrant Life in New York City,* p. 77.

4.   For novels which exploited the theme of the pitiful seamstress see Burdett, *Elliott Family;* Arthur, *The Seamstress;* English; Hampden; Judson, *Mysteries . . . of New York;* Maxwell; Burdett, *Chances and Changes;* Campbell; Buckley, *Sketch of the Working Classes;* Denison; Sikes; Judson, *G'hals of New York;* Buckley, *Amanda Willson.*

5.   Sikes, p. 85.

6.   For representative examples see Alger, *Ragged Dick; Ben; Fame and Fortune; Mark;* Gayler; S. Robinson; E. Smith; Neal, *Peter Ploddy;* St. Clair; Duganne, *Tenant-House;* Ingraham, *Jemmy Daily.*

7.   For examples of the way in which popular literature saluted the mechanic see Bradbury, *Jane Clark;* Lippard, *Quaker City;* Ingraham, *Harry Harefoot; Mary Beach;* McDougall; Lee, *Master-Builder;* Judd; Burnham; Bradbury, *Banker's Victim.*

8.   Good examples are Ingraham's *Harry Harefoot* and D. Lee's *Master-Builder.*

9.   Knights, *Plain People of Boston,* p. 120.

10.   Lippard, *Nazarene,* p. 178; Tyler, pp. 25–30; Benedict, *Miss Van Kortland,* pp. 108–16.

11.   Williamson and Swanson, "The Growth of Cities in the American Northeast," pp. 33, 55.

12.   Charvat, *Literary Publishing in America,* p. 73.

13.   Lippard, *New York,* p. 206.

14.   Thoreau, p. 24.

15.   *Ellen Merton,* p. 32.

16.   Cummings, pp. 47–48.

17.   Hilbourne, *Effie,* p. 227.

18.   Quoted in Bender, *Toward an Urban Vision,* p. 19.

19. Compare Hilbourne's *Effie*, p. 228 with Melville's "Tartarus," pp. 200–05, 208–09.

20. Lee, *Merrimack*, pp. 87, 98, 101, 177, 345; Judd, pp. 10, 64; Talcott, pp. 207–13.

21. Haven, *Gossips*, p. 219.

22. For representative examples see *Anna Archdale; Ellen Merton;* Cummings; Lee, *Merrimack;* Hawthorne, *Mosses from an Old Manse.*

7: CITIES WITH PERSONALITY

1. McCabe, *Secrets of the Great City*, p. 151; Foster, *New York in Slices*, p. 124.

2. Paulding, *Merry Tales*, p. 11.

3. Cooper, *Redskins* 1: 54–55.

4. Bradbury, *Gamblers' League*, p. 7; E. Smith, p. 8; Gayler, p. 113; Foster, *Fifteen Minutes around New York*, p. 39.

5. M. H. Smith, p. 706.

6. Vose, *Fresh Leaves*, p. 72.

7. Vose, *Seven Nights in Gotham*, p. 8.

8. See lithographs in Foster, *New York in Slices*, pp. 6, 11, 12, 17, 112, 116; S. Robinson, pp. 25, 96, 288, 337; Browne, pp. 121, 177, 310, 344; M. H. Smith, pp. 87, 217, 277, 361, 515, 523; McCabe, *Secrets of the Great City*, pp. 40, 48, 52, 74, 92, 168, 200, 234, 412, 440.

9. Cooper, *Redskins*, I, 17.

10. Vose, *Fresh Leaves*, p. 97.

11. Caffrey, p. 3.

12. For representative examples see Ritner, p. 73; Lippard, *Quaker City*, pp. 43–65, 155–56, 174–74, 189–90, 320, 324, 341, 343; Arthur, *Bell Martin*, pp. 13, 20, 22; Duganne, *Knights of the Seal*, pp. 73–74, 153, 165; Tartan, pp. 5, 81; *Mysteries of Philadelphia*, pp. vii–viii, 65, 76; Thompson, *Mysteries . . . of Philadelphia*, pp. 17, 81.

13. Foster, "Philadelphia in Slices," pp. 28–29.

14. W. W. Howe, pp. 280–81.

15. Watterson, pp. 116, 205.

16. Badeau, pp. 228–29.

17. For representative examples see M. Smith, I, 16, 26–29, 37; *Brisée*, p. 6; Benedict, *My Daughter Elinor*, p. 211; T. Greene, p. 14; *Ella Cameron*, p. 13; Walworth, pp. 238–39; W. Smith, pp. 35–36, 191–92; Badeau, p. 230; Tuel, pp. 29, 40; Lasselle, *Annie Grayson*, pp. 41–42; Lasselle, *Hope Marshall*, p. 90.

18. Washington *Star*, October 3, 1859.

19. For varied assessments of New Orleans' Janus-like character, see Durell, p. 44; Bartlett, *Clarimonde*, pp. 20–23; Summerton, pp. 453–54; Judson, *Mysteries . . . of New Orleans;* Simms, *Marie de Bernière*, pp. 15, 34–35; Ingraham, *Alice May*, p. 18; Pugh, p. 33; *Isabella Gray*, p. 141; Townsend, p. 47.

20. Glaab and Brown, *A History of Urban America*, p. 54.

21. Hill, pp. 242, 255–56; Eastman, p. 183; Young, p. 201; Jones, *Spanglers and Tinglers*, p. 37; Fitch, p. 182; Rulison, pp. 9, 12.

8: PERSONALITIES OF THE CITY

1. This stock character can be found in some of the following representative novels: Judson, *Charley Bray*, p. 3, *Three Years After*, p. 124, *Mysteries . . . of New Orleans*, pp. 11, 20; Bradbury, *Female Depravity*, p. 40; Lippard, *New York*,

p. 39; Swan, p. 96; Judson, *Mysteries . . . of New York*, p. 278; Stimson, p. 229; Curtis, *Trumps*, p. 376; Duganne, *Tenant-House*, p. 376; *Mary Beach*, pp. 51–53, 96–97; *Ellen Merton*, p. 7; English, pp. 5, 30; Ingraham, *Jemmy Daily*, p. 19; Rosewood, pp, 5, 11; Cooke, p. 51; *Florence De Lacey*, p. 106; Townsend, p. 417.

2.   For representative examples see St. Clair, p. 14; Williams, *Gay Life*, pp. 16–18; Foster, *New York in Slices*, pp. 78–79; Neal, *Peter Ploddy*, pp. 166–81; Buchanan, p. 10; Judson, *Mysteries . . . of New Orleans*, p. 28; E. Smith, pp. 303–04; Arthur, *Bell Martin*, p. 3; Young, pp. 153–54; Ritchie, *Fortune Hunter*.

3.   *Nick Bigelow*, p. 6; McCabe, *Secrets of the Great City*, pp. 276–82; Foster, "Philadelphia in Slices," p. 53; Neal, *Charcoal Sketches*, p. 160.

4.   See Ingraham, *Ellen Hart*, p. 13; Thompson, *City Crimes*, p. 36; Averill, *Secrets of the Twin Cities*, pp. 9–10; Burdett, *Convict's Child*, p. 19; Judson, *Charley Bray*, p. 6; Thompson, *Harry Glindon*, pp. 29–34; Thompson, *Mysteries . . . of Philadelphia*, p. 18; *Mysteries . . . of San Francisco*, pp. 54–56.

5.   Kimball, *Undercurrents of Wall-Street*, p. 259.

6.   See descriptions in Abbott, *Matthew Caraby*, pp. 232, 236–37, 262–63, 471; Gayler, pp. 21–22; Scoville, pp. 12–13; Lippard, *New York*, pp. 177–78; *Herbert Tracy*, pp. 26–28; Kimball, *Was He Successful?*, p. 123; Boucicault, pp. 12–13, 18; Bradbury, *Gamblers' League*, p. 50; Gould, *John Doe and Richard Roe*, pp. 20–26; Edwards, *Poor of New York*, p. 9; Lippard, *Quaker City*, p. 343; Barker, *Mary Morland*, pp. 5–6; Jackson, *Week in Wall Street*, p. 43.

7.   For representative delineations see Sikes, pp. 219–20; St. Clair, p. 40; Foster, *New York in Slices*, p. 32; McCabe, *Secrets of the Great City*, p. 489; Wright, *Our Chatham Street Uncle*, pp. 5–6, 69, 138, 141; Ritner, p. 18; *Old Haun*, p. 31.

8.   Hammond, pp. 103–04. For other books which caricatured lawyers as rapacious thieves see Cooper, *Home As Found*, p. 22; Arthur, *Rising in the World*, p. 114; Lippard, *Quaker City*, p. 24; *Pennimans*, p. 273; Cooke, pp. 108–09; Stephens *Fashion and Famine*, pp. 367–75.

9.   See *Old Haun*, p. 459; Huet, pp. 44–46; *Pennimans*, pp. 243, 282–84; Stimson, p. 115; Fay, I, 210; Greeley, p. 261.

10.   Ingraham, *Jemmy Daily*, p. 16.

11.   W. W. Howe, p. 80.

12.   For representative descriptions of sordid journalists see Judson, *B'hoys*, pp. 13–14; Rulison, pp. 83–85; Arthur, *Heiress*, p. 66; Foster, *New York in Slices*, p. 57; Jones, *Spanglers and Tinglers*, pp. 104–05; Thompson, *Outlaw*, p. 32; Judson, *Mysteries . . . of New Orleans*, pp. 53–54.

13.   For cameo portraits see S. Hale, pp. 84–85; Brougham, *Temptation*, p. 9; Gunn; Sikes, p. 78; Alger, *Fame and Fortune*, p. 52; Caffrey, pp. 13–14; Browne, pp. 206–13; M. Hankins, pp. 195–96; Ingraham, *Herman de Ruyter*, p. 10.

9: THE UNMELTED POT

1.   For representative samples of books which utilized derisive Irish characters see *Easy Nat*, pp. 22–23; Gunn, pp. 49–57; Lippard, *Nazarene*, p. 168; Stimson, pp. 274–75; Royall, p. 209; Sargeant, p. 147; Dixon, p. 261; E. Smith, pp. 418–19; St. Clair, pp. 28–29; Corcoran, pp. 67, 125; *Match Girl*, pp. 56–58; McCabe, *Secrets of the Great City*, pp. 109–16; Durell, p. 16; *Mysteries . . . of San Francisco*, pp. 21–23, 47; Young, pp. 43, 150–51; Binder, *Madelon Hawley*, pp. 3–4; Alger, *Ragged Dick*, p. 123.

2.   For favorable images of the Irish see McCorry, p. 166; Maitland, p. 64; *Florence De Lacey*, p. 44; McDougall, p. 31; Lee, *Rosanna*, p. 13; Smith, II, 13–14; *Old Haun*, p. 43; Judson, *B'hoys*, p. 113; *Match Girl*, p. 27; Maxwell,

p. 117; Elliott, pp. 22–25; Brougham, *Temptation,* pp. 11–12, 18; Brougham *Lottery of Life,* pp. 15, 30, 36.

3. For books which furthered these stereotypes see Judson, *Rose Seymour,* p. 43; Summerton, pp. 148–49; Ritner, pp. 12–13; Wright, *Our Chatham Street Uncle,* pp. 34, 40, 70, 123, 132; Jones, *Adventures of a Country Merchant,* pp. 338. Duganne, *Tenant-House,* pp. 159–61; Thompson, *Outlaw,* p. 7; Lippard, *Nazarene,* pp. 64–65; S. Robinson, pp. 16–17; Durell, p. 46; Brougham, pp. 8–9; Sikes, pp. 67–83.

4. Rosenberg, *The Cholera Years,* p. 140.

5. Lippard, *Quaker City,* p. 91.

6. For representative examples see Morford, *Shoulder-Straps,* pp. 103, 107; Thompson, *Locket,* pp. 3–4; *Mysteries of New York,* pp. 31–32; Foster, "Philadelphia in Slices," p. 63; Lippard, *Nazarene,* p. 160; Lippard, *New York,* p. 118; Brisbane, p. 38; Burnham, pp. 95, 120.

7. Wilkes, p. 7; Averill, *Cholera-Fiend,* pp. 69, 100; Corcoran, pp. 68–69, 127–28; Raux, p. 5; Duganne, *Tenant-House,* p. 424.

8. Judson, *Charley Bray,* p. 21.

10: THE PAGEANTRY OF CITY LIFE

1. Browne, p. 339.

2. Badeau, pp. 31–32.

3. Foster, *New York in Slices,* p. 3.

4. Gayler, p. 112.

5. Gunn, p. 12.

6. For representative descriptions of urban balls see Coolidge, pp. 58–59; *Florence De Lacey,* p. 17; Bartlett, *Clarimonde,* p. 29; Keeler, pp. 53–54; Simms, *Marie de Bernière,* p. 23; Franklin, p. 7; Lasselle, *Annie Grayson,* p. 127; Kimball, *To-Day,* p. 283; Maxwell, pp. 169–70.

7. Foster, *Celio,* pp. 80–81.

8. For descriptions of city shops see Morford, *Days of Shoddy,* p. 35; Haven, *Loss and Gain,* p. 18; John Neal, *True Womanhood,* p. 18; Williams, *Gay Life,* p. 26; Kimball, *Undercurrents of Wall-Street,* p. 147; Alger, *Ragged Dick,* pp. 58, 156.

9. For books which broadcast the rustic retreats within the city see Poe, *Doings of Gotham,* p. 40; Alger, *Ragged Dick,* p. 73; Alger, *Rough and Ready,* p. 140; Child, pp. 45–46, 49, 212; Browne, p. 59; M. H. Smith, pp. 361–62; McCabe, *Secrets of the Great City,* pp. 232–40; Foster, *Fifteen Minutes Around New York,* p. 102; English, p. 4.

10. For representative descriptions of the cultural amenities within the city see Foster, *New York in Slices,* p. 62; I. A. Smith, pp. 17–22; Arthur, *Out in the World,* p. 28; Moore, pp. 7, 15, 24–25, 27; Taylor, p. 281; Greeley, p. 271; Browne, p. 442; McCabe, *Secrets of the Great City,* pp. 135–40; St. Clar, p. 77; Badeau, pp. 35–41, 42–48, 56–63, 65, 71, 217.

11. For a roster of books which paid tribute to the city for its educational facilities see Roddan, pp. 237–41; Alger, *Fame and Fortune,* p. 66; "Guilty, or Not Guilty," p. 34; Abbott, *Matthew Caraby,* pp. 216, 220; Hale, *If, Yes, and Perhaps,* pp. 1–57; *John Norton's Conflict,* p. 3; Thompson, *The Locket,* p. 89; Bouton, pp. 95, 397; Ingraham, *Harry Harefoot,* p. 27.

12. For representative descriptions of the entertainments available to the urban masses see McCabe, *Secrets of the Great City,* pp. 388–92; *Mary Beach,* pp. 42–43; Alger, *Ragged Dick,* pp. 43, 49, 54; Foster, *New York Naked,* pp. 143, 147, 149; Judson, *Three Years After,* p. 43; E. Smith, pp. 25–26; Alger, *Ben,* pp. 12, 165; Sikes, pp. 208–13; Vose, *Seven Nights in Gotham,* p. 48.

11: THE AMERICAN DREAM FULFILLED

1. Kimball, *Henry Powers*, p. 331.
2. For examples of other novels which spun urban Cinderella yarns see Denison; English; Hammond; Burdett; Thompson, *The Locket*.

12: "AS A CITY UPON A HILL"

1. Beecher, "Prosperity and the Importance of Efforts to Evangelize the Nation," p. 154.
2. Stryker, *The Lower Depths of the Great American Metropolis*, pp. 9–10.
3. Lubove, "The New York Association for Improving the Condition of the Poor," p. 322.
4. For representative descriptions see Morford, *Shoulder-Straps*, p. 103; Stimson, pp. 173–74; Ingraham, *The Beautiful Cigar Girl*, p. 7; Sedgwick, *Married or Single?*, I, 103; M. Hankins, pp. 17–18.
5. For sample descriptions of the dwellings of the urban poor see Bradbury, *The Banker's Victim*, p. 15; S. Robinson, pp. 213–16; Hale, *Sybaris*, p. 172; Burdett, *Three Percent a Month*, pp. 48–49; Duganne, *Knights of the Seal*, pp. 5–6; Duganne, *Tenant-House*, pp. 33, 192, 373; *Florence De Lacey*, p. 10; Bradbury, *Old Distiller*, p. 18; *Oran*, p. 84.
6. Ingraham, *Ellen Hart*, p. 36.
7. For representative novels see Wright, *Corner Stall*, pp. 114, 187; Alger, *Ragged Dick*, p. 148; Phelps, *A Peep at "Number Five,"* p. 29; *Herbert Tracy*, pp. 62–63; Belmont, pp. 89, 157; Kimball, *Undercurrents of Wall-Street*, pp. 348–49; Kimball, *Was He Successful?*, pp. 183–91.
8. Foster, *Fifteen Minutes around New York*, p. 31; Stimson, p. 409.
9. Quoted in Glaab, *The American City*, p. 128.
10. Quoted in Schneider, *The History of Public Welfare in New York State*, p. 328.
11. Lee, *The Master-Builder*, p. 317.
12. *Life in Rochester*, p. 4.
13. M. and L. White, *Intellectual versus the City*, p. 47.
14. Lee, *The Master-Builder*, pp. 313, 316.
15. Storrs, *A Plea for the Preaching of Christ in the Cities*, pp. 9, 14.

BIBLIOGRAPHY

CONTEMPORARY LITERATURE AND OTHER PRIMARY SOURCES
[Bracketed dates indicate original publication.]

Abbott, Benjamin Vaughan; Abbott, Austin; and Abbott, Lyman [Benauly]. *Cone Cut Corners: The Experiences of a Conservative Family in Fanatical Times.* New York, 1855.
———. *Matthew Caraby. A Narrative of His Adventures during the Autumn of 1848.* New York, 1859.
Adams, John Stowell. *Sam Squab, The Boston Boy: Containing a Sketch of His Early Life, and Wonderful Adventures.* Boston, 1844.
Alden, Joseph. *Elizabeth Benton.* New York, 1846.
Alger, Horatio. *Ben, The Luggage Boy.* Philadelphia, 1870.
———. *Fame and Fortune.* Boston, 1868.
———. *Mark, The Match Boy.* New York, 1967 [1869].
———. *Ragged Dick.* Boston, 1868.
———. *Rough and Ready.* Philadelphia, 1869.
Ames, Eleanor Maria. *Up Broadway, and Its Sequel, A Life Story by Eleanor Kirk.* New York, 1870.
Anna Archdale; or the Lowell Factory Girl. Boston, 185–?.
Argus [pseud.]. *A Tale of Lowell.* Lowell, 1849.
Armstrong, William. *The Aristocracy of New York.* New York, 1848.
Arrest, Confession and Suicide of Almira Cathcart, Philadelphia, 1869.
Arthur, Timothy Shay. *Bell Martin; or, The Heiress.* Philadelphia, 1843.
———. *Debtor and Creditor; A Tale of the Times.* New York, 1848.
———. *The Heiress. A Novel.* Philadelphia, 1845.
———. *Love in High Life, A Story of the "Upper Ten."* Philadelphia, 1849.
———. *The Orphan Children; A Tale of Cruelty and Oppression.* Philadelphia, 1850.
———. *Out in the World. A Novel.* New York, 1864.
———. *Rising in the World; or, A Tale for Rich and Poor.* New York, 1848.
———. *The Seamstress. A Tale of the Times.* Philadelphia, 1843.
———. *Ten Nights in a Bar-Room and What I Saw There.* Boston, 1854.
Asmodeus [pseud.]. *Sharps and Flats, or the Perils of City Life.* Boston, 1850.
Averill, Charles E. *The Cholera-Fiend; or the Plague Spreaders of New York.* Boston 1850.

———. *The Secrets of the Twin Cities; or The Great Metropolis Unmasked.* Boston, 1849.

Badeau, Adam. *The Vagabond.* New York, 1859.

[Baer, Warren.] *Champagne Charlie; or the Sports of New York.* New York, 1868.

Baker, Benjamin. *A Glance at New York. A Local Drama in Two Acts.* New York, 189-? [1848].

[Baldwin, Isaac.] *The Wonderful Adventures and Horrible Disclosures of a Louisville Policeman.* Cincinnati, 1852.

Barker, Benjamin. *Clarilda; or The Female Pickpocket.* Boston, 1846.

———. *Mary Morland: or the Fortunes and Misfortunes of an Orphan.* Boston, 1845.

Barrington, Charles F. *Emily: or, The Orphan Sisters.* Boston, 1853.

———. *Nancy Waterman; or Woman's Faith Triumphant.* New York, 1853.

[Bartlett, Napier.] *Clarimonde: A Tale of New Orleans Life, and of the Present War.* Richmond, 1863.

———. *Stories of the Crescent City.* New Orleans, 1869.

Bateman, Mrs. Sidney F. *Self: An Original Comedy in Three Acts.* New York, 1856.

The Beautiful Jewess, Rachel Mendoza. New York, 1853.

The Beauty of Baltimore: or the Fate of the Coquette. Boston, 1845.

Belden, E. Porter. *New-York. Past, Present and Future.* New York, 1849.

Belmont, Cara. *The City Side; or, Passages from a Pastor's Portfolio.* Boston, 1854.

Benedict, Frank Lee. *Miss Van Kortland.* New York, 1870.

———. *My Daughter Elinor. A Novel.* New York, 1869.

Bennett, Emerson. *Alfred Morland; or, the Legacy.* Cincinnati, 1855.

Binder, William Earle. *Madelon Hawley, or, The Jesuit and His Victim.* New York, 1857.

———. *Viola; or, The Triumph of Love and Faith.* New York, 1858.

Bird, Robert Montgomery. *The Adventures of Robin Day.* Philadelphia, 1839.

Bolokitten, Oliver [pseud.]. *A Sojourn in the City of Amalgamation in the Year of Our Lord 19-.* New York, 1835.

Boucicault, Dion. *The Poor of New York.* New York, 1857.

[Bouton, John Bell.] *Round the Block.* New York, 1864.

[Bowen, Mrs. Sue King.] *Gerald Gray's Wife.* Augusta, Ga., 1864.

Bowline, Charley. *The Iron Tomb, or The Mock Count of New York.* Boston, 1852.

Bradbury, Osgood. *The Banker's Victim; or, The Betrayed Seamstress.* New York, 1857.

———. *The Belle of the Bowery.* Boston, 1846.

———. *Ellen Grant: or Fashionable Life in New York.* New York, 185-?.

———. *Ellen: The Pride of Broadway.* New York, 1865.

———. *Female Depravity; or, The House of Death.* New York, 1857.

———. *The Gamblers' League: or, The Trials of a Country Maid.* New York, 1857.

———. *Jane Clark; or, Scenes in Metropolitan Life.* New York, 1855.

———. *Louise Martin, The Village Maiden, or The Dangers of City Life.* Boston, 1853.

———. *Mysteries of Lowell.* Boston, 1844.

———. *The Mysterious Foundling, or, The Gamester's Fate.* New York, 1857.

———. *The Old Distiller; A Tale of Truth.* New York, 1851.

———. *The Rival Lovers, or, The Midnight Murder.* New York, 1857.

Brisbane, William Henry. *Amanda: A Tale for the Times.* Philadelphia, 1848.

Brisée. Philadelphia, 1862.

Bristed, Charles Astor. *The Upper Ten Thousand: Sketches of American Society.* New York, 1852.

Brougham, John. *Life in New York: or, Tom and Jerry on a Visit. A Comic Drama in Five Acts.* New York, 1856.

———. *The Lottery of Life. A Story of New York. An Original Local Drama in Five Acts.* New York, 1867.

―――. *The Musard Ball; or, Love at the Academy. A Contemporaneous Extravaganza in One Act.* New York, 1858.

―――. *Temptation: or, The Irish Immigrant. A Comic Drama, in Two Acts.* New York, 1856.

Browne, Junius Henri. *The Great Metropolis; a Mirror of New York.* Hartford, 1869.

Buchanan, Harrison Gray. *Asmodeus: or Legends of New York.* New York, 1848.

Buckley, Mrs. Maria L. *Amanda Willson; or the Vicissitudes of Life.* New York, 1856.

―――. *A Sketch of the Working Classes of New York.* New York, 1856.

Burdett, Charles. *Chances and Changes; or Life As It Is.* New York, 1846.

―――. *The Convict's Child.* New York, 1846.

―――. *Dora Barton: The Banker's Ward; A Tale of Real Life in New York.* New York, 1860.

―――. *The Elliott Family; or The Trials of New-York Seamstresses.* New York, 1850 [1845].

―――. *The Gambler; or the Policeman's Story.* New York, 1848.

―――. *Lilla Hart: A Tale of New York.* New York, 1846.

―――. *Never Too Late.* New York, 1845.

―――. *Three Percent a Month; or The Perils of Fast Living.* New York, 1856.

[Burnham, George Pickering.] *The Rag-Picker; or Bound and Free.* New York, 1855.

[Caffrey, Andrew.] *The Adventures of a Lodger.* Boston, 1868.

Campbell, Jane C. *The Money-Maker, and Other Tales.* New York, 1854.

[Cannon, Charles James.] *Bickerton; or, The Immigrant's Daughter.* New York, 1855.

Caroline Tracy; the Spring Street Milliner's Apprentice. New York, 1849.

Caruthers, William A. *The Kentuckian in New-York, or, The Adventures of Three Southerns. By a Virginian.* New York, 1834.

Child, Lydia Maria. *Letters from New York.* New York, 1845 [1843].

Choat, J. F. *George Welding; or, Crime and Its Consequences.* Cincinnati, 1859.

Clarke, E. G. H. [Hewes Gordon]. *Lovers and Thinkers.* New York, 1865.

Cooke, John Esten. *Ellie: or, The Human Comedy.* Richmond, 1855.

[Coolidge, Sara E.] *Ambition.* Boston, 1856.

Cooper, James Fenimore. *Home As Found.* New York, 1961 [1838].

―――. *Notions of the Americans: Picked Up By A Travelling Bachelor.* Philadelphia, 1843 [1828].

―――. *The Redskins; or, Indian and Injin.* New York, 1846.

Corcoran, D. *Pickings from the Portfolio of the Reporter of the New-Orleans "Picayune."* Philadelphia, 1846.

Cummings, Ariel Ivers. *The Factory Girl: or Gardez La Coeur.* Lowell, 1847.

Cummins, Maria Susanna. *The Lamplighter.* Boston, 1854.

―――. *Mabel Vaughan.* Boston, 1857.

[Curtis, George William.] *The Potiphar Papers.* New York, 1853.

―――. *Trumps. A Novel.* New York, 1861.

Cutler, Mrs. Lizzie. *Light and Darkness; or The Shadow of Fate.* New York, 1855.

Daly, Augustine. *Under the Gaslight: A Totally Original and Picturesque Drama of Life and Love in These Times in Five Acts.* New York, 1867.

Davis, Mrs. Rebecca. "Life in the Iron-Mills." *Atlantic Tales.* Boston, 1866.

[―――.] *Margret Howth. A Story of To-Day.* Boston, 1862.

Denison, Mrs. Mary. *Edna Etheril, The Boston Seamstress.* New York, 1847.

Dexter, Henry Martyn. *Street Thoughts.* Boston, 1859.

Dickens, Charles. *Pictures from Italy and American Notes.* London, 1850 [1842].

Dixon, Edward H. *Scenes in the Practice of a New York Surgeon.* New York, 1855.

Donaldson, John. *Jack Datchett, The Clerk: An Old Man's Tale.* Baltimore, 1846.

Drake, Benjamin. *Tales and Sketches from the Queen City.* Cincinnati, 1838.

Duganne, Augustine Joseph Hickey. *The Daguerreotype Miniature; or Life in the Empire City.* Philadelphia, 1846.

–––. *The Knights of the Seal; or the Mysteries of the Three Cities.* Philadelphia, 1846.

[–––.] *The Tenant-House or Embers from Poverty's Hearthstone.* New York, 1857.

–––. *The Two Clerks, or The Orphan's Gratitude.* Boston, 1843.

Durell, Edward Henry. *New Orleans As I Found It.* New York, 1845.

Eastman, Mrs. Mary. *Fashionable Life.* Philadelphia, 1856.

Easy Nat: or Boston Bars and Boston Boys. Boston, 1844.

Edwards, Henry. *Annie, A Story of New York Life.* New York, n.d.

–––. *The Belle of Central Park.* New York, 186–?.

–––. *The Poor of New York.* New York: Hilton and Co., 1865.

Ella Cameron or The Maid, Wife and Widow of a Day. Philadelphia, 1861.

Ellen Merton, The Belle of Lowell: or, the Confession of the "G.F.K." Club. Boston, 1844.

[Elliott, Charles Wyllys.] *Wind and Whirlwind.* New York, 1868.

Ellis, John B. *The Sights and Secrets of the National Capital.* New York, 1871 [1869].

English, William B. *Gertrude Howard, The Maid of Humble Life.* Boston, 1843.

The Factory Girl. By a Friend. Providence, 1854.

The Family of the Seisers. A Satirical Tale of the City of New-York. New York, 1844.

Fay, Theodore S. *Hoboken: A Romance of New-York.* New York, 1843.

Fisher, Sidney George. "The Diary of Sidney George Fisher 1859–1860." *Pennsylvania Magazine of History and Biography,* 87 (April 1963): 189–225.

Fitch, Anna M. *Bound Down, or Life and Its Possibilities.* Philadelphia, 1870.

Florence De Lacey; or, The Coquette: A Novel. New York, 1845.

Foster, George G. *Celio: or New York Above-Ground and Under-Ground.* New York, 1850.

–––. *Fifteen Minutes Around New York.* New York, 1853.

–––. *New York by Gas-Light; with Here and There a Streak of Sunshine.* New York, 1850.

–––. *New York in Slices; By an Experienced Carver.* New York, 1849.

–––. *New York Naked.* New York, 1850.

–––. "Philadelphia in Slices." Edited by George Rogers Taylor. *Pennsylvania Magazine of History and Biography,* 93 (January 1969): 23–72. (Originally published in the New York *Tribune* between October 21, 1848, and February 15, 1849.)

Foster, Henri. *Ellen Grafton; or the Den of Crime.* Boston, 1850.

Franklin, Augustus. *Anne Melbourne: or, The Return to Virtue.* Boston, 1846.

Gayler, Charles. *Out of the Streets, A Story of New York Life.* New York, 1869.

[Gazlay, Allen W.] *Races of Mankind; with Travels in Grubland.* Cincinnati, 1856.

Gould, Edward Sherman. *John Doe and Richard Roe; or, Episodes of Life in New York.* New York, 1862.

–––. *The Sleep-Rider; or, The Old Boy in the Omnibus.* New York, 1843.

Grayson, William J. *The Hireling and the Slave.* Charleston, S.C., 1856.

Greeley, Robert F. *Violet: The Child of the City.* New York, 1854.

Greene, Asa. *The Perils of Pearl Street. Including a Taste of the Dangers of Wall Street.* New York, 1834.

Greene, Talbot. *American Nights' Entertainments: Compiled from Pencilings of a United States Senator.* Jonesborough, Tenn., 1860.

Griscom, John H. *The Sanitary Condition of the Laboring Population of New York With Suggestions for Its Improvement.* New York, 1845.

[Griswold, V. M.] *Hugo Blanc, The Artist.* New York, 1867.

"Guilty, or Not Guilty" The True Story of Manhattan Well. New York, 1870.

Gunn, Thomas Butler. *The Physiology of New York Boarding-Houses.* New York, 1857.

Hale, Edward Everett. *If, Yes, and Perhaps. Four Possibilities and Six Exaggerations.* Boston, 1868.

———. *Sybaris and Other Homes.* Boston, 1869.

Hale, Sarah Josepha. *"Boarding Out." A Tale of Domestic Life.* New York, 1846.

Hammond, William Alexander. *Robert Severne, His Friends and His Enemies.* Philadelphia, 1867.

Hampden, Allen. *Hartley Norman. A Tale of the Times.* New York, 1859.

Hankins, Colonel. *Dakota Land; or, The Beauty of St. Paul.* New York, 1868.

Hankins, Marie Louise. *Women of New York.* New York, 1861.

Haven, Alice Emily Neal. *The Gossips of Rivertown.* Philadelphia, 1850.

———. *Loss and Gain; or Margaret's Home.* New York, 1860.

Hawthorne, Nathaniel. *The Blithedale Romance.* Boston, 1852.

———. *Mosses from an Old Manse.* Boston and New York, 1854.

Hazelton, Frank. *The Mysteries of Troy: Founded Upon the Incidents Which Have Taken Place in the City.* Troy, 1847.

Helen Leeson: or The Belle of New York. Philadelphia, 1855.

Hentz, Mrs. Caroline Lee. *The Victim of Excitement. The Bosom Serpent.* Philadelphia, 1853.

Herbert Tracy; or The Trials of Mercantile Life. New York, 1851.

Hilbourne, Mrs. Charlotte S. *Effie and I; or, Seven Years in a Cotton Mill.* Cambridge, 1863.

———. *Modern Aristocracy, or Money Worship.* Providence, 1857.

Hill, Alonzo F. *John Smith's Funny Adventures on a Crutch, or The Remarkable Peregrinations of a One-Legged Soldier after the War.* Philadelphia, 1869.

The History of the Bottle. New York, 1848.

Hone, Philip. *The Diary of Philip Hone 1828-1851.* Edited by Allan Nevins. New York, 1927.

Howe, Mary A. *The Merchant-Mechanic. A Tale of the "New England Athens."* New York, 1865.

[Howe, William Wirt.] *The Pasha Papers. Epistles of Mohammed Pasha.* New York, 1859.

Huet, M. M. *Silver and Pewter. A Tale of High and Low Life in New York.* New York, 1852.

Ingraham, Joseph Holt. *Alice May, and Bruising Bill.* Boston, 1845.

———. *The Beautiful Cigar Girl, or, the Mysteries of Broadway.* New York, 1849.

———. *Ellen Hart: or The Forger's Daughter.* Boston, 1844.

———. *Frank Rivers; or, The Dangers of the Town.* New York, 1843.

———. *Harry Harefoot; or The Three Temptations,* Boston, 1845.

———. *Herman de Ruyter; or, The Mystery Unveiled.* Boston, 1844.

———. *Jemmy Daily: or, the Little News Vendor.* Boston, 1843.

———. *The Miseries of New York, or the Burglar and Counsellor.* Boston, 1844.

———. *Paul Perril, The Merchant's Son.* Boston, 1847.

Isabella; or Filial Affection. A Tale. Boston, 1828.

Isabella Gray. A Novel. By a Lady. Philadelphia, 1858.

Jackson, Frederick. *The Victim of Chancery: or A Debtor's Experience.* New York, 1841.

———. *A Week in Wall Street. By One Who Knows It.* New York, 1841.

John Norton's Conflict. A Story of Life in New York City. Buffalo, 1866.

Johnson, Samuel D. *The Fireman, A Drama in Three Acts.* New York, 1856.

Jones, John Beauchamp. *Life and Adventures of a Country Merchant. A Narrative of His Exploits at Home, During His Travels and in the Cities.* Philadelphia, 1854.

———. *The Spanglers and Tinglers; or, The Rival Belles.* Philadelphia, 1852.
Jones, Justin. *The Belle of Boston: or, The Rival Students of Cambridge.* Boston, 1844.
———. *Big Dick, The King of the Negroes.* Boston, 1846.
———. *The Nun of St. Ursula, or, The Burning of the Convent.* Boston, 1845.
———. *Tom, Dick and Harry or the Boys and Girls of Boston.* Boston, 1849.
Joseph [pseud.]. *New-York Aristocracy; or, Gems of Japonica-Dom.* New York, 1851.
Judd, Sylvester. *Richard Edney and the Governor's Family.* Boston, 1880 [1850].
Judson, Edward Zane Carroll [Ned Buntline]. *The B'hoys of New York. A Sequel to the Mysteries and Miseries of New York.* New York, 1850.
———. *Charley Bray, or The Fireman's Mission.* New York, 1870.
———. *Ella Adams: or, The Demon of Fire.* New York, 1862.
———. *The G'hals of New York. A Novel.* New York, 1850.
———. *The Mysteries and Miseries of New Orleans.* New York, 1851.
———. *The Mysteries and Miseries of New York.* Dublin, 1849 [1848].
———. *Rose Seymour; or The Ballet Girl's Revenge.* New York, 1865.
———. *Three Years After: A Sequel to the Mysteries and Miseries of New York.* New York, 1850.
Keeler, Ralph Olmstead. *Gloverson and His Silent Partners.* Boston, 1869.
Kimball, Richard Burleigh. *Henry Powers; (Banker.) How He Achieved Fortune, and Married.* New York, 1868.
———. *To-Day: A Romance.* New York, 1869.
———. *Undercurrents of Wall-Street, A Romance of Business.* New York, 1862.
———. *Was He Successful? A Novel.* New York, 1863.
Lamas, Maria. *The Glass: or, The Trials of Helen More.* Philadelphia, 1849.
Lasselle, Mrs. Nancy Polk. *Annie Grayson; or, Life in Washington.* New York, 1853.
———. *Hope Marshall, or, Government and Its Offices.* Washington, 1859.
Lee, Day Kellogg. *The Master-Builder; or, Life at a Trade.* New York, 1852.
———. *Merrimack or Life at the Loom.* New York, 1854.
Lee, Mrs. Hannah Farnham. *Rosanna or Scenes in Boston.* Cambridge, 1839.
Life in Rochester, or Sketches from Life. New York, 1848.
Life in Town, or The Boston Spy. Boston, 1844.
Life of Paddy O'Flarrity Who From a Shoe Black Has By Perserverance and Good Conduct Arrived To A Member of Congress. 1834.
Lippard, George. *The Empire City, or New York by Day and Night.* New York, 1850.
———. *The Life of a Man of the World, or, Leaves from New York Life.* New York, 1853.
———. *Margaret Dunbar, or, Leaves from New York Life.* New York, 1853.
———. *The Midnight Queen; or, Leaves from New York Life.* New York, 1853.
———. *The Nazarene; or, The Last of the Washingtons.* Philadelphia, 1846.
———. *New York: Its Upper Ten and Lower Million.* Cincinnati, 1853.
———. *The Quaker City.* Philadelphia, 1845.
McCabe, James Dabney [pseud. Edward Winslow Martin]. *Behind the Scenes in Washington.* 1873.
———. *Lights and Shadows of New York Life; or, The Sights and Sensations of the Great City.* Philadelphia, 1872.
———. *The Secrets of the Great City.* Philadelphia, 1868.
McCorry, Peter [Con O'Leary]. *The Lost Rosary; or, Our Irish Girls.* Boston, 1870.
McCracken, J. L. H. *Earning a Living: A Comedy in Five Acts.* New York, 1849.
McDougall, Mrs. Francis Harriet Green. *The Mechanic.* Providence, 1842.
[Maitland, James A.] *The Watchman.* New York, 1855.
Martineau, Harriet. *Society in America.* London, 1837.

Mary Beach: or, The Fulton Street Cap Maker. New York, 1849.

The Masked Lady of the White House: or the Ku Klux Klan. Philadelphia, 1868.

The Match Girl; or Life Scenes As They Are. Philadelphia, 1855.

Mathews, Cornelius. *Big Abel and Little Manhattan.* New York, 1845.

———. *The Career of Puffer Hopkins.* New York, 1870 [1842].

Maxwell, Maria. *Ernest Grey; or The Sins of Society.* New York, 1855.

Medbury, James K. *Men and Mysteries of Wall Street.* Boston, 1870.

Melville, Herman. *The Complete Stories of Herman Melville.* Edited by Jay Leyda. New York, 1949.

———. *Israel Potter: His Fifty Years of Exile.* New York, 1855.

———. *Pierre, Or, The Ambiguities.* New York, 1964 [1852].

———. *Redburn. His First Voyage.* New York, 1963 [1849].

Miles, Henry Adolphus. *Lowell, As It Was, And As It Is.* Lowell, 1846.

Montaigne, Miss M. C. "The Fireman." In M. M. Ballou, *The Sea-Witch.* New York, 1855.

Moore, Horatio Newton. *Fitzgerald and Hopkins; or, Scenes and Adventures in Theatrical Life.* Philadelphia, 1847.

Morford, Henry. *The Coward. A Novel of Society and the Field in 1863.* Philadelphia, 1864.

———. *The Days of Shoddy. A Novel of the Great Rebellion in 1861.* Philadelphia, 1863.

———. *Shoulder-Straps. A Novel of New York and the Army, 1862.* Philadelphia, 1863.

Myers, P. Hamilton. *The Miser's Heir; or The Young Millionaire.* Philadelphia, 1854.

The Mysteries and Miseries of San Francisco. By a Californian. New York, 1853.

Mysteries of New York. Boston, 1845.

Mysteries of Philadelphia; or Scenes of Real Life in the Quaker City. By an Old Amateur. Philadelphia, 1848.

Neal, John C. *True Womanhood; a Tale.* Boston, 1859.

Neal, Joseph Clay. *Charcoal Sketches; or, Scenes in a Metropolis.* Philadelphia, 1838.

———. *Peter Ploddy, and Other Oddities.* Philadelphia, 1853 [1844].

Newell, Robert Henry [Orphan C. Kerr]. *Avery Glibun; or, between Two Fires.* New York, 1867.

Nichols, Thomas Low. *Ellen Ramsey; or the Adventures of a Greenhorn, in Town and Country.* New York, 1843.

Nick Bigelow: and the Female Burglar; and Other Leaves from a Lawyer's Diary. By a Member of the New York Bar. New York, 1846.

Nunes, Joseph A. *Aristocracy: or, Life Among the "Upper Ten."* Philadelphia, 1848.

Old Haun. The Pawnbroker or The Orphan's Legacy. New York, 1857.

Oran, The Outcast; or, A Season in New-York. New York, 1833.

The Orphan Seamstress, A Narrative of Innocence, Guilt, Mystery and Crime. New York, 1850.

Otis, Mrs. Eliza Henderson. *The Barclays of Boston.* Boston, 1854.

Our "First Families." A Novel of Philadelphia Good Society by a Descendant of the "Pens." Philadelphia, 1855.

Paine, Susanna. *Wait and See.* Boston, 1860.

[Palfrey, Sara Hammond.] *Agnes Wentworth.* Philadelphia, 1869.

Paulding, James Kirke. *Chronicles on the City of Gotham From the Papers of a Retired Councilman.* New York, 1830.

———. *The Merry Tales of the Three Wise Men of Gotham.* New York, 1826.

Penn, A. Sylvan. *My Three Neighbors in the Queen City.* Cincinnati, 1858.

The Pennimans; or, The Triumph of Genius. Boston, 1862.

Phelps, Mrs. Elizabeth [H. Trusta]. *A Peep at "Number Five": or, A Chapter in the Life of a City Pastor.* Boston, 1852.

———. "The Tenth of January." *Atlantic Monthly*, 21 (March 1868): 345–62.

Picton, Thomas [Paul Preston]. *The Bootmaker of the Fifth Avenue.* New York, 1866.

Poe, Edgar Allan. *Doings of Gotham.* Pottsville, Pa., 1929.

[Potter, Eliza.] *A Hairdresser's Experience in High Life.* Cincinnati, 1859.

Preuss, Henry Clay. *Fashions and Follies of Washington Life. A Play in Five Acts.* Washington, D.C., 1857.

The Price of a Glass of Brandy. By a Lady of Baltimore. Baltimore, 1841.

Prime, Samuel Irenaeus. *Life in New York.* New York, 1847.

Pugh, Mrs. Eliza Lofton. *Not A Hero. A Novel.* New York, 1867.

[Putnam, Mrs. Ellen Tryphosa Harrington.] *Where Is the City?* Boston, 1868.

Raux, Eugene. *The Road to Fortune, A New American Comedy in Five Acts.* Philadelphia, 1846.

Rees, James. *Mysteries of City Life.* Philadelphia, 1849.

Reflections and Tales. By a Lady of Philadelphia. Philadelphia, 1830.

Remington, E. F. *The City of Sin, and Its Capture by Immanuel's Army.* New York, 1857.

Revelations of Asmodeus, or Mysteries of Upper Ten-Dom. New York, 1849.

Ritchie, Anna Cora (Ogden) Mowatt. *Evelyn: or A Heart Unmasked.* Philadelphia, 1845.

———. *Fashion! or, Life in New York, A Comedy with Music in Five Acts.* New York, 1845.

———. *The Fortune Hunter: A Novel of New York Society.* Philadelphia, 1848 [1844].

Ritner, William D. *The Great Original and Entrancing Romance.* Philadelphia, 1858.

The River Pirates; A Tale of New York. New York, 1853.

Roberts, Edwin R. *The Road to Ruin; or, The Dangers of the Town.* Cincinnati, 1854.

Robinson, John Hovey. *Ella Montfield: or, The Three Disguises!!!* Boston, 1846.

Robinson, Solon. *Hot Corn: Life Scenes in New York Illustrated.* New York, 1854.

Roddan, John T. *John O'Brien; or, the Orphan of Boston.* Boston, 1850.

Roe, Azel Stevens. *Like and Unlike.* New York, 1862.

———. *Looking Around. A Novel.* New York, 1865.

———. *To Love and To Be Loved. A Story.* New York, 1851.

Rosewood, Emma. *The Virtuous Wife, or The Libertine Detected.* Boston, 1845.

Royall, Mrs. Anne. *The Tennessean; A Novel Founded on Facts.* New Haven, 1827.

[Rulison, H. M.] *The Mock Marriage; or the Libertine's Victim.* Cincinnati, 1855.

St. Clair, Frank. *Six Days in the Metropolis, or Phases of Life in Town.* Boston, 1854.

St. Clar, Robert. *The Metropolites; or Know Thy Neighbor. A Novel.* New York, 1864.

Sargeant, Lucius Manlius. *An Irish Heart. Founded on Fact.* Boston, 1836.

Savage, Sarah. *The Factory Girl. By a Lady.* Boston, 1814.

Schemil, Peter [pseud.]. "Lights and Shadows of Fashionable Life." *The Knickerbocker*, 27 (February 1846): 128–38.

Scoville, Joseph Alfred. *Clarence Bolton: A New York Story with City Society in all Its Phases.* New York, 1852.

Sealsfield, Charles. *Rambleton; A Romance of Fashionable Life in New-York during the Great Speculation of 1836.* New York, 1846 [1844].

Sedgwick, Catharine Maria. *Home Scenes and Characters Illustrating Christian Truth.* Boston and Cambridge, 1832.

———. *Married or Single?* New York, 1858.

———. *The Poor Rich Man and The Rich Poor Man.* New York, 1864.

———. *Tales of City Life.* Philadelphia, 1850.

[Seemueller, Mrs. Anne Moncure]. *Emily Chester, A Novel.* Boston, 1864.

Shepard, Isaac Fitzgerald. *Scenes and Songs of Social Life. A Miscellany.* Boston, 1846.

Shortfellow, Tom [pseud.]. *Annie, the Orphan Girl of St. Mary; or, the Golden Marriage.* Boston, 1846.

[Shubrick, Mrs. Harriet Cordelia.] *Violet; or, The Times We Live In.* Philadelphia, 1858.

Sikes, William Wirt. *One Poor Girl: The Story of Thousands.* Philadelphia, 1869.

Simms, William Gilmore. *Marie de Bernière: A Tale of the Crescent City.* Philadelphia, 1853.

———. *The Prima Donna; A Passage from City Life.* Philadelphia, 1844.

Skinner, P. H. *The Little Ragged Ten Thousand.* New York, 1853.

Sly, Costard [pseud.]. *Sayings and Doings at the Tremont House. In the Year 1832.*

[Smith, Mrs. Elizabeth Oakes.] *The Newsboy.* New York, 1854.

Smith, I. Anderson. *Blanche Vernon, The Actress. A Romance of the Metropolis.* New York, 1846.

Smith, Mrs. Margaret. *What Is Gentility? A Moral Tale.* Washington, D.C., 1828.

———. *A Winter in Washington; or, Memoirs of the Seymour Family.* New York, 1824.

Smith, Matthew Hale. *Sunshine and Shadow in New York.* Hartford, 1868.

Smith, Seba [Major Jack Downing]. *May-Day in New-York: or House-Hunting and Moving.* New York, 1845.

———. *My Thirty Years Out of the Senate.* New York, 1859 [1830].

Smith, Mrs. Thomas P. "Fashion." In Mrs. M. G. Clarke, *Sunshine and Shadow Along the Pathway of Life.* Chicago, 1865.

[Smith, William Russell.] *As It Is.* Albany, 1860.

Soule, Mrs. Caroline Augusta. "The Poor Washerwoman." In J. V. Watson, *Tales and Takings.* New York, 1857.

Spofford, Harry. *The Mysteries of Worcester.* Worcester, 1846.

Squints Through An Opera Glass By a Young Gent. Who Hadn't Any Thing Else To Do. New York, 1850.

The Startling Confessions of Eleanor Burton; A Thrilling Tragedy from Real Life. Philadelphia, 1852.

Stephens, Mrs. Ann Sophia. *Fashion and Famine.* New York, 1854.

———. *High Life in New York.* New York, 1843.

———. *The Old Homestead.* New York, 1855.

Stimson, Alexander Lovett. *Easy Nat; or, The Three Apprentices.* New York, 1854.

Strong, George Templeton. *The Diary of George Templeton Strong.* Edited by Allan Nevins and Milton Halsey Thomas. New York, 1952.

Stryker, Peter. *The Lower Depths of the Great American Metropolis.* New York, 1866.

Summerton, Winter [pseud.]. *Will He Find Her? A Romance of New York and New Orleans.* New York, 1860.

[Swan, Charles Red.] *Minny Lawson: or, The Outlaws League.* New York, 185–?.

[Talcott, Mrs. Hannah Elizabeth Goodwin.] *Madge; or, Night and Morning.* New York, 1863.

Tartan [pseud.]. *Philadelphia Malignants.* Philadelphia, 1863.

Taylor, Bayard. *John Godfrey's Fortunes. Related by Himself.* New York, 1864.

Thompson, George. *The Brazen Star: or the Adventures of a New-York M.P.* New York, 1853.

———. *City Crimes; or, Life in New York and Boston.* Boston, 1849.

———. *The Gay Girls of New-York: or, Life on Broadway.* New York, 1854.

———. *Harry Glindon: or, The Man of Many Crimes.* New York, 1851.

——— [William Darlington]. *Life and Exploits of "Bristol Bill," the Notorious Burglar.* New York, 1851.

———. *The Locket; A Romance of New York.* New York, 1855.

———. *Mysteries and Miseries of Philadelphia.* New York, 185-?.

———. *The Outlaw; or The Felon's Fortunes. By Greenhorn.* New York, 186-? [1851].

———. *Venus in Boston: A Romance of City Life. By Greenhorn.* New York, 1849.

Thoreau, Henry David. *Walden and Other Writings of Henry David Thoreau.* Edited by Brooks Atkinson. New York, 1950.

The Three Golden Balls, or, The Diary of a Pawnbroker. New York, 1849.

The Three Widows; or The Various Aspects of Life in Gotham. By A Member of the New York Bar. New York, 1849.

Torrey, Mrs. Mary. *City and Country Life; or Moderate Better Than Rapid Gains.* Boston, 1853.

Townley, Arthur. *Clifton; or, Modern Fashion, Politics, and Morals. A Novel.* Philadelphia, 1852.

Townsend, Mrs. Mary Ashley [Xariffa]. *The Brother Clerks; A Tale of New Orleans.* New York, 1857.

Trollope, Mrs. Frances. *Domestic Manners of the Americans.* London, 1832.

Tuel, John E. *St. Clair, or The Protegé; A Tale of the Federal City.* New York, 1846.

Tyler, Mrs. Martha W. *A Book Without a Title.* Boston, 1855.

The Victims of Gaming; Being Extracts from the Diary of An American Physician. Boston, 1838.

Victor, Metta V. Fuller. *Fashionable Dissipation.* Philadelphia, 1854.

Vose, John Denison. *Fresh Leaves from the Diary of a Broadway Dandy.* New York, 1852.

———. *Seven Nights in Gotham.* New York, 1852.

Walworth, Mansfield, Tracy. *Lulu. A Tale of National Hotel Poisoning.* New York, 1863.

Watterson, George. *Wanderer in Washington.* Washington, D.C., 1827.

Webb, Charles Henry. *The Wickedest Woman in New York.* New York, 1868.

Wharton, George M. [Stahl]. *The New Orleans Sketch Book.* Philadelphia, 1853.

[White, Mrs. Rhoda Elizabeth.] *Mary Staunton; or the Pupils of Marvel Hall.* New York, 1860.

Whitman, Walt. *Leaves of Grass.* New York, 1950 [1855].

Whitmore, Walter. *Ella Winston; or, The Adventures of an Orphan Girl. A Romance of Cincinnati.* Cincinnati, 1850.

Wilkes, J. Wimpleton. *The Mysteries of Springfield: A Tale of the Times.* Springfield, 1844.

Williams, Catherine Read. *Annals of the Aristocracy.* Providence, 1845.

———. *Aristocracy, or The Holbey Family: A National Tale.* Providence, 1832.

[Williams, Henry Llewellyn.] *Gay Life in New York: or, Fast Men and War Widows.* New York, 1866.

———. *The Steel Safe. The Stains and Splendors of New York Life.* New York, 1868.

Wilmer, Lambert A. *The Confessions of Emilia Harrington.* Baltimore, 1835.

Wilson, Thomas L. V. *The Aristocracy of Boston.* Boston, 1848.

Woods, Caroline H. [Belle Otis]. *The Diary of a Milliner.* New York, 1867.

Wright, Mrs. Julia. *The Corner Stall: A New York Story.* Boston, 1868.

———. *Our Chatham Street Uncle; or, The Three Golden Balls.* Boston, 1869.

Young, Samuel. *The Smoky City. A Tale of Crime.* Pittsburgh, 1845.

SECONDARY SOURCES: Books and Magazine Articles

Abbott, Edith. *Women in Industry. A Study in American Economic History.* D. Appleton and Co., 1913.

Abell, Aaron I. "The Catholic Factor in Urban Welfare: The Early Period, 1850–1880." *The Review of Politics,* 14 (1952): 289–324.

Albion, Robert Greenhalgh. *The Rise of New York Port, 1815–1860.* Charles Scribner's Sons, 1939.

Albrecht, Milton C. "The Relationship of Literature and Society." *American Journal of Sociology,* 59 (March 1954): 425–36.

Anderson, Nels. "The Urban Way of Life." *International Journal of Comparative Sociology,* 3 (December 1962): 175–88.

Arden, Eugene. "The Evil City in American Fiction." *New York History,* 35 (July 1954): 259–79.

Asbury, Herbert. *All Around the Town.* Alfred A. Knopf, 1934.

———. *The Gangs of New York.* Garden City Publishing Co., 1927.

Ashbee, Herbert Spencer. *Catena Liborum Tacendorum.* London, 1885.

Austin, James C. and Koch, Donald A., eds. *Popular Literature in America.* Bowling Green University Press, 1972.

Baldwin, Leland D. *Pittsburgh: The Story of a City.* University of Pittsburgh Press, 1937.

Baltzell, E. Digby. *Philadelphia Gentlemen: The Making of a National Upper Class.* The Free Press, 1958.

Barclay, Morgan J. "Images of Toledo's German Community 1850–1890." *Northwest Ohio Quarterly,* 45 (fall 1973): 133–43.

Bender, Thomas. "James Fenimore Cooper and the City." *New York History,* 51 (April 1970): 287–305.

———. *Toward an Urban Vision: Ideas and Institutions in Nineteenth-Century America.* The University Press of Kentucky, 1975.

Berger, Max. "British Impressions of New York a Century Ago." *New York History,* 27 (1946): 141–53.

Billington, Ray Allen. *The Protestant Crusade 1800–1860: A Study of the Origins of American Nativism.* Quadrangle Books, 1964.

Binder, Frederick Moore. "Gas Light." *Pennsylvania History,* 22 (October 1955): 359–73.

Blake, Fay M. *The Strike in the American Novel.* The Scarecrow Press, 1972.

Blake, Nelson Manfred. *Water for the Cities. A History of the Urban Water Supply Problem in the United States.* Syracuse University Press, 1956.

Blayney, Glenn H. "City Life in the American Drama, 1825–1860." *Studies in Honor of John Wilcox.* Edited by A. Dayle Wallace and Woodburn O. Ross. Wayne State University, 1958.

Boas, George, ed. *Romanticism in America.* Johns Hopkins Press, 1940.

Bode, Carl. *The Anatomy of American Popular Culture, 1840–1861.* University of California Press, 1959.

Boorstin, Daniel J. *The Americans. The National Experience.* Vintage Books, 1967.

———. *The Image; or, What Happened to the American Dream.* Atheneum, 1962.

Boulding, Kenneth E. *The Images.* University of Michigan Press, 1956.

Boynton, Henry Walcott. *Annals of American Bookselling 1638–1850.* John Wiley and Sons, 1932.

Branch, E. Douglas. *The Sentimental Years, 1836–60.* D. Appleton-Century Co., 1934.

Bremner, Robert H. *From the Depths: The Discovery of Poverty in the United States.* New York University Press, 1967.

Brown, Herbert Ross. *The Sentimental Novel in America 1789–1860.* Duke University Press, 1940.

Browne, Ray B., et al, editors. *Frontiers of American Culture*. Purdue University Studies, 1968.

Browne, Ray B., ed. *Popular Culture and the Expanding Consciousness*. John Wiley and Sons, 1973.

Brownell, Blaine A. "The Agrarian and Urban Ideals." *Journal of Popular Culture*, winter 1971, pp. 576-85.

Callow, Alexander B., Jr. *American Urban History: An Interpretive Reader with Commentaries*. Oxford University Press, 1969.

———. *The Tweed Ring*. Oxford University Press, 1966.

Carman, Harry J., and Luthin, Reinhard H. "Some Aspects of the Know-Nothing Movement Reconsidered." *South Atlantic Quarterly*, 39 (April 1940): 213-34.

Cawelti, John G. *Adventure, Mystery, and Romance*. University of Chicago Press, 1976.

———. *Apostles of the Self-Made Man*. University of Chicago Press, 1965.

———. "The Concept of Formula in the Study of Popular Literature." *Journal of Popular Culture*, 3 (winter 1969): 381-90.

———. "Myth, Symbol, and Formula." *Journal of Popular Culture*, 8 (summer 1974): 1-9.

———. "Notes toward an Aesthetic of Popular Culture." *Journal of Popular Culture*, 5 (fall 1971): 255-68.

Charvat, William. *Literary Publishing in America 1790-1850*. University of Pennsylvania Press, 1959.

Churchill, Allen. *The Upper Crust. An Informal History of New York's Highest Society*. Prentice-Hall, 1970.

Commons, John R., and Associates. *History of Labour in the United States*. The Macmillan Co., 1918.

Coolidge, John. *Mill and Mansion. A Study of Architecture and Society in Lowell, Massachusetts 1820-1865*. Columbia University Press, 1942.

Costello, Augustine E. *Our Firemen. A History of the New York Fire Department*. Augustine E. Costello, 1887.

Cowie, Alexander. *The Rise of the American Novel*. American Co., 1948.

Cross, Robert D. "The Changing Image of the City among American Catholics." *The Catholic Historical Review*, 48 (April 1962): 33-52.

Dalziel, Margaret. *Popular Fiction One Hundred Years Ago: An Unexplored Tract of Literary History*. Dufour Editions, 1958.

Davis, David Brion. *Homicide in American Fiction, 1798-1860: A Study in Social Values*. Cornell University Press, 1957.

Derby, James C. *Fifty Years among Authors, Books and Publishers*. G. W. Carleton and Co., 1885.

Donaldson, Scott. "City and Country: Marriage Proposals." In James T. Richardson, ed., *The American City. Historical Studies*. Xerox College Publishing, 1972.

Dublin, Thomas. *Women at Work. The Transformation of Work and Community in Lowell, Massachusetts, 1826-1860*. Columbia University Press, 1979.

Duffy, John. *A History of Public Health in New York City, 1625-1866*. Russell Sage Foundation, 1968.

———. *Sword of Pestilence. The New Orleans Yellow Fever Epidemic of 1853*. Louisiana State University Press, 1966.

Dulles, Foster Rhea. *Labor in America. A History*. Thomas Y. Crowell Co., 1963.

Duncan, Beverly; Sabagh, George; and Van Arsdol, Maurice D., Jr. "Patterns of City Growth." *The American Journal of Sociology*, 47 (January 1962): 418-29.

Dunlap, George Arthur. *The City in the American Novel, 1789-1900*. Russell and Russell, Inc., 1965.

Dyos, H. J. and Wolff, Michael, eds. *The Victorian City: Images and Realities*. Routledge and Kegan Paul, 1973.

Eco, Umberto. "Rhetoric and Ideology in Sue's *Les Mystères de Paris.*" *International Social Science Journal,* 19 (1967): 351-69.

Eliade, Mircea. *The Myth of the Eternal Return.* Pantheon Books, 1954.

Ernst, Robert. *Immigrant Life in New York City, 1825-1863.* Kings Crown Press, 1949.

Exman, Eugene. *The Brothers Harper: A Unique Publishing Partnership and Its Impact upon the Cultural Life of America from 1817 to 1853.* Harper and Row, 1965.

Farley, Reynolds. "The Urbanization of Negroes in the United States." *Journal of Social History,* 1 (spring 1968): 241-58.

Fiedler, Leslie A. *Love and Death in the American Novel.* The World Publishing Co., 1962.

Flory, Claude Reherd. *Economic Criticism in American Fiction, 1792 to 1900.* University of Pennsylvania, 1936.

Foner, Eric. *Free Soil, Free Labor, Free Men; The Ideology of the Republican Party before the Civil War.* Oxford University Press, 1970.

Foner, Philip S. *History of the Labor Movement in the United States from Colonial Times to the Founding of the American Federation of Labor.* International Publishers, 1947.

Ford, George H. *Dickens and His Readers. Aspects of Novel-Criticism Since 1836.* Princeton University Press, 1955.

French, Stanley. "The Cemetery As Cultural Institution. The Establishment of Mt. Auburn and the 'Rural Cemetery' Movement." *American Quarterly,* 26 (March 1974): 37-59.

French, Warren Graham. "A Sketch of the Life of Joseph Holt Ingraham." *The Journal of Mississippi History,* 11 (July 1949): 155-71.

Fried, Marc. "Grieving for a Lost Home." *The Urban Condition: People and Policy in the Metropolis.* Edited by Leonard J. Duhl. Basic Books, 1963.

Friedman, Lawrence M. *Government and Slum Housing. A Century of Frustration.* Rand McNally and Co., 1968.

Gelfant, Blanche Housman. *The American City Novel.* University of Oklahoma Press, 1954.

Gilchrist, David T. *The Growth of the Seaport Cities 1790-1825.* The University Press of Virginia, 1967.

Ginger, Ray. "Labor in a Massachusetts Cotton Mill, 1853-60." *The Business History Review,* 28 (March 1954): 67-91.

Ginsberg, Stephen F. "Above the Law: Volunteer Firemen in New York City, 1836-1837." *New York History,* 50 (April 1969): 165-86.

―――. "The Police and Fire Protection in New York City: 1800-1850." *New York History,* 52 (April 1971): 133-50.

Glaab, Charles N. "The Historian and the American Urban Tradition." *Wisconsin Magazine of History,* 57 (autumn 1963): 12-25.

―――, and Brown, A. Theodore. *A History of Urban America.* The Macmillan Co., 1967.

Goldstein, Israel. *A Century of Judaism in New York.* Congregation B'nai Jeshurun, 1930.

Goodman, Paul. "Ethics and Enterprise: The Values of a Boston Elite, 1800-1860." *American Quarterly,* 18 (fall 1966): 437-51.

Green, Constance McLaughlin. *The Rise of Urban America.* Harper and Row, 1965.

―――. *Washington: Village and Capital, 1800-1878.* Princeton University Press, 1962.

Griffen, Clyde. "Making It in America: Social Mobility in Mid-Nineteenth Century Poughkeepsie." *New York History,* 51 (October 1970): 478-99.

Griffin, Clifford S. *Their Brothers' Keepers: Moral Stewardship in the United States, 1800-1865.* Rutgers University Press, 1960.

———. "Religious Benevolence as Social Control 1815-1860." *Mississippi Valley Historical Review*, 44 (December 1957): 423-44.

Grinstein, Hyman B. *The Rise of the Jewish Community of New York 1654-1860.* The Jewish Publication Society of America, 1945.

Guérard, Albert. *Literature and Society.* Lethrop, Lee and Shepard Co., 1935.

Gutman, Herbert G. "Workers' Search for Power, Labor in the Gilded Age." In H. Wayne Morgan, ed., *The Gilded Age, A Reappraisal.* Syracuse University Press, 1963.

Hall, Stuart and Whannel, Paddy. *The Popular Arts.* Pantheon Books, 1965.

Handlin, Oscar. *Boston's Immigrants: A Study in Acculturation.* The Belknap Press of Harvard University, 1959.

Handlin, Oscar and Burchard, John, eds. *The Historian and the American City.* The M.I.T. Press, 1966.

Hansen, Marcus Lee. *The Atlantic Migration 1607-1860.* Harper and Row, 1940.

Hart, James D. *The Popular Book: A History of America's Literary Taste.* Oxford University Press, 1950.

Hawes, Joseph M. *Children in Urban Society: Juvenile Delinquency in Nineteenth-Century America.* Oxford University Press, 1971.

Higham, John. "Another Look at Nativism." *Catholic Historical Review*, 44 (April 1958-January 1959): 147-58.

———. *Strangers in the Land: Patterns of American Nativism 1860-1925.* Rutgers University Press, 1955.

Hofstadter, Beatrice K. "Popular Culture and the Romantic Heroine." *American Scholar*, (winter 1960-61), pp. 98-116.

Holbrook, Stewart H. "Life and Times of Ned Buntline." *The American Mercury*, 44 (May 1947): 599-605.

Holsti, Ole R. *Content Analysis for the Social Sciences and Humanities.* Addison-Wesley Publishing Co., 1969.

Hoover, Dwight. "The Diverging Paths of American Urban History." *American Quarterly*, 20 (summer supplement 1968): 296-317.

Howe, Irving. "The City in Literature." *Commentary*, 51 (May 1971): 61-68.

———. "Notes on Mass Culture." *Politics*, (spring 1948), pp. 120-23.

Hughes, Glenn. *A History of the American Theatre, 1700-1950.* Samuel French, 1951.

Hugins, Walter. *Jacksonian Democracy and the Working Class: A Study of the New York Workingmen's Movement 1829-1839.* Stanford University Press, 1960.

Jackson, Kenneth T. and Schultz, Stanley K. *Cities in American History.* Alfred A. Knopf, 1972.

Jacobs, Norman. *Culture for the Millions? Mass Media in Modern Society.* D. Van Nostrand Co., 1959.

James, Louis. *Fiction for the Working Man 1830-1850: A Study of the Literature Produced for the Working Classes in Early Victorian Urban England.* Oxford University Press, 1963.

Jones, Howard Mumford. *Ideas in America.* Harvard University Press, 1944.

Jones, Maldwyn Allen. *American Immigration.* University of Chicago Press, 1960.

Josephson, Hannah. *The Golden Threads: New England's Mill Girls and Magnates.* Duell, Sloan and Pearce, 1949.

Kaser, David. *Messrs. Carey and Lea of Philadelphia: A Study in the History of the Booktrade.* University of Pennsylvania Press, 1957.

Kaul, A. N. *The American Vision: Actual and Ideal Society in Nineteenth-Century Fiction.* Yale University Press, 1963.

Keating, Peter J. *The Working Classes in Victorian Fiction.* Barnes and Noble, 1971.

Kelly, A. Gordon. "Literature and the Historian." *American Quarterly*, 26 (May 1974): 141-59.

Kennedy, Charles J. "Commuter Services in the Boston Area, 1835–1860." *Business History Review*, 36 (summer 1962): 153–70.

Kennedy, Julia. *George Watterson, Novelist, "Metropolitan Author" and Critic.* Catholic University Press of America, 1933.

Kern, Alexander. "The Sociology of Knowledge in the Study of Literature." *Sewanee Review*, 51 (October–December 1942): 505–14.

King, Doris Elizabeth. "The First-Class Hotel and the Age of the Common Man." *The Journal of Southern History*, 23 (May 1957): 173–88.

Kissane, James. "Imagery, Myth, and Melville's Pierre." *American Literature*, 26 (January 1955): 564–72.

Klebaner, Benjamin J. "Poverty and Its Relief in American Thought, 1815–61." *The Social Service Review*, 38 (December 1964): 382–99.

Klein, Alexander. *The Empire City: A Treasury of New York.* Rinehart and Co., 1955.

Knights, Peter R. *The Plain People of Boston, 1830–1860: A Study in City Growth.* Oxford University Press, 1971.

Kramer, Paul and Holborn, Frederick L., eds. *The City in American Life: A Historical Anthology.* G. P. Putnam's Sons, 1970.

Kuklick, Bruce. "Myth and Symbol in American Studies." *American Quarterly*, 24 (October 1972): 435–50.

Kwiat, Joseph J., and Turpie, Mary C., eds. *Studies in American Culture: Dominant Ideas and Images.* University of Minnesota Press, 1960.

Lane, Roger. *Policing the City: Boston 1822–1885.* Harvard University Press, 1967.

Larsen, Lawrence H. "Nineteenth-Century Street Sanitation: A Story in Filth and Frustration." *Wisconsin Magazine of History*, 52 (spring 1969): 239–47.

Laurenson, Diana T., and Swingewood, Alan. *The Sociology of Literature.* Schocken Books, 1972.

Lehmann-Haupt, Hellmut. *The Book in America.* R. R. Bowker Co., 1939.

Leonard, Ira M., and Parmet, Robert D. *American Nativism, 1830–1860.* Van Nostrand Reinhold Co., 1971.

Lesser, Simon O. *Fiction and the Unconscious.* Vintage Books, 1962.

Lewis, R. W. B. *The American Adam: Innocence, Tragedy and Tradition in the Nineteenth Century.* University of Chicago Press, 1955.

Limpus, Lowell M. *History of the New York Fire Department.* E. P. Dutton and Co., 1940.

Lingelbach, William E., ed. *Approaches to American Social History.* D. Appleton-Century Co., 1937.

Lipset, Seymour Martin, and Bendix, Richard. *Social Mobility in Industrial Society.* University of California Press, 1959.

Litwack, Leon F. *North of Slavery: The Negro in the Free States, 1790–1860.* The University of Chicago Press, 1961.

Lockwood, Charles. "The Bond Street Area." *The New-York Historical Society Quarterly*, 56 (October 1972): 309–20.

Lowenthal, Lee. *Literature, Popular Culture, and Society.* Prentice-Hall, Inc., 1961.

Lubove, Roy. "The New York Association for Improving the Condition of the Poor: The Formative Years." *The New-York Historical Society Quarterly*, 43 (July 1959): 307–27.

Lynch, Kevin. *The Image of the City.* The M.I.T. Press, 1960.

McKelvey, Blake. *American Urbanization: A Comparative History.* Scott, Foresman and Co., 1973.

———. *The City in American History.* George Allen and Unwin, 1969.

———. *The Urbanization of America, 1860–1915.* Rutgers University Press, 1963.

Madison, Charles A. *Book Publishing in America.* McGraw-Hill Book Co., 1966.

Mandelbaum, Seymour J. *Boss Tweed's New York.* John Wiley and Sons, 1965.

Markun, Leo. *Mrs. Grundy: A History of Four Centuries of Morals . . .* D. Appleton and Co., 1930.

Marraro, Howard R. "Italians in New York during the First Half of the Nineteenth Century." *New York History,* 26 (July 1945): 278-306.

Martin, Terrence. "Social Institutions in the Early American Novel." *American Quarterly,* (spring 1957): 72-84.

Marx, Leo. *The Machine in the Garden: Technology and the Pastoral Ideal in America.* Oxford University Press, 1964.

Matthiessen, F. O. *American Renaissance: Art and Expression in the Age of Emerson and Whitman.* Oxford University Press, 1941.

Maurice, Arthur Bartlett. *New York in Fiction.* Dodd, Mead and Co., 1899.

Meier, Richard L. *A Communications Theory of Urban Growth.* The M.I.T. Press, 1962.

Mellard, James M. "Racism, Formula, and Popular Fiction." *Journal of Popular Culture,* 5 (summer 1971): 10-37.

Mendelsohn, Harold. *Mass Entertainment.* Yale University Press, 1966.

Messbarger, Paul R. *Fiction with a Parochial Purpose: Social Uses of American Catholic Literature 1884-1900.* Boston University Press, 1971.

Meyers, Marvin. "The Jacksonian Persuasion." *American Quarterly,* 5 (spring 1953): 3-15.

Miller, Douglas T. "Immigration and Social Stratification in Pre-Civil War New York." *New York History,* 49 (April 1968): 157-68.

———. *Jacksonian Aristocracy: Class and Democracy in New York 1830-1860.* Oxford University Press, 1967.

Miller, Zane L. *The Urbanization of Modern America: A Brief History.* Harcourt Brace Jovanovich, Inc., 1973.

Mohl, Raymond A. "Poverty, Pauperism, and Social Order in the Preindustrial American City, 1780-1840." *Social Science Quarterly,* 52 (March, 1972): 934-48.

———, and Richardson, James F. *The Urban Experience: Themes in American History.* Wadsworth Publishing Co., 1973.

Monaghan, Jay. *The Great Rascal: The Life and Adventures of Ned Buntline.* Little, Brown and Co., 1952.

Moncada, Francesco. "The Little Italy of 1850." *Atlantica,* (January 1933): 160-62.

Montgomery, David. *Beyond Equality: Labor and the Radical Republicans 1862-1872.* Alfred A. Knopf, 1967.

———. "The Working Classes of the Pre-Industrial American City, 1780-1830." *Labor History,* 9 (winter 1968): 3-22.

Moody, Richard. *The Astor Place Riot.* Indiana University Press, 1958.

Moorman, Charles. "Melville's Pierre in the City." *American Literature,* 27 (1956): 571-77.

———. "Melville's Pierre and the Fortunate Fall." *American Literature,* 25 (March 1953): 13-30.

Morris, John V. *Fires and Firefighters.* Little, Brown and Co., 1953.

Morris, Lloyd. *Incredible New York: High Life and Low Life of the Last Hundred Years.* Random House, 1951.

Mott, Frank Luther. *Golden Multitudes: The Story of Best Sellers in the United States.* The Macmillan Co., 1947.

Myers, Andrew B., ed. *The Knickerbocker Tradition: Washington Irving's New York.* Sleepy Hollow Restorations, 1974.

Myers, Gustavus. *History of Bigotry in the United States.* Random House, 1943.

———. *The History of Tammany Hall.* Burt Franklin, 1917.

Noel, Mary. *Villains Galore: The Heyday of the Popular Story Weekly.* The Macmillan Co., 1954.

North, Douglass C. *Growth and Welfare in the American Past: A New Economic History.* Prentice-Hall, 1966.

Nye, Russel Blaine. "Notes for an Introduction to a Discussion of Popular Culture." *Journal of Popular Culture,* 4 (spring 1971): 31–38.

———. *Society and Culture in America 1830–1860.* Harper and Row, 1974.

———. *The Unembarrassed Muse: The Popular Arts in America.* The Dial Press, 1970.

Oberholtzer, Ellis Paxson. *The Literary History of Philadelphia.* George W. Jacobs and Co., 1906.

O'Connor, William Van. "The Novel As a Social Document." *American Quarterly,* 4 (1952): 169–75.

Papashvily, Helen Waite. *All the Happy Endings.* Harper and Row, 1956.

Park, Robert. *The City.* University of Chicago Press, 1925.

Pattee, Fred Lewis. *The Feminine Fifties.* D. Appleton-Century Co., 1940.

Pearson, Edmund. *Dime Novels; or, Following an Old Trail in Popular Literature.* Little, Brown and Co., 1929.

Pessen, Edward. "The Egalitarian Myth and the American Social Reality: Wealth, Mobility, and Equality in the 'Era of the Common Man.'" *American Historical Review,* 76 (October 1971): 989–1034.

———. *Jacksonian America. Society, Personality, and Politics.* The Dorsey Press, 1969.

———. *Riches, Class, and Power before the Civil War.* D. C. Heath and Co., 1973.

———. "The Workingmen's Movement of the Jacksonian Era." *Mississippi Valley Historical Review,* 43 (December 1956): 428–43.

Pickett, Robert S. *House of Refuge. Origins of Juvenile Reform in New York State, 1815–1857.* Syracuse University Press, 1969.

Pope, Jesse Eliphalet. *The Clothing Industry in New York.* University of Missouri Press, 1905.

Pred, Allan. "Manufacturing in the American Mercantile City, 1800–1840." *Annals of the American Association of Geographers,* 56 (June 1966): 307–25.

Quinn, Arthur Hobson. *A History of the American Drama: From the Beginning to the Civil War.* F. S. Crofts and Co., 1946.

Raleigh, John Henry. "The Novel and the City: England and America in the Nineteenth Century." *Victorian Studies,* 11 (1967/68): 291–328.

Rayback, Joseph G. *A History of American Labor.* The Free Press, 1966.

Ressequie, Harry E. "A. T. Stewart's Marble Palace—The Cradle of the Department Store." *The New-York Historical Society Quarterly,* 48 (April 1964): 131–62.

Reynolds, Quentin. *The Fiction Factory; or, From Pulp Row to Quality Street.* Random House, 1955.

Richardson, James F. *The New York Police: Colonial Times to 1901.* Oxford University Press, 1970.

———. "The Struggle To Establish a London-Style Police Force for New York City." *New-York Historical Society Quarterly,* 49 (April 1965): 175–97.

Ridgway, Whitman. "Measuring Wealth in Ante-Bellum America: A Review Essay." *Historical Methods Newsletter,* 8 (March 1975): 74–78.

Riegel, Robert E. *Young America 1830–1840.* University of Oklahoma Press, 1949.

Rosenberg, Bernard, and White, David Manning. *Mass Culture: The Popular Arts in America.* The Free Press, 1954.

Rosenberg, Carroll Smith. *Religion and the Rise of the American City: The New York City Mission Movement 1812–1870.* Cornell University Press, 1971.

Rosenberg, Charles E. *The Cholera Years: The United States in 1832, 1849, and 1866.* The University of Chicago Press, 1962.

Rossman, Kenneth R. "The Irish in American Drama in the Mid-Nineteenth Century." *New York History,* 21 (January 1940): 39–53.

Rothman, David J. *The Discovery of the Asylum: Social Order and Disorder in the New Republic.* Little, Brown and Co., 1971.

Schlesinger, Arthur M. *Learning How To Behave: A Historical Study of American Etiquette Books.* The Macmillan Co., 1946.

———. *The Rise of the City 1878-1898.* The Macmillan Co., 1933.

———. "Social History in American Literature." *Yale Review,* 18 (autumn 1928): 135–47.

Schmitt, Peter J. *Back to Nature: The Arcadian Myth in Urban America.* Oxford University Press, 1969.

Schneider, David M. *The History of Public Welfare in New York State 1609-1866.* University of Chicago Press, 1938.

Schneider, Robert W. *Five Novelists of the Progressive Era.* Columbia University Press, 1965.

Schultz, Stanley K. *The Culture Factory: Boston Public Schools 1789-1860.* Oxford University Press, 1973.

Shove, Raymond Howard. *Cheap Book Production in the United States 1870 to 1891.* University of Illinois Library, 1937.

Shryock, Richard Harrison. *Medicine and Society in America 1660-1860.* New York University Press, 1960.

———. "Public Relations of the Medical Profession in Great Britain and the United States, 1600-1870." *Annals of Medical History,* 2 (1930): 308–39.

Smith, Timothy L. *Revivalism and Social Reform in Mid-Nineteenth-Century America.* Abingdon Press, 1957.

Smuts, Robert W. *Women and Work in America.* Columbia University Press, 1959.

Spearman, Diana. *The Novel and Society.* Routledge and Kegan Paul, 1966.

Spiller, Robert E. *Literary History of the United States.* The Macmillan Co., 1948.

Stern, Madeleine B. "Dick and Fitzgerald, The Troupers of Ann Street." *Publishers' Weekly,* 150 (November 23, 1946), 2919-2925.

———. "G. W. Carleton: His Mark." *Publishers' Weekly,* 150 (August 17, 1946): 710-15.

Still, Bayrd. *Mirror for Gotham: New York As Seen by Contemporaries from Dutch Days to the Present.* New York University Press, 1956.

———. *Urban America.* Little, Brown and Co., 1974.

Stout, Janis. *Sodoms in Eden: The City in American Fiction before 1860.* Greenwood Press, 1976.

Strauss, Anselm L. *Images of the American Cities.* The Free Press of Glencoe, 1961.

Sykes, Richard E. "American Studies and the Concept of Culture: A Theory and Method." *American Quarterly,* 15 (summer supplement 1963): 253-70.

Taylor, George Rogers. "American Urban Growth Preceding the Railway Age." *Journal of Economic History,* 27 (September 1967): 309-39.

———. "The Beginnings of Mass Transportation in Urban America." *Smithsonian Journal of History,* 1 (summer and autumn 1966): 31-52.

———. *The Transportation Revolution, 1815-1860.* Rinehart, 1951.

Taylor, Walter Fuller. *The Economic Novel in America.* University of North Carolina Press, 1942.

Thernstrom, Stephan, and Knights, Peter R. "Men in Motion: Some Data and Speculations about Urban Population Mobility in Nineteenth-Century America." *Journal of Interdisciplinary History,* 1 (autumn 1970): 17-35.

Thernstrom, Stephan, and Sennett, Richard, eds. *Nineteenth-Century Cities: Essays in the New Urban History.* Yale University Press, 1969.

Thernstrom, Stephan. "Notes on the Historical Study of Social Mobility." *Comparative Studies in Society and History,* 10 (January 1968), 162–72.

———. "Reflections on the New Urban History." *Historical Studies Today.* Edited by Felix Gilbert and Stephen R. Graubard. W. W. Norton and Co., 1972.

Trachtenberg, Alan. "The American Scene: Versions of the City." *Massachusetts Review,* (spring 1967): 281-95.

Tryson, W. S. "Book Distribution in Mid-Nineteenth-Century America: Illustrated by the Publishing Records of Ticknor and Fields, Boston." *The Papers of the Bibliographical Society of America,* 41 (1947): 210-30.

Tyler, Alice Felt. *Freedom's Ferment: Phases of American Social History from the Colonial Period to the Outbreak of the Civil War.* Harper and Row, 1944.

Van Doren, Carl. *The American Novel 1789-1939.* The Macmillan Co., 1940.

Vicinus, Martha. *The Industrial Muse: A Study of Nineteenth-Century British Working-Class Literature.* Croom Helm, 1974.

Wade, Richard C. *The Urban Frontier: Pioneer Life in Early Pittsburgh, Cincinnati, Lexington, Louisville, and St. Louis.* University of Chicago Press, 1959.

———. *Urban Violence.* University of Chicago Center for Policy Study, 1969.

Walker, Robert H. "The Poet and the Rise of the City." *Mississippi Valley Historical Review,* 49 (June 1962): 85-99.

Waples, Douglas; Berelson, Bernard; and Bradshaw, Franklyn R. *What Reading Does To People: A Summary of Evidence on the Social Effects of Reading.* University of Chicago Press, 1940.

Ward, David. *Cities and Immigrants: A Geography of Change in Nineteenth-Century America.* Oxford University Press, 1971.

———. "The Emergence of Central Immigrant Ghettoes in American Cities, 1840-1920." *Annals of the American Association of Geographers,* 58 (June 1968): 343-51.

Ware, Caroline. *The Early New England Cotton Manufacture: A Study of Industrial Beginnings.* Russel and Russel, 1966.

Ware, Norman. *The Industrial Worker 1840-1860. The Reaction of American Industrial Society to the Advance of the Industrial Revolution.* Peter Smith, 1959.

Warner, Sam Bass, Jr. *The Private City: Philadelphia in Three Periods of Its Growth.* University of Pennsylvania Press, 1968.

———. *The Urban Wilderness: A History of the American City.* Harper and Row, 1972.

Weber, Adna Ferrin. *The Growth of Cities in the Nineteenth Century.* The Macmillan Co., 1899.

Wecter, Dixon. *The Saga of American Society: A Record of Social Aspiration 1607-1937.* Charles Scribner's Sons, 1937.

Weimer, David R. *The City As Metaphor.* Random House, 1966.

Welsh, Alexander. *The City of Dickens.* Clarendon Press, Oxford, 1971.

Welter, Barbara. "The Cult of True Womanhood: 1820-1860." *American Quarterly,* 18 (summer 1966): 151-74.

Wertheimer, Barbara Mayer. *We Were There: The Story of Working Women in America.* Pantheon Books, 1977.

White, Morton and Lucia. *The Intellectual versus the City: From Thomas Jefferson to Frank Lloyd Wright.* The New American Library, 1964.

Williamson, Jeffrey G. "Antebellum Urbanization in the American Northeast." *Journal of Economic History,* 25 (December 1965): 592-608.

———, and Swanson, Joseph A. "The Growth of Cities in the American Northeast 1820-1870." *Explorations in Entrepreneurial History.* Supplement Second Series, 4 (1966): 3-101.

Wirth, Louis. "Urbanism as a Way of Life." *The American Journal of Sociology,* 44 (July 1938): 1-24.

Wittke, Carl. *The Irish in America.* Louisiana State University Press, 1956.

———. *We Who Built America: The Saga of the Immigrant.* Prentice-Hall, 1945.

Wohl, Richard R. "The 'Country Boy' Myth and Its Place in American Urban Culture: The Nineteenth-Century Contribution." Edited by Moses Rischin. *Perspectives in American History*, 3 (1969): 77–156.

———, and Strauss, Anselm L. "Symbolic Representation and the Urban Milieu." *American Journal of Sociology*, 63 (March 1958): 523–32.

Wright, Louis. *Middle Class Culture in Elizabethan England*. University of North Carolina Press, 1935.

Wright, Lyle. *American Fiction 1774-1850: A Contribution toward a Bibliography*. The Huntington Library, 1969.

———. *American Fiction 1851-1875: A Contribution toward a Bibliography*. The Huntington Library, 1965.

———. "A Few Observations on American Fiction, 1851-75." *Proceedings of the American Antiquarian Society*, 65 (April–October 1955): 75–104.

Wyllie, Irvin C. *The Self-Made Man in America: The Myth of Rags to Riches*. Rutgers University Press, 1954.

Zuckerman, Michael. "The Nursery Tales of Horatio Alger." *American Quarterly*, 24 (May 1972): 191-209.

INDEX